COME TO THIS COURT AND CRY

COME TO THIS COURT AND CRY

How the Holocaust Ends

LINDA KINSTLER

BLOOMSBURY CIRCUS
LONDON · OXFORD · NEW YORK · NEW DELHI · SYDNEY

BLOOMSBURY CIRCUS
Bloomsbury Publishing Plc
50 Bedford Square, London, WC1B 3DP, UK
29 Earlsfort Terrace, Dublin 2, Ireland

BLOOMSBURY, BLOOMSBURY CIRCUS and the Diana logo are trademarks of
Bloomsbury Publishing Plc

First published in Great Britain 2022

A catalogue record for this book is available from the British Library

ISBN: HB: 978-1-5266-1259-5; TPB: 978-1-5266-1258-8; EBOOK: 978-1-5266-1262-5;
EPDF: 978-1-5266-4896-9

2 4 6 8 10 9 7 5 3 1

Typeset by Newgen KnowledgeWorks Pvt. Ltd., Chennai, India
Printed and bound in Great Britain by CPI Group (UK) Ltd, Croydon CR0 4YY

To find out more about our authors and books visit www.bloomsbury.com
and sign up for our newsletters

Once, in a moment of inexcusable curiosity, I went to the trouble of hunting up Riga in the Encyclopedia Britannica. That fount of current information describes it as a thriving port on the Baltic Sea, from which agricultural products, chiefly oats, are exported to England. Obviously, it was an old edition of the Encyclopedia. By this time the rumors far outnumber the oats.

The Drifter, *Nation* magazine, 25 January 1928[1]

Contents

1933

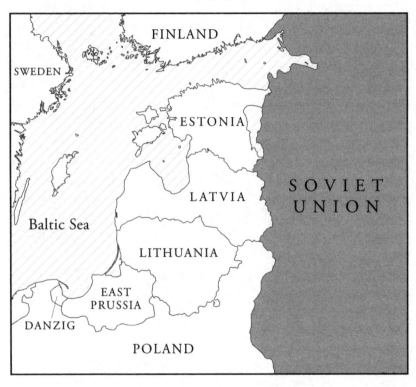

1945

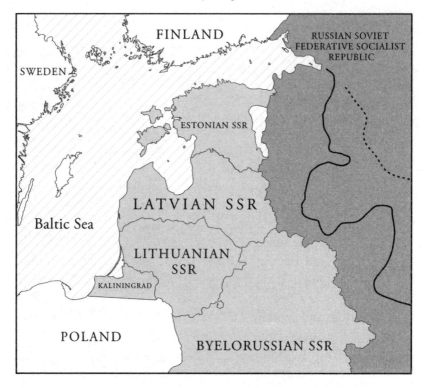

FINLAND

SWEDEN

RUSSIAN SOVIET
FEDERATIVE SOCIALIST
REPUBLIC

ESTONIAN SSR

LATVIAN SSR

Baltic Sea

LITHUANIAN
SSR

KALININGRAD

POLAND

BYELORUSSIAN SSR

- - - - - - - - FRONT LINE DECEMBER 1941

─────────── FRONT LINE NOVEMBER 1942

Author's Note

This book takes place largely in Latvia, a nation that has known many foreign rulers and foreign tongues. Since the thirteenth century, it has been claimed at different times by the Germans, Poles, Swedes and Russians. The modern nation of Latvia came into existence on 18 November 1918, when it declared independence from Russian imperial rule. It enjoyed twenty-two years of tumultuous sovereignty until the summer of 1940, when it was occupied by the Soviet Union and became the Latvian Soviet Socialist Republic. From 1941 to 1944, Latvia was under German control, referred to by its rulers as a province of Ostland. In 1944, Latvia returned to Soviet rule, and remained a Soviet Socialist Republic until the collapse of the Soviet Union in 1991.

The story in this book emerges from the upheavals wrought by these successive occupations and their aftermaths. It also reflects the rich and varied linguistic culture of the land: I have done my best to preserve spellings as they are presented in the original primary and secondary source texts. As a result, the reader may note discrepancies in the spellings of several names and proper nouns. Many of these discrepancies stem from the grammatical rules of the Latvian language, in which almost all male names end in "s", while female names usually in "e" or "a". Herbert, in English, becomes Herberts in Latvian, Viktor becomes Viktors. My surname, in Latvian, is not Kinstler but Kinstlere.

But this is also a global story, one that traces the search for war criminals and Holocaust survivors across several continents. It was a frenzied and plurilingual effort: correspondence issued in German was sometimes answered in Yiddish; witnesses who gave testimony in Russian later had their accounts translated into Latvian, German, English, Hebrew and Portuguese. Wherever possible, I have remained faithful to the spellings I encountered in the archive, in the hope that this will both enrich the prose and serve future researchers who may venture down this path.

Prologue

THE NOVEL

It is March 1965. Two men stand facing one another in a Riga cemetery. They are there on official business, their meeting hurried, clandestine. Elsewhere in the city, celebrations marking twenty-five years of Soviet rule are underway.[1] The whole year had been dedicated to commemorating the anniversary. Never mind the fact that the anniversary itself was something of a fiction. To count twenty-five years of Soviet rule meant strategically omitting the three years of Nazi occupation that punctuated the period 1941 to 1944. Three years when blood ran down Riga's streets like summer rain.[2]

The man who poses the question is identified as 'Boris Karlovics'. He asks his colleague why it was necessary to kill and butcher the target; the plan had been to bring him back to Riga alive. It was supposed to be a kidnapping, not an assassination. His colleague demurs and hands Boris a package. 'It just happened,' the man says. 'Boris Karlovics, please understand, it wasn't planned … one member of the group went too far.'

Boris returns to his apartment and reflects on his poor luck. It was his job to ensure that the mission went smoothly, the most important assignment of his decades-long career in the KGB, the crowning achievement of a lifetime of evasion, duplicity and deceit. Now, he cannot see a way out of the 'whirlpool of revanchism' in which he is trapped. Inside the package, he finds news clippings announcing a murder in Montevideo. A separate envelope contains photographs of the crime scene: a trunk smeared with blood, a disfigured corpse crumpled inside. 'Is it possible that this is Herberts Cukurs?' he thinks. Herberts Cukurs, a man who had once seemed larger than life, a pioneering aviator known as the 'Latvian Lindbergh', more famous and more beloved than the last Latvian prime minister. Boris had known Cukurs during the war. They both belonged to the Arājs Kommando, one of the most brutal killing brigades under Nazi command, composed exclusively of local volunteers. Boris had embedded in the unit as a double agent, relaying news of the brigade's actions back to Moscow. He had won the trust of Cukurs and his colleagues, and then, one by one, he had betrayed them.

There is a knock on the apartment door. A KGB general is outside – Boris's boss, holding a bottle of vodka. Together, the two men go over the crime scene photos, they discuss why the operation went wrong. His boss had asked Boris to see the mission through, to supply whatever was necessary to incriminate Cukurs and bring him back to Riga. Boris had falsified testimonies, embellishing the accounts of Jewish survivors. He had doctored interrogation records of Arājs Kommando members to underscore Cukurs's cruelty, depicting him as someone who took ruthless pleasure in destroying human lives. He had sent Soviet agents to South America to keep watch over his target. And still he had failed.

Boris leaves the general alone for a moment to go to the toilet. He cannot shake the suspicion that the body in the photographs does not actually belong to Cukurs. Something about the mission went awry. But it is too late. At the table, the general has drawn his gun. When Boris emerges, it will all be over.

*

If this sounds like the plot of a cheap spy novel, that is because it is. The spy novel is a seductive genre, one that offers an alluring release from mystery, ambiguity and unknowns. 'To the spy, no choice is accidental; everything is deliberate,' the literary scholar Nicholas Dames writes. Spy novels speak to a base desire for clarity and conservation, an assurance that a small army of agents is somewhere out there, that they not only possess the truth but also nobly shield the rest of us from it. They offer an escape from the cascading uncertainties of past, present and future. They assure us that the mistakes and close calls of history were committed in the service of the status quo. Dames argues that the genre of the spy novel stands for a 'pessimistic, fatal nationalism', the kind of nationalism that operates in the service of vanished ideals: 'Spies are devoted to the old world – whatever old world one believes in – once it becomes clear the old world is setting.'[3] The most important function of the spy novel is, perhaps, to provide us with a discernible, comforting plot. Immersed in its pages, readers may momentarily indulge in the belief that, no matter how many twists and turns the narrative may take, or how many deaths and disappearances there may be, all will be explained in the end.

I encountered this particular spy novel for the first time while browsing through a bookshop in the old city of Riga in 2016. The novel was propped up on the 'new releases' display. It was called *Jūs Nekad Viņu Nenogalināsiet*, or, in English, *You Will Never Kill Him*.[4]

I asked the shopkeeper if it was a popular title, and she said yes, of course. Why else would it be up there on the wall? I cracked the spine open, and there on the first page of the first chapter found my dead, disappeared grandfather's name and patronymic: Boris Karlovics.

It is hard to describe the sense of disorientation brought about by this encounter. One can reasonably expect to find dead relatives and familiar surnames in photo albums, cemeteries, letters, mementos, deeds, maybe even historical texts. But novels are another story. It was not quite vertigo that overcame me, seeing his name, but a certain unsteadiness, a feeling of being in two places at once. It felt like encountering an anachronism in the flesh – like an ambush. The writer Maria Tumarkin describes the past as 'vortex-like', something that cannot be confined to 'little zoo enclosures', that 'cannot be visited like an aging aunt'. Once it grabs hold of you it does not let go. 'At least in certain places,' Tumarkin writes, 'it is like a criminal's mark burned into your family's skin.'[5]

Growing up, I had been told that my paternal grandfather had disappeared after the Second World War, and until very recently that had seemed like explanation enough. Millions vanished over the course of that terrible decade, and I had always thought of him as just another one among them, a man buried anonymously in an unmarked grave, a dead citizen of a dead country, like so many others. He did not come up in family conversations, and there were no photographs of him on display. It was only later that I learned there was good reason for the silence: Boris had indeed been a member of the same killing brigade that Cukurs had belonged to, the Arājs Kommando. He had become a KGB agent after the war, and then he had vanished. My father had dedicated much of his life to finding out what really happened to his own father, to no avail. One day, he had called me in distress. He wasn't making any progress, the archives were turning up no answers. He delegated the search to me: 'You're a journalist,' he said. 'Why don't you find out?'

I told him I would try, but I wasn't sure I wanted to. My parents and older sister had emigrated from Soviet Latvia in 1988, and my parents divorced a few years after arriving in the United States. I grew up among my mother's circle of Soviet Jews and spent years in Jewish day school, where every day began with the recitation of the American national anthem, followed by the Israeli one. The only grandfather I ever thought of was my mother's father, Misha, a man who nearly lost his foot fighting for the Soviet army and danced through his old age. The absence on the other side of the family did not concern me – indeed, it rarely crossed my mind.

All that changed in 2016, when, as a graduate student at the University of Cambridge, I came across a series of curious old headlines in the Latvian newspapers. I had taken an interest in familiarising myself with the contours of my family's abandoned life. I said it was scholarly research: I made their Soviet past into an object of academic intrigue. That was how I came to read a 2011 article in one of the major Latvian news outlets, *Delfi*, reporting that the Latvian Prosecutor General's office was investigating whether a dead man named Herberts Cukurs had been involved 'in the killing of Jews'.[6] Cukurs is remembered, by some, as the 'Butcher' or the 'Hangman' of Riga, though neither of these monikers is quite right. He bears the ignominious honour of being the only Nazi whom the Israeli Intelligence Agency, Mossad, is known to have assassinated. The same agent that orchestrated the logistics of Adolf Eichmann's kidnapping, in 1960, flew back to South America five years later with a new mission: court-martial and kill Cukurs and leave his rotting body behind for the police.

That spring, I wrote to the Latvian Prosecutor General's office asking for more information about the case. I read the newspaper reports and tried to piece together the story: how could a dead man be the subject of a criminal investigation? Why had the press secretary, in one article, said that it was impossible to 'confirm or deny' his participation in the Holocaust?[7] On what legal basis was the investigation proceeding, and where could it possibly lead? My curiosity about the legal particulars acted as a kind of cover: I also couldn't help but wonder if my grandfather's name might turn up somewhere among the files.

I received a detailed response from the prosecutor in charge: the case remained open, no decision had been issued. In a long, dense paragraph, the prosecutor enumerated the potential legal outcomes of the case. It was a thicket of conditional clauses, an avalanche of 'ifs' and 'coulds'. His office had been searching the world for evidence, they had petitioned all the relevant nations – Russia, Israel, Brazil, Uruguay, Germany, the United Kingdom – for supporting documents. There would be a decision, and theoretically, the letter explained, a trial. A trial over the misdeeds and memory of a dead man. A ghost in the dock.

The prosecutor's explanation was accompanied by a postscript written in italics: '*The surname "Kinstler" which belongs to the person requesting this information is more or less significant in the Herberts Cukurs case. This is due to the fact that one of the flamboyant members*

*in [the] so called "Arājs team" where Herberts Cukurs was a member
– Boris Kinstler had the same surname (who also had other alias[es]
and was closely related to Arājs himself in this team). Maybe it is not
only a case of similar surnames?"*[8]

If only he knew. I wrote back, confirming his suspicion about
my relation, and asked that his office keep me apprised of any
developments. The press secretary responded, relaying a question
and a recommendation from the prosecutor. The question was: did
I have any family documents that might pertain to the case? Any
official papers from Boris's wartime service? I told them the truth: we
had nothing. The recommendation was more intriguing: a novel
called *You Will Never Kill Him* had recently come out in Riga.
The book 'was presented as a literary not documentary work',
the prosecutor explained, but it nevertheless contained a wealth
of information about both my grandfather and Cukurs, and the
connection between their two stories. He suggested that I read the
novel and reach out to the author to learn more.

Soon enough, I began my own investigation. I bought the books,
I read the conspiracy theories. Every lie contains a sliver of
truth, I reminded myself. Every lie is an index of desire. I started
to become familiar with the major protagonists in my grandfather's
life. What began as a family story quickly became an investigative
journey through the archives of ten nations, across three continents.

To probe the past is to submit the memory of one's ancestors
to a certain kind of trial. In this case, the trial came to me, or at
least the spectre of one. I found myself retracing the prosecutor's
steps, following the origins and evolution of this unexpected case.
I learned all I could about Cukurs, the man at the centre of the
criminal investigation. He died a spectacular death, the target of an
assassination aimed at expanding the limits of law, his body left to
rot in a place called Shangrilá.

*

This book is not a spy novel. Though spies, security agents and
their circles do play their role, this book does not explain away the
gaps of history. Instead, it leans into the great unknown. I have

tried to gaze down into the abyss of the past and pull out what I can, to understand how the stories we tell about ourselves, our families, and our nations are passed down, preserved and altered along the way.

The subtitle – *How the Holocaust Ends* – is neither prediction nor, God forbid, prescription. It is a warning. The stories that make up the heart of this work are the testimonies of Jewish survivors and their descendants, people who are repeatedly asked to reiterate what they have seen and experienced, whose remembrances and inheritances are challenged at every turn. Following the prosecutor's investigation meant that I was forced to confront the fragility of survivor testimony in the twenty-first century, to observe the ease with which it can be – and is being – dismissed and undermined. The literary scholar Marc Nichanian documented this phenomenon long ago, in his work on the Armenian genocide. 'Genocide is not a fact because it is the very destruction of the fact, of the notion of fact, of the factuality of fact,' he wrote in 2006.[9] Genocide is not just the murder of a people or nation. The genocidal will destroys the evidence of its crimes as it is committing them. It 'seizes testimony at the very moment it is uttered,' Nichanian writes.[10] It refutes testimony, silences witnesses. He warned of this impossible problem years ago, but perhaps, just as we ceased to hear the voices of the survivors, no one was listening closely enough.

What follows is an exploration into how the memory of the Holocaust extends into the present and acts upon it, and what it means to guard and honour that memory in this new and uncertain century. It is a story about how every nation has its own tale of complicity and victimhood, occupation and terror. It is at once a legal genealogy and a familial one, an effort to trace the roots of law's extending claim upon the writing of history. I chart the failures, victories and silences of law alongside those of my relatives and their neighbours and friends, dead and alive.

If memory is a milieu de rencontre, a meeting place, as the French scholar Marie-Claire Lavabre argues, then so is the bookshop, and so is the courtroom.[11] In memory, literature, and law, we encounter multitudes of stories, unfamiliar and often contested accounts of the past. These stories – these inheritances, really – come with demands. To receive them is also to inherit a set of obligations and dilemmas: how much to preserve? How much to expose? How much to omit, hide away? How much to reclaim? I started out by studying all of these questions, only to find out that I was already living them. Along the way, remembering went from being an injunction to a knotted, nearly impossible question.

The verb zakhar – remember, in Hebrew – appears in the Bible at least one hundred and sixty-nine times. 'The verb is complemented by its obverse – forgetting,' the Jewish scholar Yosef Yerushalmi wrote. 'As Israel is enjoined to remember, so it is adjured not to forget.' In his canonical study of the entanglement of Jewish history and scripture, Yerushalmi traces the operation of memory across centuries of religious tradition. But when the time came, in 1987, to write the postscript to the volume, he wondered if he had approached the question of memory all wrong. Not long before he started writing, a friend had sent him a news clipping from *Le Monde* that polled French readers about whether Klaus Barbie, the butcher of Lyons, should be put on trial. 'Of the two following words, *forgetting* or *justice*, which is the one that best characterises your attitude toward the events of this period of the war and the Occupation?' the paper asked. Yerushalmi was caught off guard by *Le Monde*'s formulation of the question. 'Can it be that the journalists have stumbled across something more important than they perhaps realized?' he wondered. 'Is it possible that the antonym of "forgetting" is not "remembering," *but justice*?'[12]

This book is an investigation into that possibility. In it, I follow an improbable and occasionally fantastical series of events in an effort to explore what 'justice' means. Doing so requires considering something that Yerushalmi leaves unsaid – that the Hebrew word zakhar shares the same root as the word zecher – to pierce, to puncture. To kill.[13]

PART I

For since we are the outcomes of earlier generations, we are
also the outcome of their aberrations, passions and errors,
and indeed of their crimes. It is not possible wholly to free
oneself from this chain. If we condemn these aberrations and
regard ourselves as free of them, this does not alter the fact
that we originate in them.

Friedrich Nietzsche, 'On the Uses and
Disadvantages of History for Life'[1]

For quite a while it was the height of style to die in that
manner, freed from any concern for providing clothing or a
coffin for yourself.

Aleksandrs Pelēcis, 'The Siberia Book'[2]

The Police Academy, December 2019

The hum of a small motorcade of cadets announced our arrival at the lush campus of the Uruguayan Police Academy. It was early December, the height of summer, and a trio of police dogs lazed about the entrance. I watched as young men dismounted from their scooters and filed towards a set of buildings whose facades bore the motto of the national police: Saber, Honor, Deber. Knowledge, Honour, Duty. A van pulled up behind them, and out stepped a woman in a blue worker's jumpsuit, her dark hair pulled up in a bun. This was Beatriz Almeida, director of the state police archive. She waved in the direction of my small group and announced that she would get changed before showing us around.

Marcelo Silva, a federal judge and my companion for the day, suggested that we walk the grounds in the meantime. His father had been a policeman, Silva told me, and he used to accompany him to the academy for shooting practice. Silva was a tall, sturdy man with a thick shock of dark hair. He dressed elegantly, in dark jeans and a blue Oxford shirt, a golden crucifix hanging around his neck. Outside the courtroom, Silva dabbled in painting. When I first reached out to let him know I would be visiting Montevideo, he wrote back with one request: could I bring some North American oil paints along with me? The pigment was richer and better for mixing than the ones he could find in South America, he explained. He had an eye for detail and a passion for art that, I quickly learned, extended to his legal work and writing. Over the course of our conversations, he slid easily between references to literature, physics and the criminal code. 'Confiá en el tiempo, que suele dar dulces salidas a muchas amargas dificultades,' he told me over lunch, quoting Cervantes. 'Trust in time; it usually gives sweet endings to many bitter challenges.' He was full of legal aphorisms. 'It is very important to inhabit the mind of the murderer, before, during, and after the "fact"' of a crime, he told me. As we strolled, we circled around the subject that had brought us together, biding our time until Almeida re-emerged. 'I have a defect,' Silva told me. 'I cannot let go of a case.'

I found him through his writing. With the Uruguayan journalist Linng Cardozo, Silva had written one of the most objective accounts of the case that I had flown twelve hours to Montevideo to investigate. This was the case that Silva could not let go of. The book, called *El Baúl de Yahvé* ('The Trunk of God'), is effectively a crime scene investigation. It is subtitled *El Mossad y La Ejecución de Herberts Cukurs en Uruguay* ('Mossad and the Execution of Herberts Cukurs in Uruguay'). A quartet of nouns which would not seem to belong in the same sentence, each of which requires explanation. As an epigraph, Silva had chosen a short passage from the Book of Exodus, in which God orders Moses to assemble the elders of Israel, to tell them that the God of their fathers had appeared before him, that he had anointed Moses as his messenger.[1]

Silva had discovered the case in 2007, in the pages of a historical atlas that he had received for his birthday. The execution of Herberts Cukurs was listed among other curiosities and events visited upon Uruguay in 1965. The atlas noted that the exact circumstances of the murder had never been clarified. Silva's interest was piqued, and he began to investigate further. At the time, he was working as a criminal prosecutor, spending his workdays dealing with the ugliest crimes. He had the skills and the government connections to probe into the recent past. He started making enquiries, and soon the circumstances of this anomalous execution began to unfurl before him, though he quickly found that the narrative remained riddled with question marks and ambiguities. Silva recalled an old police maxim: a homicide that is not cleared up in the first few days will never be solved. Four decades had already elapsed since the event. He got to work.

The crime scene was discovered in the first week of March 1965, after the Montevideo police received a call from a journalist with a wire service in Germany. The journalist asked if the police had dispatched anyone to investigate a murder in Shangrilá, a small neighbourhood of bungalows on the outskirts of the city, right on the shore. A few days earlier, German bureaus of AP and Reuters had received identical telegrams from a single anonymous source, which were written in the form of a legal ruling:

> VERDICT: Considering the gravity of the crimes of which HERBERT CUKURS is accused, notably his personal responsibility in the murder of 30,000 men, women and children, and considering the terrible cruelty shown by HERBERT CUKURS in carrying out his crimes, we condemn the said CUKURS to death. He was executed on 23 February 1965 by 'Those Who Will Never Forget'. His body can be found at Casa Cubertini Calle Colombia, Séptima Sección del Departamento de Canelones, Montevideo, Uruguay.

At first, the wire services dismissed the telegram as a hoax – the reporters had never heard of a man named Herberts Cukurs, and thus had little reason to be concerned about his supposed fate. In the meantime, the men who called themselves 'Those Who Will Never Forget' quickly escaped from Uruguay. Among them was Yaakov Meidad, a Mossad agent who, in an infamous 1960 operation, had helped abduct Eichmann from Buenos Aires and deliver him for trial in Jerusalem.

It was not until the anonymous source followed up with a phone call to the Reuters bureau in Bonn that the journalists reconsidered casting aside the tip: 'I am one of those who will never forget', a man's voice said over the receiver. 'Did you get our letter?'[2]

Only after that cryptic phone call did the German reporters get in touch with the Montevideo police. Alejandro Otero, the chief of police intelligence in Uruguay, went to Calle Colombia to investigate. Otero had a reputation as an upstanding officer, a disciplined man who carefully ironed his shirts every day. He was not someone who could be easily shaken.

When Otero and a small team of policemen arrived at the house identified in the telegram on 6 March 1965, they found a key jammed into the front door, the entrance locked.[3] A putrid smell surrounded the single-storey bungalow. They peered through the windows and saw blood on the walls and floors, bullet casings on the ground. They broke the window and entered the property. In the living room, they found a travelling trunk with blood seeping out from beneath it. A corpse lay crumpled inside, the face swollen and battered almost beyond recognition. This was Herberts Cukurs, a man once celebrated for his record-breaking trans-continental flights, but now remembered for the facts of his extrajudicial execution and all that he did to deserve it.

*

I first met Silva a few days prior, when he came to greet me outside my hotel in the old city of Montevideo. He handed me a list of places of interest and told me to circle the ones I wanted to see. On his typed itinerary: the Hotel Nogaro, Hotel London and Hotel Victoria Plaza, where the Israeli agents had stayed; the petrol station off of La Rambla where the lead agent, Yaakov Meidad, and his target had stopped to fill up; the car rental agency they used; the restaurant in the resort town of Punta del Este where the agents allowed themselves to unwind, if only for a moment. I looked over his list with a translator and together we circled the most critical places, including the Hotel Victoria Plaza, where Meidad and Cukurs had both rented rooms in the days leading up to the murder. (How exactly assassin and target ended up together in a hotel in the Uruguayan capital will soon be explained.) Also on the agenda: Casa Cubertini, the house where the murder took place, and the National Police Academy, where the crime scene evidence remained.

We piled into Silva's car and set off, first to the Hotel Victoria Plaza, now the Radisson. In the lobby, the hotel's original name was still on display. Out front, graduates of a local culinary school celebrated with their families and posed for pictures on the stairs. Silva reminded me that the Israelis had deliberately chosen Uruguay as the site of the execution – if they were caught red-handed, the country had no death penalty for murder. 'Killing someone here is easier than in other places,' he explained.

From there we drove several miles down La Rambla, the city's placid seaside avenue, past the Holocaust memorial, the naval museum and the salvaged rangefinders of the *Admiral Graf Spee*, a German pocket battleship scuttled off the coast of Montevideo in 1939. Silva mentioned that the stone eagle figurehead that had adorned the ship had been retrieved from the ocean floor in 2006, the diving mission financed by wealthy investors. The eagle, and the bronze swastika wreath clutched in its talons, would soon go up for auction, but for the time being it was hidden away in a government warehouse outside the city. One potential buyer had said he hoped to display the Nazi eagle at the next World Cup.[4]

When we got to Shangrilá, Silva slowed the car. The sea breeze filtered through the windows. It was a calm and quiet area worthy of its paradisiacal name, its streets lined with modest family homes tucked between tall trees. Casa Cubertini, where Cukurs was killed, had once been one of the only homes on the street. Now, it sat among a dense row of flat-roofed dwellings. Silva told me that the current occupants, a woman and her two young children, hated that people sometimes came to gawk at their house. We drove by slowly, back and forth, trying not to make a disturbance. A low red wall and two small jacaranda trees in bloom guarded the entrance, the front door marked by ornamental sconces. It looked like any other humble home, its history thoroughly erased. There was nothing more the house could tell me; I snapped a photograph and took a video on my phone, and told Silva that he could drive away.

After seeing the house, we took a lunch break in the neigh-bourhood on a street lined with palms, the sea crashing on the other side of the road. The Cukurs case, Silva told me, was just a curiosity of Uruguayan history. 'Here, it's part of the past,' he

said. 'For Latvia, it's the present. It's like relativity.' He cited Albert
Einstein, describing how time passes more quickly for a couple in
love, and slower for a man in jail. I guess in this analogy the man
in jail is Latvia, stuck in the past. Memory can be a special kind
of prison, one from which there can be no easy escape, no path to
parole.

I asked Silva about the documents found on Cukurs's body.
In other accounts of the murder, including the assassin's own
telling, I had read that it was the text of the telegram, the 'verdict'
announcing the reason for his execution.[5] Silva corrected me. It
was not the verdict, but something far more interesting: a folder
containing an excerpt from the published Nuremberg diary of
Gustave Mark Gilbert, the prison psychologist who attended to
the major German war criminals while they awaited sentencing.[6]
The entry was dated 27 July 1946 – day 188 of the Nuremberg trial
– the day that Sir Hartley Shawcross, the chief British prosecutor,
delivered his closing argument.

Shawcross's speech is remembered as one of the most chilling
moments of the tribunal. This final speech of the British prosecution
was devoted to addressing 'the murder of the Commandos'.
Shawcross specifically detailed the horrific crimes committed in
the Baltic states, where the 'Holocaust by bullets' took hundreds
of thousands of lives. He urged the Allied judges to remember
how many had been lost, how many families extinguished, how
brutally and needlessly they were killed. 'Day by day, over years,
women were holding their children in their arms and pointing
to the sky while they waited to take their place in blood-soaked,
communal graves,' he said. 'What right has any man to mercy
who has played a part – however indirectly – in such a crime?'[7]
A video of his address shows the war criminals – among them
the Reichsmarschall Hermann Goering, Nazi foreign minister
Joachim von Ribbentrop, Wehrmacht commander Wilhelm
Keitel and SS Chief Ernst Kaltenbrunner – shifting in their seats
on the dock.[8]

Shawcross ended his speech by reminding the judges of the monumental task before them. He recalled the testimony of Hermann

Friedrich Graebe, an engineer who had told the court of how, on a business trip to Dubno, Ukraine, he had witnessed a mass murder. 'I watched a family of about eight persons, a man and a woman, both about fifty with their children of about one, eight and ten, and two grown-up daughters of about twenty to twenty-four,' Graebe said. 'An old woman with snow-white hair was holding the one-year-old child in her arms and singing to it, and tickling it. The child was cooing with delight. The couple were looking on with tears in their eyes. The father was holding the hand of a boy about ten years old and speaking to him softly, the boy fighting his tears. The father pointed towards the sky, stroked his head, and seemed to explain something to him.' A minute later, the whole family was killed.

Shawcross told the judges that it was their job to seek justice for the father who had cradled and comforted his son as they stood in the execution line in Dubno, and millions of others who waited in the same terrible lines across Eastern Europe. The judges had to remember this father's story, and all the stories just like it that would never be told. 'You will remember when you come to give your decision the story of Graebe, but not in vengeance – in a determination that these things shall not occur again,' he said. 'The father – do you remember? – pointed to the sky, and seemed to say something to his boy.'

Above all, Shawcross encouraged the judges to imagine that it was not just lawyers, journalists and military police staring back at them in the Nuremberg courtroom, but all of humanity, bedraggled and wounded from the long years of war. The judges, he argued, had to imagine that 'mankind itself' stood before them, crying out a single, simple plea:

> [A]fter this ordeal to which mankind has been submitted,
> mankind itself – struggling now to re-establish in all the
> countries of the world the common simple things – liberty,
> love, understanding – comes to this Court and cries: 'These are
> our laws – let them prevail!'

These forceful words, the assassins left upon the body.

*

The police academy was the last stop on our tour of Montevideo. When Otero and his team ended their investigation of the murder, the trunk was transferred to the police archive, where it had remained ever since in a state of prolonged decay. Technically, however, it was still a piece of evidence.

Almeida, the director of the police archive, re-emerged in a flowing green silk shirt, lipstick and snakeskin flats, her dark hair carefully combed. She spoke a mile a minute, barely pausing for breath as she apologised for the slightly crumbling state of the academy. The entire police archive was in the process of being moved out of a central building in downtown Montevideo, she explained. The plan was to give important historic artefacts to different police bureaus all over the country, so that every station would be able to put Uruguayan history on display. But in the meantime, it was all here, piled up in a regal building that used to be the national police commander's office. The trunk, she warned me, had not been adequately preserved – only the top of it remained. A few years ago, during yet another move, some staff had mistaken the bottom for a piece of trash and had thrown it away. It's a shame that history could be dispensed with so casually, she lamented. She was doing her best.

Finally, she unlocked the doors to the commander's old office, its entrance lined with imposing white columns. When I glimpsed inside, I understood why she had felt the need to warn me. It looked like a scrap furniture storage house: stacks of boxes lined the walls, office chairs were piled on top of each other, empty display cases were shoved together towards the walls. In an adjacent room there were old police signs and abandoned crime scene evidence – Almeida showed me a pair of bullet-ridden wooden doors that were being temporarily stored next to the toilet.

The trunk, or what was left of it, sat atop a large wooden conference table in what was once an airy reception room. The bloodstains were still clearly visible, dried dark brown patches colouring the frayed cloth exterior. There were paint splatters on it, from when the walls of the police museum were repainted, Almeida explained. Silva gestured towards its rusting lock, as if to emphasise how much time had passed since its last use. He and Almeida insisted on taking it outside so that I could see it in the light, and I watched as they carefully lifted it up and shuffled towards the door. They leaned it up against one of the grand white columns and stepped back. 'There is DNA here,' Silva said. He confessed that when he first saw the trunk, in 2010, he was tempted to take a bit of it for DNA testing, but refrained. On the inside face, I could see where the bloodstains had seeped through the wood and cloth. There used to be a horrible smell, Almeida told me. For many years, the museum kept the trunk firmly closed.

'Touch it!' Almeida said. I demurred – evidence was evidence, and I did not want to contaminate it any further. 'No, really, touch it!' she said. It felt like an order. The bloodied spots felt damper than the others, even sixty years on, a side effect of the humid summer air, or perhaps of my own imagination. 'It is a privilege,' Almeida told me. 'It is very important, emotionally, for the Jewish people, for the German people, and for us as well. It gives me goosebumps. It is to contact a formative moment for all of humanity.'

We stood together and looked at what was left of the trunk. Cukurs was a person for whom there was 'more than one reading', Almeida explained. His family had one version of the story, while those whose relatives he had helped kill and imprison had quite another, she said. She was proud that the Uruguayan investigators who had responded to the scene had produced what she called an 'objective tabula rasa' of the execution. 'Sin emociones,' she said. Without emotion.

2

Boris

In one photograph of my grandfather Boris, he stands in the centre of a family wedding photo, a boutonnière pinned to his lapel, glaring at the camera over the heads of the bride and groom. His hair is carefully slicked back, his pocket square perfectly folded. He has an expansive forehead and a narrow nose and mouth, features which he passed on to my father, who passed them on to me. He is twenty-four years old: fighting age. To the far right of the photo sits his own father, Kārlis. His features are sharper than his son's – Kārlis has the kind of cavernous eyes one sees in Egon Schiele canvases, his suit slightly twisted, his necktie askew. His wife, my great-grandmother Leontine, stands beside him in profile, her hair bundled into a low chignon, her fist resting on her husband's shoulder. The photograph is dated 26 April 1942. Ten months into the German occupation of Latvia, four months after the Wannsee Conference, where Hitler's deputies met to coordinate the 'Final Solution to the Jewish Question'.[1] Roughly 57,500 Jews had by then been killed in occupied Latvia. The murders were still ongoing in nearby streets and forests as my grandfather and his relatives gathered to celebrate the newlyweds.

Kārlis and Leontine had fled the territory of Latvia during the First World War, joining the waves of people ordered to evacuate the area and head east as the Germans approached. They settled in Rybinsk, a trading city on the Volga, north-east of Moscow. In May

1918, Leontine gave birth to Boris. Two years later, after years of agitation and war, the fledgling government of Soviet Russia halted its attempts to bring Latvia under its control. For the first time in history, Latvia was under the dominion of no imperial order. From their exile in Rybinsk, Kārlis and Leontine must have joined their compatriots in toasting to the birth of their long-awaited nation. They started making preparations to return to their homeland, now a country of its own.

The very idea of the modern nation, and the concept of nationalism, was born in the Latvian countryside. In the late eighteenth century, a young German pastor named Johann Gottfried von Herder rode from farm to farm collecting the local folksongs. A student of Immanuel Kant, he had secured a position as a visiting teacher at the Riga Cathedral School.[2] In Latvian villages, he heard folksongs, what the Latvians call dainas, four-line poems that blend stories of pagan myth and earthly life. They were curious songs, different from ones he had heard in Germany or Königsberg. They seemed unique to the people who lived in the area, who seemed to him to be a 'people', in that they shared a culture, and that culture was tied to the land. Some of them were innocent tales of agricultural life, while others appealed to the pagan gods. Poring over these poems, Herder began to formulate a theory of the ties that bind peoples, cultures and states, of what makes a nation. The Latvian songs, in particular, seemed to him to possess a 'living presence that nothing written on paper can ever have'.[3]

As Herder explored the Baltic countryside, new nations were emerging around the world, and old nations were making new demands. He wondered about the causes and virtues of these new national formations, about what held them together and what made them distinct: 'What sorts of virtues or unvirtues have governed human beings at all times, and has the tendency of human beings been improved or worsened with time, or always remained the same?' he asks in an early draft.[4] Were humans getting worse, or better? He began to discern how much beauty lies in one nation, but he also worried that the source of all that beauty could also lead a nation to its own demise. He warned that the formation of national identities could lead nations to clash with one another, that it could give way to prejudice, to 'Mob-thinking! Limited nationalism!' His warning was the first known use of the word 'nationalism'.

In 1870, a hundred years after Herder rode through the Latvian farmland, a group of young men studying at the University of Tartu formed the first Latvian student fraternity. They called it Lettonia, invoking their still-nascent nation's Latin name. It would become Latvia's most elite student corporation. Only ethnic Latvians were allowed to join. Russians, Jews and Germans formed their own groups.[5] The fraternity, like the nation, would define itself by excluding those who were not savējie – not one of their own. Anti-Semitism was nothing new: in 1766, the Riga Town Council had issued an edict limiting the economic activities of Jewish merchants; in 1810, the Riga Jewish Community wrote a letter to their Christian neighbours, asking to be recognised as 'competent members of society'. In 1861, German papers carried reports of the persecution of the Riga Jews. Things got marginally better before they got worse: more than 20,000 Jews from Poland and Ukraine fled to Latvia at the end of the nineteenth century, escaping pogroms in their hometowns. Anti-Semitic sentiment rose in response to this influx of newcomers, but some Latvian national figures pushed back against it. Krišjānis Valdemārs, a writer and scholar who became the figurehead of the Latvian National Awakening, wrote that Latvians could learn from their successful Jewish neighbours, rather than wasting time envying and deriding them. In 1866, a Riga newspaper argued that the Jews belonged in Latvia more than anywhere else, because they served as 'living proof of how much a small, despised nation can be strengthened, and in them we clearly see what can be achieved through attention, patience, and close fellowship'.[6] Yet even these conciliatory efforts marked the Jewish and Latvian peoples as unmistakably distinct.

When, in 1938, it came time for my grandfather to head to the University of Latvia he presented himself to Lettonia and applied to join the brotherhood. The fraternity still exists: I have scrolled

through its Facebook page[7] and website, both full of photographs
of celebrations, marches, lectures, fencing matches and 'literary
evenings'.[8] The website promises that the group offers 'shelter and
protection for Latvian students who gather to grow in the national
spirit and love of the homeland'.[9]

Nearly everything that I know about Boris derives from his
Lettonia application materials: a curriculum vitae, a strip of head
shots and a small application fee. In his letter to the brotherhood,
he provides a brief life history, starting with his family's return to
Latvia in 1920 to reclaim their land. During the First World War,
Kārlis had narrowly evaded capture by German forces because of
his mastery of the German language, and he wanted his son to have
the same protection. So he and Leontine sent the young Boris to
a German school in the small town of Saldus, where he evidently
struggled to fit in. 'Those were seven hard years for me, which
I still proudly remember,' Boris wrote in his application. 'Being
a Latvian boy, I suffered there a lot.' He had already learned to fit
his personal experiences into the broader narrative of his nation,
which had also suffered, fought and prevailed. Kārlis worked as
a farmer and Leontine ran the household. Later, they sent their
son to the local gymnasium in Liepāja, a bustling seaside port city.
According to the Latvian newspaper archive, there he won third
place in a digging competition,[10] and by his own account he had
an unfortunate incident with the German teacher, one Frau Recke,
which almost led to his expulsion. It was also there that he first met
a girl named Biruta, who wore her hair in two long, blonde braids.
My grandmother, the woman who would one day silently guard
the many unanswered questions Boris would leave behind.

Boris's application to Lettonia was accepted. He joined the
brotherhood in the autumn of 1938, when he enrolled in the
agricultural department of the university. Two years prior, another
ambitious Latvian man with severe features had been formally
accepted into its ranks. His name was Viktors Arājs. He was the son
of a single mother who struggled to make ends meet. He had won
a full scholarship to enrol in the law school, but it was not enough
to support himself and his family. 'Looking for part-time work, he

fatefully joined the police reserve,' the historian Richards Plavnieks writes. 'This side-occupation gradually took more and more time away from his studies, eventually causing him to suspend his studies altogether several times.' In 1939, however, Arājs returned to the university, and to Lettonia one last time, determined to finish his law degree. He eventually did in 1941, graduating as a 'Soviet jurist', as he would one day describe himself.[11] The first Soviet occupation of Latvia meant that he, and the rest of the brotherhood, had to follow Soviet codes and laws if they wanted to survive. 'Indubitably, I was then a communist,' Arājs remarked, decades later, facing trial for war crimes. But if he was a communist then, he would soon switch allegiances entirely – above all, Arājs was an opportunist.[12] During his university career, he and Boris must have encountered one another in the Lettonia clubhouse, the centre of Latvia's old-boys network. It was the start of their lasting, infamous association.

In 1940, the Soviet Union occupied Latvia and almost immediately banned the student fraternities, viewing them as strongholds of nationalists and class enemies. Lettonia went underground as Latvia found itself, once again, under the control of Moscow. The brotherhood continued to meet clandestinely, sometimes in a restaurant in the city centre, sometimes in members' apartments.[13] This period marked the start of what Latvians refer to as the Baigais Gads, the Year of Horror. Banks were nationalised, homes seized and redistributed, libraries gutted, schools revolutionised, church attendance discouraged. 'Thus the inhabitants of the Baltic states became Soviet citizens,' the great Polish writer Czesław Miłosz wrote of this moment. 'In the eyes of the new authorities this mass of people, who were so well off that they put the rest of the Union to shame, represented a scandalous relic of the past.'[14]

The Soviets rounded up and deported well-to-do Latvian and Jewish families, piling them into cattle trucks and sending them to camps in Siberia. Two per cent of the nation's population was killed and removed in this manner. Among them were my great-aunt Velta, her sister Maija, their mother and grandmother. Velta's father was killed before he even got to the train. 'They were looking for father; they shot their rifles into the oak tree and the chestnut tree because they thought he might be hiding in the branches,' she recalled, years later. They struggled to survive upon arrival in Siberia. 'Mother died in 1943, and I had nothing to wear on my feet then. I think I may have been near death myself,' Velta remembered. Today, her village of Bauska is marked with plaques honouring the deportees. 'June–July 1941: To Those Who Never Came Back', the signs read. It is the same phrasing that, in other countries and elsewhere in Latvia, is used to honour those who never returned from the Nazi concentration camps and ghettos. For some of the Jewish families among the deportees – only those who managed to survive the cold, hunger and hard labour – the forced relocation to Siberia would seem, in hindsight, a macabre stroke of good luck.

It took just thirty minutes for the village of Bauska to change hands in July 1941; the Soviets left town at 3.00 in the afternoon, and German forces arrived at 3.30.[15] On 1 July, SS-Brigadier Walter Stahlecker, the commander of Einsatzgruppe A, arrived in Riga. Arājs was the first person he met.[16] The German tasked the young Latvian lawyer with forming his own police unit. Arājs's appointment to lead a unit was confirmed the next day.

The meeting meant that Arājs's career would take a dramatic turn – it was the kind of success that he had joined Lettonia hoping to secure.[17] On 4 July, he published an announcement in the new nationalist newspaper *Tēvija* calling for 'all nationally-thinking Latvians' who might 'wish to take an active part in the cleansing of our country from harmful elements', to present themselves at the 'Headquarters of the Security Kommando at Valdemārs Street 19'. His aim was to 'command a unit composed of radical nationalists and the cream of pre-war Latvian society', Plavnieks writes. Arājs drew heavily upon the membership of Lettonia for his new recruits.[18] Seven of the forty founding members were his fraternity brothers. One of them was almost certainly my grandfather Boris.

My grandmother did not want to believe that Boris joined the Kommando of his own accord. She told my father that the men of Lettonia drew lots to see who would join Arājs's murderous unit, because none of them had been particularly eager to do so.

She hadn't known Boris during the war – at the time, she was married to someone else – and, later, chose not to ask too much. Technically, all the men were volunteers, but the choice to join the Kommando was sometimes 'affected by pressures and threats that had placed the person's physical existence at risk', as the historian Rudīte Vīksne writes. 'In the conditions of a twice-occupied country, it is difficult to establish a clear criterion of voluntary choice.'[19] The Holocaust scholar Lawrence Langer coined the term 'choiceless choices' to describe this kind of moral calculus.[20] 'During the war, the situation in Nazi-occupied territory was such that it was impossible for civilians not to come into contact with the occupation regime,' the historian Franziska Exeler writes. 'The German administration depended heavily on the employment of Soviet citizens – in particular, as policemen, town mayors and village heads – and willingly or unwillingly, individuals became entangled or complicit in German crimes.'[21]

After the newspaper announcement went out, Arājs and his fraternity brothers set up tables in front of the Lettonia headquarters and began signing up the new recruits who answered the call. In the evening, Arājs and his 'nationally-thinking' colleagues stormed the streets of Riga. I do not know, and cannot know, if my grandfather Boris was among them, but I figure it is safer to assume the worst. The men converged upon the Great Choral Synagogue, on Gogol Street, the largest synagogue in the city. Lithuanian Jews who had fled to Riga from Vilnius, Kaunas, Siauliai and elsewhere had taken shelter in the basement. The Arājs Kommando attacked. 'Holy writings were torn up and thrown into the flames. Guards with machine guns surrounded the synagogue and shot anyone who tried to escape,' the historian Bernhard Press writes in *The Murder of the Jews in Latvia*. 'The screams of the burning victims could be heard over a great distance and filled the souls of the people in the neighboring houses with horror. Some of them soon left their homes forever, because at night it seemed to them that they could still hear the cries of the burning human victims.'[22] A Nazi newsreel captured the conflagration; the clip begins with scenes of Jewish men being dragged off the streets, and ends with footage of the Choral Synagogue's stained-glass windows straining to contain the fire, the wooden roof destroyed, flames pouring out of the congregation hall and erupting into the heavens. Soon, all but one of the synagogues in Riga had been destroyed.

3

Cukurs

Another man, a Latvian with a formidable reputation, would soon join the Arājs Kommando. He was broad-shouldered and athletic, with carefully parted blond hair and the weathered skin of an adventurer. Born in 1900 and raised in Liepāja, where Boris had also gone to school, the man built his own planes and was known for his improbable trans-continental journeys, feats of aviation which won him international admirers. He had fought in the Latvian war of independence, studied in the military aviation school and served in the country's newly-established air force, which he left with the rank of captain.[1] Over the course of the 1930s, his flight paths were eagerly tracked by his countrymen; with every new exotic locale he visited, he seemed to expand the imaginary bounds of his small nation. At the height of his aviation career, he flew to Shanghai, Hong Kong, Tokyo, Rome, Serbia, India, Dakar, Senegal, The Gambia and Jerusalem, sending short dispatches and photographs to newspapers back home, where loyal readers anxiously followed his progress across the globe. His 1937 dispatches include accounts of a 'Dangerous encounter in the jungle', 'Crocodile hunting at night', 'Holy evening in Hanoi cathedral' and 'Lunch with the sons of the Indian Maharaja'. He was known as the 'Latvian Lindbergh'. His name was Herberts Cukurs.

Cukurs won a Harmon trophy, one of the top aviation prizes, for Latvia in 1933, the same year that Anne Morrow Lindbergh,

Charles's wife, won the prize for the United States. 'Latvian Lindbergh expected to-day', the *Shanghai Times* reported on 25 May 1937, heralding Cukurs's arrival in the city. Two days later, the *China Press* featured a photograph and interview with the 'Latvian "Lindbergh" In Shanghai', in which Cukurs, 'with a broad grin', 'assured the reporter that the head-hunting natives of Borneo are friendly fellows. They only indulge in the sport of cutting people's heads off "when they don't like you".' The 'Borneo head-hunters,' he said, were the 'gentlemen of the jungle'. His photograph appeared in newspapers around the world – there he was, in Jakarta, disembarking from his trusted C-3 two-passenger plane, or in Osaka, being greeted by a small group of dignitaries. Upon returning from his tour of British Palestine, Cukurs gave a lecture at the Jewish Club of Riga extolling the virtues of the Zionist project. The audience listened to him raptly, imagining their promised homeland.[2]

Like the American Lindbergh, he courted fame and followers. He was the kind of man who wanted people to tell stories about him, to know his name, to recognise him on the street and in the cinema, which sometimes showcased newsreels from his journeys. Cukurs loved being photographed next to his plane, and he loved how his flights became fodder for the papers. By the thirties, when both men were active in the skies, the figure of the aviator had come to stand for order, achievement and exertion. The man in the sky stood for the 'new age' of mankind; he was the 'aviator hero' who pushed humanity closer towards modernity with every flight. 'No machine requires as much concentration of the human mind, as much human will to power, as the flying machine does,' Guido Mattioli wrote in his 1935 book *Mussolini Aviatore*, which documents the aviation exploits of il Duce, who got his pilot's licence as a young man. 'Hence there appears to be a necessary, inner spiritual affinity between aviation and fascism. Every aviator is born a fascist.'[3] That same year, another Italian writer, the futurist Cristoforo Mercati, wrote that the flights of *il Duce* were the 'quintessence of our Fascist age'. They signalled the arrival of the fascist future to come: 'The instinct of Icarus, the human instinct to fly ... has spread in no generation with such strong roots, with such strength and passion, as it has in ours.'[4] The entanglement of aviation and fascism was certainly true of the American Lindbergh: he and his wife travelled to Nazi Germany, accepted its honours and ardently tried to prevent the US from entering the war.[5] But while Lindbergh militated in favour of Hitler's regime in the US and abroad, Cukurs would come to serve it.

Cukurs's aviation career had flourished alongside the nation's short-lived bout of self-determination; the higher and further Cukurs flew, the higher and further Latvia would go. Upon returning from The Gambia, a former short-lived Latvian colonial outpost, in 1935, Cukurs was awarded a modest farmhouse in Bukaisi, a village near the Lithuanian border.[6] His book about the journey, *My Flight to Gambia*, complete with photographs from his cockpit, became a collector's item, giving Latvians the bird's-eye view of the Spanish Sierra Nevadas, of Casablanca, of the French Alps. In 1937, Kārlis Ulmanis, the authoritarian prime minister of the interwar years, awarded Cukurs the Order of Three Stars for meritorious service to the nation, the highest state honour. It came with a white cross inscribed "Par Teviju", "For the Fatherland", and "per aspera ad astra" – "through hardship to the stars".

When the Year of Horror came in 1941 and the Soviet army quickly took over the city, Cukurs's fame, and his reputation as a skilled pilot and mechanic, ensured a modicum of protection. That year, he was briefly summoned to Moscow, where authorities sought his help building the Soviet air fleet.[7] Rumours circulated that the Soviets tried to woo him by gifting him a brand-new Cadillac. But then the tide of war turned. 'At the end of June 1941, the gigantic struggle between two colossi broke,' Cukurs wrote after the war. 'Hitler's Germany chased the shattered Red Army eastward with such tremendous blows that it was thought that the Red Colossus would collapse at any moment and never get up again. In a few weeks, Latvia was cleared of Red troops for the first time in 700 years. Latvians greeted the Germans with flowers and joy. The whole nation took a deep breath and believed that now, after a difficult year of Soviet occupation, when Latvia lost its independence, it would again become a free state in the family of nations.'

Cukurs's way of contributing to this effort was to join Arājs's new professional killing unit.[8] The Latvian Sicherheitsdienst (SD) units, the 'intelligence' divisions of the SS, were 'initially made up of volunteers who sought revenge for relatives who had been tortured to death or deported to Siberia by the Soviet occupants, as well as by those who wanted to continue their military career,' writes the Latvian historian Uldis Neiburgs.[9] In the Riga ghetto, the Jews came to recognise the members of Lettonia, calling them the *Arājsen Burschen*, Arājs's Fraternity Fellows.[10] Because of his fame, Cukurs was the most recognisable of them all.

There are various accounts of the role he assumed in the Kommando. He retained his Latvian military rank, going by *Kapteinis*, Captain Herberts Cukurs. But his precise duties have been the subject of historical and legal debate. In court documents from after the war, he is referred to as Arājs's 'adjutant', one of his closest associates; Arājs meanwhile, once described Cukurs as a 'weapons officer'. In other accounts, he is depicted as a mechanic or chauffeur, responsible for transporting the men of the Kommando from their headquarters to the ghetto and the killing fields.

From testimonies, documents and histories, I started piecing together the fragments, trying to get a sense of my grandfather's involvement, sorting through fractured accounts of the war. In a seminal historical account by the Latvian American historian Andrew Ezergailis, *The Holocaust in Latvia*, I read of how comfortable the Kommando clubhouse was, with a fireplace, a yard, a garage. 'During the early days Kinslers taught the rudiments of German in the living room,' Ezergailis writes.[11] My grandfather's mastery of the language earned him the role of 'liaison officer' with the German command, a position that would prove instrumental to his eventual fate. 'Across the street in the park basic marching and rifle exercises were practiced by the commando,' Ezergailis writes. 'At some time during the commando's stay in the house the Anti-Semitic Institute was also established there.' They collected Jewish books and religious artefacts plundered from their missions, perhaps they even put them on display. They used the basement as a prison.

The Arājs Kommando wasn't supposed to be a permanent unit – the Germans were cautious about arming the locals, and did not want to give them too much power. 'Sonderkommando Arājs was one of the most significant inventions of the early stages of the Holocaust,' Ezergailis explains. The Nazi commanders overseeing the eastern operation – Heinrich Himmler, Reinhard Heydrich, Walter Stahlecker, Rudolf Lange, Friedrich Jeckeln – imagined that the unit's remit would be limited to 'carrying out pogroms'. It was supposed to be a quick job, a 'Holocaust by bullets' that did not require the infrastructure of trains and camps and gas chambers. And for a time, it was. There are several accounts of Cukurs participating with zeal in the killings. In the forest of Rumbula, where 25,000 Jews were killed over the course of a few weeks, Cukurs is said to have been present, to have praised the Germans' marksmanship, to have joined them in firing rounds. 'Although Arājs's men were not the only ones on the ghetto end of this operation, to the degree that they participated in the atrocities there the chief responsibility rests on Herberts Cukurs' shoulders,' Ezergailis writes.[12] An endnote accompanies this sentence. I flip the pages to see what it says, and encounter what seems to be the seed of denial: 'Although Cukurs has entered into the literature of the Holocaust in Latvia as one of the great monsters, there is very little actual evidence against him. Among the Latvian witnesses he figured hardly at all, mostly as a man who tinkered in the garage,' Ezergailis writes. 'The heaviest evidence against Cukurs pertains to the atrocities inside the ghetto on the morning of November 30.'

On 30 November, the Jews of the Riga ghetto were woken up at 4.00 a.m. and assembled for transportation to the Rumbula Forest. The killing began in the ghetto. 'The Arājs men, perhaps one hundred, were led by Herberts Cukurs,' Ezergailis writes. Frida Michelson, one of the few Latvian Jewish survivors from the Rumbula action, remembered seeing 'an unending column of people, guarded by armed policemen', passing by. 'Young women, women with infants in their arms, old women, handicapped, helped up by their neighbors, young boys and girls – all marching, marching.' An SS man opened fire on the columns. 'The Latvian policemen were shouting "Faster! Faster!" and lashing whips over the heads of the crowd.' As she watched her neighbours and friends marching to their deaths, she felt paralysed. 'My mind was aflame,' she writes. 'You must see it. You are the witness. Take it all in. There, before your window, before your eyes the tragedy of your whole nation is being played out. Remember. Do not forget!'[13]

After the war, Michelson told her tale of survival to everyone who would listen. Soviet officials, journalists, neighbours, friends – they all wanted to know how she survived. Some people did not believe her. Others told her story for her. As it began to mutate and circulate, she decided to write it down herself. 'It was impossible to tell everyone everything,' she writes. She started taking down notes, recording her experience. 'Someday I will have children. Let them read it when they grow up; let them read it and never forget it.'[14]

Cukurs, too, wrote his story, or at least one version of it. In a letter dated 26 July 1945, titled 'Latvia during the National Socialist Occupation', he writes of the disappointment of the Latvian soldiers, who, 'with weapons in hand, helped the Germans clear the country of Red troops'. Once German control was secured, they were asked to turn over their guns. 'There was no longer any talk of the Latvian Army and independence,' Cukurs writes. 'The saddest thing was the Jewish question: in the course of half a year, Latvia became a mass grave of more than 100,000 Latvian and countless *Mitteleuropean* Jews who arrived in freight cars in the Riga suburban train stations.' The destiny of the Jews, he writes, 'was so horrible that I asked myself more about this question'. In a conspicuous passive voice, he launches into an abbreviated description of the horrors of the Holocaust. 'From the very first days of the occupation, the Jews were mishandled and murdered.' The ghetto was surrounded with barbed wire and policed around the clock. 'Anyone who came into contact with Jews was allowed to shoot without warning,' he writes.[15]

Who was 'anyone'? He makes no mention of his own actions during this period. His account does not explain who put up the barbed wire around the ghetto, who drove the blue killing buses, who fired all the shots that rang through the night, and who, in the final days of the occupation, attempted to chemically destroy the mass graves. He writes only of collectives – Nazis, Latvians, Jews, Reds – not of individual lives and individual responsibility, and certainly not of his own. And yet, the letter teems with details of conditions in the ghetto, of Nazi ordinances and 'Aktions', that an ordinary civilian would not have known. 'Surely history will give its verdict of all these German acts,' Cukurs writes. 'But in the memory of the Latvian people, the German occupation will remain the most terrifying of all time.'

4

The Kommando

In a group photograph of the Arājs Kommando from 1942, the men are lined up in five rows, commanders at the front, officers at the back. Arājs sits in the middle, hands limp on his thighs, smirking. Next to him is his boss Rudolf Lange, the commander of the German security police in Latvia, formerly the deputy head of the Berlin police. Lange and Arājs are both thirty-two years old in the photo. Lange wears black leather gloves and a smile. Their visor caps, decorated with the SS eagle and a Totenkopf, a skull and crossbones, cast shadows over their eyes. Behind them, some thirty young men stand and stare at the camera, their caps tilted uniformly to the right, each one with a Totenkopf at its crown, a small sea of skulls.

Someone, perhaps an archivist, has labelled each man with a number in pen. Arājs is #3, Lange #4. They have not all been identified, and it is clear that this is a photo of a select group of members – the Arājs Kommando grew dramatically in 1942, which is also when the group began wearing standardised military uniforms. Before then, the men had just worn whatever they had on hand. That same year, the Soviets breached the German line nearby and reinforcements were needed. New recruits were sent first to an SD training camp in Fürstenberg, Germany, and then to take up posts either at concentration camps in Latvia or on the front lines near Minsk.[1] By then, virtually all Latvian Jews had been murdered, but new transports were arriving from Hanover,

Hamburg, Berlin, Leipzig, Vienna and Prague. What were Arājs's other men doing while this group sat for their portrait? Cukurs, with his recognisable face, is nowhere to be seen.

For a long time I thought that Boris somehow escaped this group photo. I scanned the men's faces, looking for a match – perhaps he was the man in the commander's hat in the third row, his face completely shadowed, or perhaps he was the Sturmführer in the second row, looking in the wrong direction, just barely in the frame – but neither seemed quite right.

And then I realised that the version of the photograph that I was looking at, the one posted on museum walls and on book covers, had been cropped. Its rightmost edge ran straight through one man's face. In the Latvian National Archive, the historian Uldis Neiburgs, a friend of my father's, finds the original image, in which six more men come into view. Their likenesses have been slightly overexposed, their faces blurred. At the very edge of the frame, a man in the first row gazes directly at the camera. The archivist has labelled him # 8. He has a familiar jawline, thin nose and lips. His cap casts a shadow over his eyes. He is dressed in a full SS uniform, his bare hands crossed neatly in his lap. Neiburgs emails the photograph to my father, along with a single, simple question: 'Please tell me if BK is No. 8?'

They were known for their method of killing, the Arājs men – for the ruthless efficiency with which they carried out the extermination of not only virtually all Latvian Jews, but also of over 10,000 Reich Jews as well. The men of the Kommando rarely acted alone – for large-scale 'Aktions', German officers were present, while for smaller-scale village killings, the local police usually joined in. They travelled to the killing sites in blue city buses, large enough to hold forty men and their rifles. The buses, manufactured in Sweden for public transport, became ubiquitous signs that a massacre was about to be unleashed. The Kommando had a standard procedure for carrying out executions: ten at a time, victims were told to line up either at the edge of, or inside, a pit. Behind them, ten Kommando members knelt, their rifles aimed at their backs. Behind this first line of executioners, another ten Kommando members stood and took aim at the victims' necks. Those who were not immediately killed were sometimes given 'mercy shots'. Officers with bolt-action rifles guarded the periphery of the killing site.[2] They were young men, usually between sixteen and twenty-one years old. They had been brought up during the authoritarian Ulmanis years, encouraged not to think for themselves. 'People of that age, particularly if they have been brought up "in law-abiding spirit", are easier to manipulate,' Vīksne writes.[3] The men joined for varied reasons: to advance their social position, to fight the Soviets, to avoid manual labour, for the food, for the guns. Some said they had been told that their property would be restituted, or that joining the Kommando was a way of avoiding being mobilised into the German army. Only a handful cited overt dislike of Jews in their applications, though they didn't have to – the propaganda of the day treated 'Jews' and 'communists' as synonymous terms.[4] The number of educated recruits decreased over time, as the actual nature of the work became clear. Some students left after they discovered they were expected to become killers. Boris, though, evidently stayed on.

To try to clarify who my grandfather was – and what he did, and for whom – is to confront endless shadows. The war created a chaotic field of shifting allegiances, names and uniforms. 'There were many families in which older brothers had been mobilized into the Latvian Legion, while younger brothers were drafted into Soviet forces,' Neiburgs writes. 'There were also men who were soldiers in both the German and the Soviet army before the end of the war.'[5] It wasn't difficult to fall through the cracks, to disappear from the record. Still, Boris did leave a few traces: I've found his name in the footnotes of historical monographs, in conspiracist comment sections and in the occasional archival document. A right-wing memorial site lists his dates of birth and death, his 'categories': 'KGB, Member of student's corporation, Nazi, Scout, spy, WWII participant', as well as a purported timeline of his life. The Latvian National Archive turns up a handful of clues: I find his signature on a 2 February 1942 record from the headquarters of the Latvian Security Police. It reads: 'We would like to ask that the following officers from the Latvian Security Police renew their gun licenses': followed by a list of twelve names and birth dates. 1. Arājs, Viktors, 6.12.1910; 3. ZUKURS, Herberts, 17.5.1900; 9. KINSTLERS, Boriss, 20.5.1918. My grandfather signs at the bottom, his role typed out: 'B. Kinstlers. Schriftleiter.' Scribe. In another letter, dated 8 October 1942, Boris petitions the commerce department for permission to allow men returning from the Eastern Front permits to buy tobacco. 'The case involves around 300–400 people a month. We kindly ask for your opinion in writing,' he concludes. His signature suggests that he's had a promotion: 'Ltn. B. Kinstlers, Deputy Head of Administration.' Both letters are signed with the stamp of the SD.

In post-war interrogation records, he comes ever so slightly into focus. The men of the Arājs Kommando – that is, those who didn't disappear, but instead turned up in displaced persons' camps or returned to Riga after the war – were interrogated by the Soviets and the West Germans for accounts of their crimes, for lists of names. The group is estimated to have numbered somewhere between 1,200 and 2,000 men at its peak; only 356 members were captured and convicted by Soviet authorities.[6] It is not known how many of Arājs's men survived the war;[7] by 1944, the unit had been dissolved, its remaining members dispatched to the front lines, including Arājs himself. In 1946, Jānis Brencis, a a former officer of the Kommando, lists the group's members for the benefit of Soviet investigators. Cukurs is the thirtieth name he comes up with.[8] Boris is the 165th. He describes my grandfather as an Untersturmführer, 'not clearly Latvian, about 26 years old, thin, on the shorter side'. Cukurs, by contrast, he remembers as being 'about 45 years old, of medium height, densely built, with a round face and a straight, massive chin, and dark blond hair'. In other testimonies of former Kommando members, I discover glimpses of Boris in action, partial and perhaps fictive recollections of a deeply troubled time: there he is, at the border of a killing trench, in conversation with a fellow soldier about the indignity and injustice of the murders. There he is, in the car with Arājs, speaking 'good German', working as an interpreter. And there he is, according to another testimony, leading a shooting campaign, his gun licence apparently renewed.

It is difficult to speculate about how truthful these accounts are, to discern the fabricated or embellished parts from the factual ones. This is the trouble that haunts all testimony, but especially testimony delivered at the behest of a hostile power, when the testifier is trying to save his own skin. 'Considering the Soviet practices of interrogation, it must not have been difficult to make witnesses testify in the way the interrogator wanted them to,' Vīksne writes. The interrogators were not concerned with specificity. In the criminal files of the captured Kommando members, Vīksne finds only vague descriptions of their complicity, such as 'took part in arrests and executions of Soviet citizens of Jewish origin' or 'volunteered for the auxiliary police service under the enemy's authorities and took part in punitive operations against Soviet citizens'. All that mattered was that they had participated, not where or when or how, if they had pulled the trigger themselves or simply guarded the periphery or stayed in the car and watched their colleagues do so. Once they had been captured and taken into Soviet custody, the former Kommando men were encouraged to confess quickly; no external witnesses were summoned, only fellow Kommando arrestees.[9] During the Stalinist period, the Soviet legal system did not prioritise 'objective proofs', preferring the easy determinations of personal confessions. 'It must also be taken into account that suspects as a rule tried to present themselves in as favorable a light as possible, except for cases when under physical or mental coercion they confessed things they had actually not done,' Vīksne explains. People said whatever they thought they needed to say in order to survive.

These glimpses of my grandfather – be they fabricated, fictional or factual – are all that remain. Even if the details and dates of these encounters are false, their context is enough to confirm his complicity. Of that there is no question. This is not a redemptive story; I have no interest in recuperating my own inheritance. Yet there are other accounts that cannot be omitted, accounts that complicate the narrative. They suggest that, at some point, by force or compulsion or choice, he changed sides. In her study of the KGB interrogation records of former Arājs Kommando members, Vīksne came across accounts that suggest that Boris may not have been quite who he appeared to be. These accounts suggest that he may have been working for the Soviets all along, or at least for some time.

'It is unlikely, despite the rumors, that agents of the Soviet security organs infiltrated the Arājs Kommando from the very beginning in 1941/2. There is no documentary evidence of this and the situation was not conducive to it,' Vīksne writes. 'However, it has occasionally been said that Boris Kinstler, who was Arājs's translator and associate, was a spy in 1941. The criminal files confirm Kinstler's collaboration with the KGB after the war. There is evidence that twelve Commando members had been recruited as agents of the state security during and after the war. Recruitment of agents took place on the basis of compromising material, as employees of state security admitted in writing.'

So he could have been a spy both 'during' and 'after' the war. It is 'unlikely', yet it has 'occasionally been said'. These careful phrases give way to a world of possible meanings. From these words, a million rumours flow.

5

'The trial begins'

My mother forwards me a video on WhatsApp. The app warns me that it has been forwarded many times, that it might be spam. It has been circulating among her emigré friends, bouncing from Riga to Tel Aviv to Düsseldorf to Boston and beyond. I click and out comes the sound of a triumphant marching band and the booming voice of a German newscaster: 'For the third time since 1917, German troops arrive in Riga. This old city with seven hundred years of history has repeatedly shown its close connection to German culture. The invasion of our troops was greeted with jubilation from the people.' It appears to be a scene from July 1941, but the newsreel is undated. Crowds of civilians line the streets, they wave at the processing German soldiers and heil their new leaders. Riga has been liberated, the announcer declares. Latvian flags wave, women and children wear traditional dresses, they smile and laugh. A Wehrmacht officer cracks open a beer, onlookers pass around a block of bread and butter. Suddenly the video cuts to another crowd, standing on the same streets, only three years later. The same victorious music plays, and this crowd, too, smiles and waves, though there are no Latvian flags, no traditional dresses. This time it is the Soviet army processing through the streets. This time, men and women occasionally interrupt the orderly lines of soldiers to deliver kisses and bouquets. 'For three years, the citizens of Riga have been awaiting this meeting,' a Russian announcer declares. 'Riga has been returned to the Soviet nation.'

The video invites viewers to look at the faces in the crowd and wonder: which smiles are genuine, and which are fake? Which parade is the happier one? It acknowledges the ugly fact that both occupying armies received their own parades. That no one in either welcoming party knew what was to come. When I ask my mother about this video, she mentions that as a young boy, my father took part in a re-enactment of the Soviet victory parade for a state-sponsored historical film. He played another version of himself, a good young communist cheering and carrying the red flag.

In 1944, after that second happy parade, the atmosphere in Riga was thick with paranoia. One occupying power had been traded for another. 'The weather, streets, and homes were all gray. People's faces were gray. In the liberated city, a strange way of life took hold,' writes Musya Glants, who was ten years old at the time. 'It seemed that those who had survived the occupation of Riga were hiding behind blacked-out windows. Different people, with different fates, all had the feeling that nothing good would come of the new occupiers.'[1] Latvians remembered the horrors and deportations of the first Soviet occupation, and had good reason to fear that the second time around would be worse. Many of those who had stayed in Latvia went into exile, and those who had been exiled and interned returned to stay. One Jewish survivor, Frank Gordon, told me that he had heard of cases in which 'young Latvian women invited Soviet officers to their apartments, gave them alcohol to drink and later killed them'. I do not know if this is a true story, but perhaps the fact that it has lived on as a revenge fantasy tells us all we need to know.

The Soviets arrived wanting to take their own kind of revenge. Well before the war was over, they began putting Nazi collaborators and officers on trial. The proceedings were called show trials, yet there was a kind of justice to them. It was an ugly, perhaps perverted and certainly abbreviated approach to justice. And yet it was a kind of justice all the same. The Soviet trials were the first to publicly expose the nature of the crimes that were still ongoing, and the obedient, thoughtless nature of the criminals. The Soviets had been preparing for these procedures for some time, collecting evidence of Nazi crimes under the auspices of the 'Extraordinary Investigative Commission into the Crimes

Committed by the German Fascist Invaders and their Collaborators', comprised of 5,000 sub-commissions spread throughout the formerly occupied territory. Officers of the Extraordinary Commission interrogated bystanders, witnesses, survivors; forensic experts were dispatched to mass graves. Some of the Commission's accounts contain wild fabrications and exaggerations, often tripling the already horrifying number of victims.[2] These embellishments would make it easier, later, for Western prosecutors to discount the many truths these reports also contained.

At a computer in the US Holocaust Memorial Museum, I scroll through the commission's reports from Latvia. Some are barely legible, handwritten accounts, documenting the days and hours of the 'Aktions', how the SS and their functionaries organised and transported their victims. One witness underlines the names Arājs and 'Cukurs'. There are accounts from every town, neatly digitised and organised in a drop-down folder. The volume overwhelms. When the novelist Daša Drndić sat before the same state files, looking at testimonies from other territories and towns, she was overcome not by what they documented, but by how much. 'Everything is written in these documents: there is a record of every theft of other people's belongings ... whose house was plundered, who carried out the theft and when, what was taken, and, in some cases, what fate the victims met,' she writes. 'In other words, it is all known. It is known.'[3]

In July 1943, eleven Soviet traitors were put on trial in Krasnodar, a city in southern Russia near the coast of the Black Sea. It was a quick proceeding – in this first trial, it was only their own citizens who were being sentenced and judged, yet it laid the groundwork for the trials to come. The state prosecutor ended his closing statement with this rallying cry: the 'court of history' would deliver its verdict on the fate of the 'traitors, fascist hirelings, and bootlickers' on trial. 'Not one of them will escape stern retribution! Blood for blood, death for death!'[4] Eight defendants were hanged before an applauding crowd in the city square, the execution filmed, photographed and distributed globally.[5]

In October 1943, the Allied powers signed the Moscow Declaration, agreeing that Germans who had participated in atrocities would be put on trial wherever their crimes had been committed. Over the next two months, British Prime Minister Winston Churchill tried to push his cabinet towards adopting a harsher approach, arguing for the creation of a kill list of 'Hitler and Mussolini gangs and the Japanese war lords', who could be shot without penalty. Any of the criminals who fell into Allied hands, he suggested, would be identified by a 'Court of Inquiry' and then 'shot to death within six hours and without reference to higher authority', allowing their captors to sidestep the messy ordeal of an international trial. The 'kill list' was not adopted, but its vengeful sentiment lingered on.[6]

Once the Moscow Declaration was adopted, the Soviets wasted no time putting it to work: in Kharkov, the second largest city in Ukraine which, until 1934, had been the capital of the Ukrainian Soviet Socialist Republic, they organised a war crimes trial designed for international consumption. In December 1943, three Germans and one Soviet traitor stood beneath the Klieg lights of the Kharkov Drama Theatre and pleaded guilty to unspeakable crimes, to having participated in the systematic execution of the city's 'peaceful Soviet citizens'. From the press box, the celebrated Soviet writer Ilya Ehrenburg rejoiced at the momentousness of the trial's opening day, the first day of the first war crimes trial held by any one of the Allied powers:

> I waited a long time for this hour. I waited for it on the roads of France ... I waited for it in the villages of Belarussia, and in the cities of ... Ukraine. I waited for the hour when these words would be heard: 'The trial begins.' Today I heard them. The trial commences. On the dock, beside a traitor, three Germans. These are the first. But these are not the last. We will remember the 15th of December – on this day we stopped speaking about a future trial for the criminals. We began to judge them.[7]

The Kharkov trial began with four guilty pleas and ended, four days later, with four public hangings. It was a dramatic affair, a spectacle that was once again filmed and distributed across the Soviet Union, Britain and the US: the judges, prosecutor and attendants all in uniform, seated upon the illuminated stage; the mezzanine and orchestra packed; the wheels of justice grinding into motion. The Soviets saw the Kharkov trial, like the Krasnodar trial before it, as a model for all that was to come, the first instance of 'the great trial which shall be held of all Hitler's thugs', as the writer Konstantin Simonov put it; the first attempt to try Nazi soldiers and collaborators according to 'the laws and norms of international law'.[8]

Footage of the trial shows the audience in rapt attention; women in floral headscarves, men in Soviet military uniforms taking in the confessions of the accused.[9] From his own perch in the press box, the American journalist Edmund Stevens noticed that 'many of the people in the audience had personal knowledge or experience of the events and atrocities described, and had seen or known the defendants during the German occupation. Several times during more gruesome bits of evidence there were stifled sobs from some woman – not out of pity for the defendants.'[10] In this sense the trial had something in common with the earliest juries of medieval England, when 'jurors were for a time selected based on their pre-existing knowledge of the case and their familiarity with the defendants'.[11] For the audience at Kharkov, the crimes for which the defendants stood accused were painfully fresh. My mother's large Jewish family had been evacuated from the city in 1941, along with all the employees of my great-aunt Dora's manufacturing plant. They ended up in Shymkent, Kazakhstan, with thousands of Soviet families. I wonder what they would have thought had they been in the audience that day; but then again, if they had not been evacuated, they would have already been dead.[12]

The defence counsel at the Kharkov trial pleaded for a more lenient sentencing on the grounds that 'these men were made into assassins by, first of all, killing their souls'.[13] The defendants confessed freely and openly to their crimes, and forensic experts reported on their examination of the mass graves. Watching the confession of the German army captain Wilhelm Langheld, Ehrenburg remarked upon how ordinary he seemed, almost bored by the conclusion of his own life: 'He is used to obeying. He responds calmly, methodically: yes, he killed women, yes, he tortured prisoners. Yes. Yes. Yes.'[14] Another defendant, Second SS

Lieutenant Hans Ritz, a lawyer before the war, argued he had just been following orders, despite admitting that he had 'expressed a desire to be present' when the gas vans were loaded. Asked if the Germans had made any attempts to observe 'the standards of international law', Ritz replied succinctly: 'I must say that on the Eastern Front there was no question of international or any other law.' He had to be propped up on his way to the gallows.[15]

On 26 January 1946, the central hall of Riga's House of Soviet Officers was packed to the rafters. Formerly the home of the Riga Latvian Society, the oldest official Latvian organisation, founded in 1868, the building's gilded interior and art nouveau mosaics had been appropriated for the exclusive use of the Soviet army.[16] The war was over and, 1,600 kilometres away, the Nuremberg Trials were underway, the major war criminals imprisoned, the international press corps beginning to lose their minds with boredom over the protracted nature of the proceedings.

That day in Riga, the trial known as the 'little Nuremberg' began. Seven Nazis stood accused, all of whom had played significant roles in the occupation of Latvia and the massacre of its residents: General Lieutenants Siegfried Ruff, Wolfgang von Ditfurth, Albrecht Baron Digeon von Monteton and Generals Friedrich Werther, Bronislaw Pawel and Hans Küpper.[17] The highest ranking man was the SS *Obergruppenführer* Friedrich Jeckeln, commander for the Baltic states and Belarussia. It was Jeckeln who had been ordered to kill the 30,000 Jews of the Riga ghetto, Jeckeln who had determined how to fulfil this order most efficiently, setting the precise specifications for the construction of the death pits, the ruthless manner in which they should be 'packed'. It was Jeckeln who had ensured that the map of the region under his command sent back to Berlin was dotted with coffins.[18]

The seven defendants wore military uniforms stripped of insignia. Each one was allowed only a brief in-court examination, quickly followed by their sentencing. Most of the time was devoted to witness statements: priests, doctors, soldiers and one fourteen-year-old girl offered their statements to the court, standing up before an audience of their neighbours and speaking into a microphone. For the first three days of the proceedings, a twenty-six-year-old Soviet officer named Peter Krupnikov translated between Latvian, Russian and German for the benefit of all parties involved. Krupnikov had spent the war years as a translator for SMERSH, the Soviet counter-intelligence agency that derived its name from the Russian phrase for 'Death to Spies'.[19] His experience at the 'little Nuremberg' would change the course of his life.

By the time Jeckeln stood up in the auditorium on 3 February 1946, his face gaunt and his hands clasped behind his back, he had been interrogated twenty-nine times at all hours of the day and night. All seven men were swiftly condemned to death by hanging, shoved into black vans and transported to a wide field on the opposite bank of the Daugava River, to what is now called Victory Park.

A massive crowd had gathered to observe the hangings, the first public executions in Riga in over 300 years. Seventeen-year-old Frank Gordon stood among them, watching the seven empty nooses blowing in the wind as they waited for their victims. 'Every detail of the execution was very well orchestrated, with almost, one might add, a German meticulousness,' he writes in his memoirs. The men were driven to the scaffold on parallel truck beds, their eyes open and their hands bound. 'When the nooses were tightened around the necks of the condemned, the trucks slowly drove away and the generals were left hanging,' Gordon remembers. 'A terrible roar rose from the crowd. People were howling and ululating.' After a few minutes, the crowd closed in on the corpses, stripping them of clothes and boots. 'I felt this to be an act of barbarity, but as regards Jeckeln – I felt nothing but deep personal satisfaction,' Gordon writes. 'I felt a bit of pity towards the others – army officers who were caught in this show trial which was organized, let's say it clearly, in order to intimidate the insubordinate Latvians who did not consider themselves "liberated".'

The trial had been carefully choreographed to signal the change in political regime, a sign that the Soviets had returned to Riga and were there to stay. A detailed trial report was published in Latvian. I find a copy of it in an armoire at my father's house, and realise that he has pored over it, looking for any signs of his own surname. I do the same, and, finding none, I stare at the images: the report begins with an image of the Soviet judge-generals in epaulettes at their table and ends with an image of seven lifeless bodies hanging from the scaffold, surrounded by a staring crowd.

6

Come to This Court and Cry

What happened at Nuremberg? We know the story, we have seen the images of that world-historical trial: the carved mahogany courtroom walls, the military guards in white helmets, the defendants wearing headphones, the lawyers in smart suits. The 'Big Nuremberg', so profoundly unlike its 'little' Latvian twin. The 'Big Nuremberg' is remembered as a 'monumental' documentary proceeding, an archival triumph. The reconstitution of the liberal world order, the reinstatement of law.[1] The little Nuremberg, like the little nation in which it took place, is hardly remembered at all.

What we call 'Nuremberg' was the first trial of twenty-four major war criminals, the only trial conducted by the four-power International Military Tribunal (IMT). The official proceedings ran from November 1945 to October 1946 at the Nuremberg Palace of Justice. In his opening speech, US Chief of Counsel Robert H. Jackson underscored the validity of the 'novel and experimental' tribunal and acknowledged its unprecedented stakes: 'We must never forget that the record on which we judge these defendants today is the record on which history will judge us tomorrow. To pass these defendants a poisoned chalice is to put it to our own lips as well.'[2] He urged the court to 'dispose of the contention that to put these men to trial is to do them an injustice entitling them to some special consideration'. There was no good alternative to a trial, Jackson argued. The defendants would do well to recognise that the tribunal was their last and only hope: 'If these men are the

first war leaders of a defeated nation to be prosecuted in the name
of the law, they are also the first to be given a chance to plead for
their lives in the name of the law,' he proclaimed.

The 'twenty-odd broken men' on the prisoners' dock were
'living symbols of racial hatreds, of terrorism and violence, and
of the arrogance and cruelty of power,' Jackson said. 'They are
symbols of fierce nationalisms and militarism, of intrigue and
war-making which have embroiled Europe generation after
generation ...' But the court did not have to take his word, or
anyone else's, for it. 'If I should recite these horrors in words of
my own, you would think me intemperate and unreliable,' he
said. 'Fortunately, we need not take the word of any witness but
the Germans themselves.'[3]

Jackson was concerned about the fallibility of witness testimony.
From the very beginning, the survivors' remembrances were only
somewhat trusted. Accordingly, he did his best to ensure that
the evidence presented at trial would consist primarily of written
records rather than spoken words. 'The decision ... was to use
and rest on documentary evidence to prove every point possible,'
he would later write of his reasoning.[4] Documents, photographs
and films of the concentration camps were presented to the Allied
judges. These artefacts would tell the story of Nazi atrocities, more
so than the words of those who had managed to live through
them. The Evidence Room at the Palace of Justice was a sight to
behold.

Still, so much was as yet unknown: When the tribunal opened
in 1945, neither the prosecution nor the public had grasped the
full scale and scope of Nazi crimes, despite the mountains of
documents piling up nearby. Documentation of the killings was
scattered across Europe; Allied intelligence services were still
collecting information. In July 1945, Jackson visited Berlin; in the
Reich Chancellery, he saw that Hitler's desk 'was overturned in his
room and that letters addressed to Goering were strewn about'.[5]
Files from the Wannsee Conference, where Hitler's 'Final Solution'
was presented to the Nazi leadership, would not be found until
the spring of 1947. Despite Jackson's aspirations, the prosecutors

thus had no choice but to rely upon witnesses to make their case. 'We wanted to find out as much as possible as quickly as possible,' Robert Kempner, the assistant US chief counsel, said in an interview with the journalist Christiane Kohl in 1987. 'That meant talking to certain people with whom one might not otherwise have shared a cup of tea.'[6] Witnesses were used to contextualise the documentary evidence, to underscore the guilt of the accused. In some instances, Nazis who had already been sentenced were called to the stand to testify against their former colleagues.[7]

It also meant that the prosecution relied overwhelmingly upon the evidence that was available, the vast majority of which had to do with the genocide visited upon Eastern Europe. 'The Eastern Jew has suffered as no people ever suffered. Their sufferings were carefully reported to the Nazi authorities to show faithful adherence to the Nazi design,' Jackson said in his opening speech. He invited his audience to look at a 15 October 1941 report from Einsatzgruppe A, in which the Nazi leadership gloats about their successful actions in the Baltic states, about their ability to induce 'Native anti-Semitic forces' to 'start pogroms against the Jews during the first hours after occupation'. He quoted a passage from the report that references the Arājs Kommando and its 'extensive executions':

From the beginning it was to be expected that the Jewish problem in the East could not be solved by pogroms alone. In accordance with the basic orders received, however, the cleansing activities of the Security Police had to aim at a complete annihilation of the Jews. Special detachments reinforced by selected units in Lithuania – partisan detachments, in Latvia units of the Latvian auxiliary police – therefore performed extensive executions both in the towns and in rural areas. The actions of the execution detachments were performed smoothly.[8]

As Jackson read out these words, a detachment of Latvian guards clad in American military uniforms were helping monitor the accused and patrol the Palace of Justice complex.[9] Just as their

national identities were masked, so, too, was the full truth of the
misfortunes that had been visited upon their region.

What happened in the Baltics – the way the Soviets conspired
with Nazi Germany to invade their territory, and the deportations
and deaths that followed – was one of the central concerns of the
proceedings. There were some things – deportations, massacres,
protocols – that the Soviets did not want aired in public. The
Allies sought to expose Nazi war crimes in the Baltic states and
throughout Eastern Europe, but had to tiptoe around the subject
of Soviet atrocities and aggression in the same territories. To call
attention to them would risk undermining the collective Allied
case. When the Soviets tried to use the indictment to claim official
control over the Baltics, and to pin the massacre of 22,000 Polish
soldiers at Katyn on the Nazis, the other Allied powers had little
choice but to quietly assent and hope those matters would not
come up in court.[10] The fate of the Baltics was at once the subject
at the centre of the trial, and all too often the thing which could
not be said.

In her impressive history of the Nuremberg tribunal, Francine
Hirsch documents how the Soviet prosecution team strained to
conceal inconvenient truths about the conduct of its countrymen.
At one point during the proceedings, the Soviet delegation
requested that their fellow prosecutors refrain from bringing up
anything to do with 'the socio-political structure of the USSR'
or 'the Soviet Baltic Republics',[11] which had recently come under
their control and which they were actively trying to subdue. The
Soviet prosecutors were terrified that the existence of the secret
protocols of the 1939 Molotov–Ribbentrop Non-Aggression
Pact, in which Soviet and Nazi leadership had agreed to divvy up
Eastern Europe, would be exposed. In the secret protocols, the
Soviets had claimed Finland, Estonia and Latvia; the Germans
claimed Lithuania and a large swathe of Poland. When the
Big Nuremberg began, none of this was public information.
Unfortunately for the Soviets, the fact that Ribbentrop, Hitler's
foreign minister, sat among the accused meant that the Pact did
not stay secret for long.

The Allied prosecutors confronted a destroyed and devastated world, and through their deliberate choice of words – the four counts against the accused were 'conspiracy', 'crimes against peace', 'war crimes' and 'crimes against humanity', in that order – tried to marshal the full power of law towards its reconstitution. Robert Kempner, the assistant US chief counsel, famously described the proceedings as 'the greatest history seminar ever held'.[12]

After nearly a year of proceedings, twelve of the twenty-four original defendants were sentenced to death for crimes against peace, crimes against humanity and war crimes. One of them, Hitler's chosen successor Hermann Goering, managed to kill himself with a cyanide pill in his cell before his execution date.[13] Three of them – the Nazi minister of economics, his personal aide and deputy and the commander of the German navy – were sentenced to life in prison (only one of them, Rudolf Hess, served the full term).[14] Four were sentenced to ten to twenty years in prison. Three others – a senior propagandist, the one-time head of the Reichsbank and the former Nazi ambassador to Austria – were acquitted.

Soon afterwards, the fragile post-war accord between the Allied powers began to fray. From the very beginning of the military tribunal, Allied representatives had struggled to make the requirements of their judicial systems compatible with one another. The Americans and British had presumed that the trials would proceed according to the adversarial procedures of common law, in which accusations of guilt would have to be cross-examined and argued in court. The Soviets and the French, on the other hand, operated according to the inquisitorial system of civil law, in which evidence is collected, prepared and evaluated by an examining magistrate and prosecutor before the start of proceedings. The Soviet delegation had assumed that SS and Gestapo members would be presumed guilty, given that they were members of criminal organisations. As far as they were concerned, the men on trial were already irredeemably guilty; the tribunal was there to tell the world of their crimes and make a spectacle of their sentencing. The Americans were repulsed by this thought: 'Jackson warned that no American judge would accept this formula, which made no provision for the organization to defend itself,' Hirsch writes.[15]

In late 1946, the British, French and Soviet delegations packed up and left the court in the hands of the Americans, who would unilaterally conduct the twelve successor trials of Nazi functionaries in their custody – these, too, were little Nurembergs, though of a different kind. From 1946 to 1948, the Americans oversaw the prosecution of Nazi doctors, judges, industrialists and SS officers. On 30 July 1948, twenty-four former employees of the German chemical conglomerate IG Farben were sentenced for contributing to the waging of an aggressive war. A subsidiary of IG Farben had manufactured Zyklon B, the gas used to murder millions of concentration camp inmates. Of the twenty-four IG Farben defendants, eleven were acquitted, among them the head of chemical research and members of the SS and SA. The harshest sentences were reserved for those who had helped construct the IG Farben plants near Auschwitz, where camp inmates were sent to work on creating the materials of their own annihilation. The men who built and oversaw those factories received a maximum of eight years in prison, including time served.[16]

To repeat these paltry sentences is to contend with their abiding inadequacy. In their closing statements at the Nuremberg tribunal, the prosecutors appealed to all of humanity, defended the way the trials were conducted and begged for harsh punishments. Roman Rudenko, the Soviet prosecutor, asked for the death penalty for all defendants: 'And in the name of the sincere love of mankind which inspires the peoples who consented to the greatest sacrifices in order to save the world, freedom and culture, in memory of the millions of innocent human beings slaughtered by a gang of murderers, who are now before the Court of a progressive mankind, I appeal to the Tribunal to sentence all the defendants without exception to the supreme penalty.'[17] The French chief prosecutor, Auguste Champetier de Ribes, underscored the wide circle of culpability that enabled such ruination, and emphasised how the defendants' crimes differed from those of an ordinary criminal. 'Genocide, murder, or any other crime becomes anonymous when it is committed by the State. Nobody bears the chief responsibility. Everybody shares it – those who by their presence maintain and support the administration, those who conceived the crime and those who ordained it, as well as he who issued the order,' de Ribes said. 'As for the executioner, he says to himself, "*Befohl ist Befehl*," "An order is an order," and carries out his hangman's task.'[18]

Jackson used his closing statement to defend, once again, the fact there had been a trial at all. 'Of one thing we may be sure. The future will never have to ask, with misgiving, what could the Nazis have said in their favor. History will know that whatever could be said, they were allowed to say. They have been given the kind of trial which they, in the days of their pomp and power, never gave to any man,' he said. 'The extraordinary fairness of these hearings is an attribute of our strength.'[19]

But it was the concluding speech of the British chief prosecutor, Sir Hartley Shawcross, that roused the courtroom to attention, for it was he who conjured the perturbing image of 'mankind itself', bedraggled and struggling, taking up a seat at the courtroom, begging for justice. Shawcross quoted Goethe, the great German poet, prophesying that fate would strike the German people for their willingness to 'ingenuously submit to any mad scoundrel who appeals to their lowest instincts'. He enumerated the various roles that each of the defendants played in aiding and abetting mass murder, all the different strains of criminality represented in the dock. All of them, he said, deserved death: 'What matters it if some forfeited their lives only a thousand times whilst others deserved a million deaths?'

Over and above all, he said, the trial would ensure that 'the rights of men, made as all men are made in the image of God', would assert themselves over the prerogatives of state and nation. The Nuremberg tribunal gave us the concept of 'human rights' and laid the groundwork for the adjudication of their violation the world over. They also established bitter truths about the abiding injustices of our time: some crimes are so horrid that no punishment will suffice, no amount of reckoning can undo what has been done or prevent the same terrible crimes from recurring.

If Jackson wanted the judges to imagine that the accused stood for all that was sinful and unholy in mankind – racial hatreds, fierce nationalism, arrogance, cruelty – Shawcross wanted the judges to imagine that everyone else in the courtroom – the notetakers, clerks, guards, lawyers – represented what could still be salvaged. It was for this reason that he asked them to rule as if all of humanity had been called to the witness stand and permitted to address the court in a single, unified voice: 'And so, after this ordeal to which mankind has been submitted, mankind itself – struggling now to re-establish in all the countries of the world the common simple things – liberty, love, understanding – comes to this Court and cries: "These are our laws – let them prevail!"'

Shawcross hoped 'our laws' would prevail, yet when he uttered these words, neither he nor his colleagues on the prosecution quite understood to whom the 'our' referred. The Nuremberg tribunal was the product of a hodgepodge of legal interpretations and aspirations; much was lost in translation, literally and figuratively. It delivered a kind of justice, but that justice was not enough to avenge everyone who had been lost, not enough reconstruct the European continent, not enough to reconstitute its laws. Not enough to grant peace to the next generation, to those who had survived. No court can undo what has been done, no matter how it may try. In this light, Shawcross's closing words can only be read as a kaddish, a prayer for the dead: come to this court and cry.

7

The Committee Men

The telegrams flew all over the world. From London and Munich, on they went to New York, Manila, Toronto, Los Angeles, Rio de Janeiro and Tel Aviv. Nuremberg had inaugurated a short and swift frenzy of war crimes trials; the Tribunal had established a list of criminal Nazi organisations, setting the precedent that enabled any and all of their members to be tried. For a brief moment after the war, the Allies had hundreds of Nazis in custody. Now they needed witnesses to tell them who all these men really were, and what they had done.

Many of these missives passed through the letterbox at 55 New Cavendish Street, a Georgian townhouse in Marylebone, London, which for a time in the late 1940s served as the headquarters of both the World Jewish Congress and the Committee for the Investigation of Nazi Crimes in the Baltic Countries.[1] Its tenant was a man named Herman Michelson, an independent Jewish businessman who served as chairman and treasurer of the Committee and a leader of the World Jewish Congress. From his offices in London, Michelson was overseeing a worldwide search for evidence, sending marching orders and encouragements to Baltic refugees all around Europe. He had made it his mission to see to it that those who had been captured stood trial, and that those who were still at large would be found.

In 1949, the list of those in custody included Viktors Arājs, who had been identified in a displaced persons' camp in the British Zone of

Germany. Arājs was to be a major defendant in what British officials had begun referring to as the 'Riga Ghetto Case', a group trial of sixteen war criminals to be conducted by an Allied Control Council Court, the court of the governing body of the German occupied zones.[2] Michelson had spent years collecting evidence for the case, dispatching his friends and colleagues to provide depositions to the crimes they had witnessed. He was a central node in a vast network of Jewish refugee organisations large and small all around the world; in the late 1940s, this network was working at a furious speed to collect all the testimonies they could, to document the Holocaust while the survivors' memories were still fresh.[3]

Among those whom Michelson recruited to his cause was a young Latvian refugee named Edward Alperovitch, a man who, when I met him in his old age, recalled the details of this period with scientific specificity. Born in 1926 to Jewish parents in Liepāja, Alperovitch had grown up speaking German at home, his parents reserving Russian for conversations they did not want their two sons to overhear. His father Adolf worked in the family's grain export business; his mother Erica had worked as a clerk in the district office of the German military administration during the First World War, and later did private tutoring. They were a well-to-do family, part of the town's lively Jewish community.

The Second World War began as Alperovitch was starting to attend an all-boys technical school. 'Though Soviet troops were now swarming through the streets of my hometown, and German troops were only 70 km away, we did not anticipate the coming danger and made no effort to emigrate,' he writes in his memoir. 'There were reasons, of course: most countries were not exactly vying for immigrants (especially Jews), my father was not sure whether he could support us in a new country, his export business was going well at last, and he did not want to abandon his mother and other elderly relatives. And the Soviet-German nonaggression pact of August 1939 seemed to assure peace in our corner of the world. When Hitler in October 1939 summoned Baltic Germans "home to the Reich", we misinterpreted this signal, thinking that now he would have no reason to invade the Baltic countries.'

In June 1940, 'the first of several disasters' befell the Alperovitch family when the Soviets occupied Latvia. His father Adolf's bank accounts were frozen, and because Adolf was a businessman he was immediately branded as a class enemy. The grain business itself was seized and 'nationalised' as Soviet property – Adolf was permitted to keep only his debts and became an employee at his own company. Around this time, some of Alperovitch's acquaintances began emigrating to Nazi Germany, they feared the Soviets so much. In June 1941, the first deportations began. Families were rounded up and placed on trains bound for Siberia.

On 14 June, the Alperovitch family received a phone call telling them to pack one suitcase each. It was their turn to go. Luckily, one of their lodgers happened to be a major in the Soviet paramilitary unit patrolling the border. They asked him to intervene on their behalf, and he obligingly had their names erased from the deportation list.

Fifteen days later, the Nazis arrived in the city. 'Within hours things became harsh,' Alperovitch writes. His parents thought the war would be over within a year, so they hatched a lie to disguise their identities. Erica was to claim that as a baby she had been left on the doorstep of a Jewish family 'with a note bearing only her first name and a cross, indicating that she was Christian'. That would mean that Edward and his brother Georg, both of them blond-haired and blue-eyed, would be half-Jewish and, for the time being, exempt from Nazi race laws. They worried that people in the neighbourhood would give them away – their neighbours and friends had known Erica's parents, and knew very well that she was not a foundling – but the plan worked. 'As it turned out,' Alperovitch writes, 'the people who knew didn't want to hurt us and those who wanted to hurt us did not know.'

His father Adolf had no clever ruse to resort to. He soon went into hiding in the family home, running into the pantry whenever anyone came to the door. Then, one day in early December, ten policemen showed up and took both of Alperovitch's parents away. His mother returned six days later; Adolf did not. She later found out that he had been killed the following day, on 9 December.

On 15 December, they came for the boys. The newspaper had announced the 'Aktion' just days prior, in a few sinister lines hidden beneath an article about the price of Christmas trees: 'Jews were not allowed to leave their homes on Monday December 15, 1941 and Tuesday December 16, 1941.' Signed, the Commandant of the SS and the Liepāja police.[4] Latvian policemen woke Edward and Georg in their beds and marched them to the Women's Prison, where they stood in line and waited to be killed. They saw groups of Liepāja Jews being marched towards the beach, to the rolling dunes of Šķēde. The boys pleaded with a German policeman to let them go; they showed him the passes stating that they were only half-Jewish. 'He stared at us for a long five seconds (presumably running through his checklist of Jewish racial characteristics), and then dismissed us with a single word – 'geht' ('go') – Alperovitch recalls. For the next three days, they watched those they had stood in line with, their classmates and their parents, being driven and marched to the killing site. An SD man took photographs of the 'Aktion', capturing young children cowering behind one another, women trying to preserve their modesty and families marching towards the firing line. In groups of twenty, the Jews of Liepāja were told to undress and line up on the side of a pit dug into the sand as a firing squad took aim from behind. The last thing they saw was the bitter chop of the winter waves crashing upon the shore. Edward Alperovitch would spend the rest of his life working to preserve their memories, documenting their murders in detail, doing what he could to hold their murderers to account.

He survived the war by working odd jobs, mostly in construction, and benefiting from the protection of a man named Fritz Müller, a Stuttgart architect sent to Liepāja with the German army, who disdained Nazi rule and once told Edward that 'it would be no calamity if the German nation ceased to exist after the end of the war'. '[H]is remark made me realize that individuals are more important than nations,' Alperovitch writes. In 1944, Edward and his mother boarded a ship of refugees bound for Danzig (his brother Georg died of typhoid at the start of the year). They ended up, in October 1945, in a displaced persons' (DP) camp in Munich, where

Alperovitch was able to resume his scientific studies at a temporary university run by the United Nations Relief and Rehabilitation Association. They were greeted and processed by the Central Committee of Liberated Jews in the US Zone of Germany, which at the time 'operated very casually', he told me. The clerk who greeted the Alperovitches informed them that refugees who had survived concentration camps were entitled to better food rations and housing. Edward and his mother had never been interned, so, 'the clerk quickly invented a new camp, Stargard in Pomerania', where they had been supposedly imprisoned. (In reality, they had briefly stayed at a camp for Baltic refugees in the same region.) 'He redefined [the DP camp] as a concentration camp and issued us about ¼-sized pieces of paper claiming that we had been in KZ Stargard [*Konzentrationslager* Stargard] with consecutive, fictitious four-digit prison numbers like 1573 and 1574,' Alperovitch told me via email. 'A month or two later I had occasion to show my KZ pass to a US military government official, who already knew that such passes were given to practically all newcomers.'[5]

His mother became the secretary of a group called the Federation of Liberated Latvian Jews in the US Zone of Germany, and Edward joined as well. They lived in a single furnished room in Munich; there, Edward would draft letters and his mother would type them up. One of their group's main functions was to collect testimonies that could be used in identifying and trying war criminals. Soon, Edward became the Committee's war crimes representative. In this capacity, he regularly corresponded with Michelson in London, who sent him lists of suspects in British custody and requests for testimonies that could speak to their wartime activities. It was Edward's job to circulate these requests among survivors in German displaced persons' camps, to collect all the evidence he could find. On 19 September 1948 he wrote to the Central Committee in Munich, updating them on his progress collecting evidence against a particular suspect: Herberts Cukurs. 'In connection with your above-mentioned letter we also inform you that Harry Moglinitzky, David Fishkin, Max Tukacier can testify against the criminal Cukurs,' Alperovitch writes, in Yiddish. 'It is to be presumed that a lot more witnesses will be gathered if it were to become known that Cukurs has been arrested.'[6] The testimonies were damning: Tukacier wrote that he had seen Cukurs ruthlessly beating Jews at the headquarters of the Kommando, that he had watched as Cukurs selected detainees from the basement in groups of ten and hustled them upstairs, from where he heard the sound of gunshots echo. Fishkin reported seeing Cukurs shoot 'about 500' Jewish people in and around the Riga ghetto, describing how he shot at stragglers who could not keep up with their columns as well as at children who dared to cry out.

During this time, Alperovitch came across a call for witnesses for the last and final war crimes trial at Nuremberg, the trial of the German High Command. The court was seeking to examine the extent to which the German army had participated in the roundups and extermination of Europe's Jewish communities alongside the SS and the Gestapo. Alperovitch had one key piece of evidence to offer the prosecution, a memory of the executions in Liepāja that 'strongly implicated German Field Marshal Wilhelm Ritter von Leeb, Commander of Army Group North'. Von Leeb had overseen the German army's occupation of the Baltic states as part of Operation Barbarossa. He was the highest ranking of the thirteen army officers on trial; the suit was formally named *The United States of America* vs. *Wilhelm von Leeb et al.*

The Americans hoped that this last Nuremberg trial would help nudge Germany towards democracy by exposing the criminality and culpability of its military officers, who at the time still enjoyed a fair amount of social and political prestige.[7] Von Leeb stood accused of the same four counts as the twenty-two men tried at the International Military Tribunal: crimes against peace, war crimes, crimes against humanity and conspiracy. The prosecution sought to prove that he was aware of the confiscation and looting of Jewish property, and that he and his men knew of the mass killings and participated in the executions. When von Leeb took the stand, he claimed not to have known that Jews had been ordered to wear 'identifying insignia', not to have known of or participated in looting ('I can only say here that neither in the First World War nor in the Second World War did I take as much as a cigarette away from anybody,' he said) and not to have known that the Jews had been ordered to live in ghettos. He also claimed that it was only the SD, and none of the men under his command, who participated in the killing of Latvian Jews. Presented with documents that suggested otherwise, von Leeb and his co-defendants contorted the words on the page: the prosecutor Walter H. Rapp complained to the judge that 'when it said in a document hundreds of Jews looted; we were told that it doesn't mean a hundred Jews; that it [m]erely means one hundred Jews had gone to the doctor'.

Alperovitch had been summoned to counter von Leeb's denials. The prosecution interrogated him three times before allowing him to appear in court, asking him about what he had heard and seen during the German invasion of Liepāja, and how he had survived. Alperovitch remembered that the trucks he had seen rolling through town and rounding up Jews had been marked with the letters *WH* or *WM* – the W stood for Wehrmacht. He spent about a week living in a room with four other men, all witnesses, swapping crude and terrifying stories of survival. He was called to the witness stand in the Palace of Justice on 2 August 1948, to be cross-examined by Rapp, who was also the head of the Evidence Division. Alperovitch delighted in the reversal of fortune that the Allied victory had brought: 'It was strange to see these famous generals from the topmost ranks of the Third Reich seated in the dock, and even more so, to encounter them in the WC,' he writes. 'These wizened old men had been the terror of Europe, but now they stood at the urinals, still in their uniforms but wearing slippers instead of jackboots, each with a towering black MP [military policeman] behind him.'

By the time Alperovitch appeared on the witness stand, the trial had already reached its final stages. The prosecution hoped his testimony might be admitted as rebuttal evidence, claiming it directly contradicted von Leeb's defence. Alperovitch told the court that only forty of Liepāja's 8,000 Jews survived. 'I saw German soldiers who carried furniture, house utensils, radios and so forth away from Jewish dwellings,' he said. 'After that more than thirty men were shot in the northerly part of town, amongst them the father of one of my school friends.'

'Why was that?' Rapp asked.

'Only because they were Jews,' Alperovitch answered. He told the court that he had walked by their bodies.

At this point, von Leeb's lawyers objected to the introduction of new evidence at such a late stage. Rapp and the American prosecutor Kurt Ponger fought for two days for Alperovitch's testimony to be admitted; they told the judge that they felt they had already proven their case on the basis of documents alone, but that it wasn't enough. '[W]hen the defendants took the stand they told this Tribunal that what was in the documents wasn't really true; it doesn't mean what it says. The Court must learn to interpret the way these men have learned to interpret in their career,' Rapp said. 'They were fictitious reports; they were not really real reports. Therefore, we ought to be able now to rebut such allegations.'

The judge disagreed, chastising Rapp for not producing Alperovitch as a witness earlier in the proceedings. The defence's objection was sustained, and Alperovitch's short testimony was struck from the record. 'Too bad, because von Leeb (70) – a vicious anti-Semite since at least WWI – was sentenced to only 3 years,' Alperovitch writes in his memoir. He had arrived in Nuremberg just a few weeks too late.

The trial of the High Command did little to turn German public opinion against the military, nor did it educate civilians about the Wehrmacht's crimes. Von Leeb's three-year sentence included time served; he was released right after the trial concluded. Alperovitch, for his part, returned to Munich and spent the next few months resuming his work for the Federation of Liberated Jews. Michelson asked if he might help collect evidence for a much-anticipated 'Riga Ghetto trial', a trial of SS men, including Viktors Arājs, who had participated in the Nazi occupation in Latvia and now found themselves in British custody. Alperovitch dutifully accepted this new charge.

But on 18 May 1949, a disappointing letter came through the letterbox at 55 New Cavendish Street. It came from a prominent author: Major F. Elwyn-Jones, MP, who had served under Shawcross as one of the junior counsels for the United Kingdom at Nuremberg. He wrote with poor tidings: 'Dear Mr. Michelson, I have now received a statement from the Foreign Office about the Riga Ghetto case'. The British would not be pursuing a ghetto trial after all.

Elwyn-Jones copied out a letter from the foreign secretary, Ernest Bevin. In a Lords debate the previous week, Bevin explained, a peer had announced that 'all future cases of crimes against humanity involving allied or United Nations victims, as well as those in which the victims were of German nationality, will be tried by German courts,' Bevin wrote. Arājs's case was being 'brought to the attention of German authorities', and, as for the other men in custody, well, the evidence just did not suffice. 'There is no doubt that the crimes committed in and near Riga were ghastly,' Bevin wrote, but 'the extent to which the persons who have been apprehended participated in these crimes is, however, of course another matter, and I am informed that much of the evidence submitted concerning the notions of individuals and their participation in events is in fact hearsay.'[8]

Viktors Arājs would remain in British custody at a displaced persons' camp until West German authorities came for him. That day came on 11 October 1949, when an arrest warrant for Arājs was issued in Hamburg. But the warrant could not be served. 'For reasons that are not clear to this day and probably never will be,' Richards Plavnieks writes, 'Arājs was simply absent from the camp in which he was supposed to be interned.'[9] Amidst all the bureaucratic shuffle, he had found a way to make himself disappear.

8

The Victory Day Parade

I sat with my father at his dining-room table in California, a folder of archival documents and photographs spread out before us. He began telling me a story I had never heard before. It is an unverifiable, mysterious and almost surreal story. It goes like this:

It is 9 May 1949. Victory Day, four years since the surrender of German forces. There is a parade in the centre of Riga. The newspapers feature portraits of Stalin, covered in military medals. My grandmother Biruta joins the celebrating crowd outside. She is five months pregnant. It has been just over a month since the Soviet authorities deported 30,000 residents of Latvia – including 10,000 children – to Siberia. On that same day, 25 March 1949, she and Boris had married. It has been almost a month since her new husband left on what he said was a routine business trip. It has been only a few weeks since she was notified of his alleged suicide.

She watches the parade wind through Riga's sprawling boulevards. Out of the procession, two women emerge and walk towards her. They give my grandmother a watch and a letter. These are supposed to serve as proof of Boris's death, but my grandmother doesn't believe it. It wasn't his watch. She is summoned to KGB headquarters in Riga, a terraced art-deco building known as the 'Corner House'. The officers confiscate the letter and the watch. They tell her not to go looking for the body.

What was in the letter? I ask my father. He doesn't know. Maybe he never asked, or maybe my grandmother did not want to say. She died in 2002, before I knew anything of this story, before I knew just how many questions there were to pose. She kept no diaries, no notes. All my father knows is the version of the story that his mother told him, which he is now passing on to me. The story ends like this: one day in 1963, she is summoned back to KGB headquarters. The officers want to know: has she heard anything from Boris?

*

Biruta and Boris met outside the anatomical theatre one day in late 1947, maybe early 1948. It is an unmissable building that still stands on the bank of the Daugava River, at the intersection of three tram tracks. The exterior is almost Moorish, ornamented with sand-coloured curves and golden six-pointed stars. The stars catch my eye – how could any building glinting with Jewish stars have survived the war? I read that it was built as a Greek Orthodox Seminary, completed in 1879 – thus the stars, ancient symbols of creation. Today, it is the Institute of Anatomy and Anthropology at Riga Stradiņš University. 'This is the place where the dead help the living', its website reads. 'Hic locus est ubi mors gaudet, sucurrere vitae.'[1]

Biruta is a medical student on her way home after a day of coursework. Boris just happens to be passing by. They recognise one another from their schooldays in Liepāja. They lost track after that; each is probably happy to see that the other is alive. By then, Biruta had been married and widowed. Boris had been taken as a prisoner of war in May 1945, transferred twice before he was released a year and a half later, in January 1947. He is dressed in plainclothes; he tells her he works as an insurance salesman.

I imagine that they have a short and easy courtship, more of a reunion than a new love affair. There are only a few photographs of Biruta and Boris together as young lovers. In one, dated 1948, they stand next to each another in a large family photo on the grounds of our summerhouse in the village of Bauska. Another photograph, which I find tucked into the pages of my Baby Book, shows them alone together in a field. It looks to be from the same day as the group photo – Boris wears wide khaki trousers and an oversized suit jacket with a pocket handkerchief, a cigarette in hand. Biruta stands next to him in a floral summer dress and cardigan, her hands clasped behind her back. Their wedding is commemorated in two photographs: the first shows them sitting on a bench outside the clerk's office, my grandmother in a black dress, hands wrapped in a fur muff. Boris is in a suit and a checked tie, his hair gelled and combed. The second shows Biruta signing what must be their marriage certificate while Boris looks on. He becomes part of her family and then he disappears. My grandmother was taken care of: she would get a position at a good hospital in Riga. Soviet officials and their families found themselves in her dental chair. A decade after her death, I find her fur muff in a closet in the summerhouse. It has become rough and dehydrated with age, the animal's eyes and claws shiny and fragile; I mistake it for a carcass.

There were rumours about Boris. So many stories to sift through and choose from. One that seems plausible, even likely, is that the KGB recruited him to help identify German collaborators. Boris would walk around Riga with a pair of KGB officers on his tail. Whenever he recognised a man from his time in the Arājs Kommando, he'd walk up to him, tap him on the shoulder, greet him like an old friend. The shoulder tap was the signal that the man was a target. Another rumour: Boris shielded Biruta from the second round of Soviet deportations by taking her on a ride in his car. That way, she wouldn't be in the house when the authorities came calling. More rumours: that he had been spotted in East Germany, or in South America. That there wouldn't be a body because Boris was still alive.

Biruta never accepted the official story of her husband's death. His death notice says he killed himself in Sillamäe, in Estonia, which at the time was a 'closed' Soviet city, the site of the USSR's uranium mines. One had to have a permit to exit and enter; the town had been carefully excised from maps of the region. What had Boris been doing there? Where would he have procured a gun? Could something have happened on his trip that made him want to die?

Had he been planning it all along? Or was there more to the story? Biruta told my father that Boris took nearly every photograph of himself, every document of his life, with him when he left. All that remains are, quite literally, scraps. My father tells me that he has a photo of his father that has been 'cut off, with scissors'. The edge is uneven; someone or something was clipped from the frame. He warns me that in this image my grandfather is wearing a black leather jacket. 'Gestapo-like,' he says. He sends me the image on WhatsApp, and I see that his description was unsettlingly accurate: there is Boris in a long black leather jacket, seated on the grass in front of what is probably Biruta's country house and squinting into the sun. He cradles a bouquet of wildflowers in his leather coat sleeves.

In the archive, I find the scraps that Boris could not make disappear. The Latvian National Archives hold a copy of Boris's 'KGB Card', an index card listing his name, birthdate, address and date of registration, 14 February 1947, in elaborate Cyrillic letters. After the Soviet Union collapsed in 1991, bags full of these index cards were discovered in the basement of the abandoned KGB headquarters. They became known as the 'Cheka bags', after the original name of the KGB, and began to occupy a curious role in political life. They contained the names of KGB informers and agents throughout Latvia, many of whom held positions of influence in Latvia's new, European political system. For three decades, they were kept hidden away from the public, accessible only via the Latvian National Archives, and only to those who wanted to take a look at their own files. And then, one day in 2019, they were published online in alphabetical order, freely available for everyone with a Latvian national ID to see. It was supposed to be a kind of national exercise in repentance and confession, a ritual cleansing. One judge called it a 'matter of hygiene'.[2]

People looked up their friends, relatives and neighbors in attempts to discover who had been informing on them in the post-war period. They wondered if the archive would reveal the secrets of their pasts. Sometimes the archive spits out information, sometimes it stays silent. Both of these outcomes are devastating, each in their own way.

The KGB cards in the Latvian archive cannot be blindly trusted. It is impossible to know how many of the cards were real, and what they meant. Why had these particular cards been left behind in the basement, and not others? Were they plants, designed to foment maximum unrest and suspicion? What did it take to have a card on file? One meeting with the authorities? Two? In a film interview with documentary journalists shortly before his death, the last head of the Latvian KGB, a man named Edmunds Johansons, sits behind his old desk and tells reporters that the files that were left behind were the least important ones, the ones that the Soviets could afford to lose. 'It's like a hot potato in your mouth, understand – you can't eat it, you can't spit it out. That's how it is with the files, and that's how it's going to be,' he tells them. 'You can't prove anything, so basically it's like ... fighting with windmills.'

You can't prove anything. What does it take to 'prove' that a crime was committed fifty years ago, or seventy, or a hundred? What does 'proof' even mean, in a twice-occupied nation, a nation that has had its people and property killed, burned and stolen, displaced and discredited? The state has changed its language, its legal system, its way of thinking and speaking and ruling. The national narrative had been radically altered one too many times. If evidence is the grammar of the trial, under these circumstances one can hardly begin to form a sentence.[3]

Nevertheless, one has to try. The archive still has some things to reveal. Uldis Neiburgs, the Latvian historian and family friend, asks an Estonian colleague if there might be any records of Boris's journey north, any documents or newspaper announcements mentioning a suicide in Sillamäe. 'Dear Uldis, The story – if it is true in all its components – seems like a typical intelligence fiction novel,' the colleague, a historian named Toomas Hiio, responds. He could not find anything about Boris in the KGB records from that era, but said that it would have been easy for Boris to obtain a pistol if he had wanted to. 'A classmate of my father's once told me that at the end of the 1940s, almost all teenage schoolboys in his village school had their own rifles hidden somewhere. The forests in the vicinities of Tallinn were full of arms and explosives,' he writes. But given Boris's KGB connections, he wasn't sure that the suicide story should be taken at face value: 'Did he really commit suicide, or did he simply disappear for some other purpose? Secondly, if he really died in April 1949, did he commit suicide or was he simply liquidated? Thirdly, why was he sent to Sillamäe three weeks after the mass deportations? Fourthly, if he was sent there to identify his former colleagues in the Arājs Kommando, perhaps something about Kinstlers might be found in one of their files?'

The Estonian National Archives, in Tartu, contain a trove of once-classified KGB counter-intelligence reports.[4] One day, via email, a friend and fellow scholar sends me a zip file of these documents, which were all labelled 'top-secret' The reports, authored by officers of the Second Department of the Ministry of State Security of the Estonian Soviet Socialist Republic, detail the activities of the Soviet security services in the Estonian SSR between March and April 1949. These are some of the reports Hiio was talking about – if Boris's job after the war really did involve identifying German collaborators and spies, he thought that perhaps his signature might be found on one of them.

The documents are at once cryptic and categorical. There is no trace of Boris upon them, no mentions of a suicide, but plenty of hints about the world that he inhabited. Each report begins with a neat table that claims to list exactly how many spies were apprehended that month and from where they hailed. In April 1949, Soviet counter-intelligence reported that in the Estonian SSR, two English spies, two American spies, five French spies, two German spies and thirty-six 'unidentified' spies had been detected. A report from May begins with a similar table, and goes on to detail a particular case: 'In the process of further undercover work on PIIP, Johannes through Agent "48", information was obtained that PIIP was connected to and aware of the espionage activities of VIIPAS Raivo Vrunovich, arrested by the MGB in 1947 for belonging to British intelligence and the Estonian bourgeois-nationalist underground.' There are hundreds of these reports, each one with a new agent-hunting story. Who was Agent 48, I wonder? Another document mentions one 'Agent Rome'; another an agent code-named 'Helgisoo', who in May 1949 was assigned the case of an Estonian woman named Ilse who had cooperated with the SD and had recently returned to Estonia with orders to meet a British intelligence officer. The reports reflect a culture of suspicion and cynicism, a world where counter-intelligence officers could decide that virtually anyone was really an 'unidentified' spy.

It was a world where it was easy to disappear, to swap one identity for another, to sneak across a border and slip into a new life, a new story. It was also a world in which it was easy to die.

9

A Deposition

On 4 August 1950, an urgent letter from Brazil arrives through the letterbox at 55 New Cavendish Street, with the heading: 'Re: War Criminal Herbert Cukurs'. Sent by two prominent members of the Jewish community in São Paulo, Drs Israel Scolnicov and A. Gartenberg, the letter contains a time-sensitive request.

The Federation of Brazilian Jews was engaged in an intense legal effort to expel Cukurs from their country. They had abandoned hope of arresting him, but after a series of public relations stunts they had successfully brought his presence in the country to the attention of the Brazilian ministers of justice and foreign affairs. The authors of the urgent letter explain that because Cukurs could not be extradited, they were militating for his 'expulsion in an administrative way'.

Scolnicov and Gartenberg reported that the Brazilian ministers had asked them to supply 'all evidences for the charges we lifted against Cukurs', but the Federation only had photocopies of the testimonies of the four Jewish survivors that Alperovitch had previously sent over: Rafael Schub, Abram Shapiro, Max Tukacier and David Fishkin. 'We need urgently some more substantial evidences', they wrote. Could Michelson send the original declarations of the four testimonies, and, if that was not possible, copies of them 'written on *your* sheets, duly legalized by a competent British authority or by the Brazilian consulate'. Without 'public legalized documents', they warned, the Brazilians could throw out the case.[1] They needed all the first-hand testimonies they could get. Copies would not suffice.

Over a month later, Michelson responded in the form of a one-line telegram: 'LEGALISED DOCUMENTS AIRMAILED.'[2]

Luckily, the Federation of Brazilian Jews had also discovered that a first-hand witness to Cukurs's crimes lived nearby. They hoped that she could save their case. On 14 August, this witness, a young woman with curled hair and brown eyes, arrived at the Federation's headquarters. Her name was Miriam Kaicners, and she was there to give a deposition. Seated before an 'ad-hoc' judicial committee, she began to recount the story of her young life and improbable survival.[3]

Miriam was born in 1920 to a Jewish family in the Latvian village of Bērzpils, some fifty kilometres from the Russian border. Her parents were shopowners; when she was fourteen years old, they sent her to study in Riga, and after that she returned to her village only on holidays. When the Soviet army occupied Latvia in 1939, Miriam stopped her studies and began working for a shoe manufacturer in the capital. When the German army took over, she was fired from her job and began living with various Jewish families. She lost touch with her parents; at the time of her 1950 deposition, she hadn't heard from them in years. A few weeks after the German occupation, she was arrested and sent to what she described as the 'Gestapo headquarters at 19 Waldemar St'. The headquarters of the Arājs Kommando.

When she arrived at the forbidding building, one of the young men who worked there happened to recognise her from school. He seemed surprised to see her there, Miriam recalled. Perhaps he had not realised she was Jewish, or perhaps he had just never given a thought to her ethnic identity. He told her she was lucky that she knew him, 'otherwise bad moments awaited her'. She stayed in the prison overnight. In the morning, this schoolmate told her to go and sweep the courtyard, to get some fresh air, and Miriam did as she was told. Outside, she saw a man who looked familiar, a famous man; he had given talks at her school and had lived near her in Riga. Cukurs recognised Miriam, too. He approached her and asked how she had ended up there. Evidently, he quickly took an interest in preserving her life: 'After a little while, Mr. Cukurs told her to leave through the gate without looking to the sides or behind her, moving straight ahead, and that he would follow behind her,' she recalled. He told her to go to the house where he was living at the time, a house he had forcibly appropriated from its Jewish residents, the Shapiros. Miriam was told that 'Mr. Shapiro was dead, his wife was under arrest, and that he [Cukurs] was keeping their son for his own personal services'. The Shapiros' son, Abram, waited on Cukurs and occasionally entertained him on the piano.

According to her own account, Miriam only stayed at Cukurs's appropriated apartment for a few days before he moved her in with a Jewish family, the Blumenaus. 'There, I would hide every time that the Nazis would come to raid the house in search of young women,' she told the committee. In late November 1941, she moved with the Blumenau family to the newly formed Jewish ghetto. 'One day, Mr. Cukurs, wearing an SS military uniform and a leather coat, accompanied by other Gestapo officers, came to visit the ghetto,' she recalled. Cukurs quietly stopped by the Blumenau residence to give them butter, and told them not to tell anyone of his kindness. Not long afterwards, Miriam reports that Cukurs told the Blumenaus that the residents of the ghetto would be going on a trip to an unknown location, for which they could only prepare twenty kilograms of luggage. They would travel '1,000 persons at a time'. Miriam watched the first group depart. She remembered seeing corpses on the streets of the ghetto, belongings and blood littering the ground.

Cukurs saved her from the same fate. Before the Blumenaus were "deported" to their deaths, he arrived and offered to take Miriam and the Blumenaus' daughter, Shelly, away with him. Mrs Blumenau refused to be separated from her daughter; Miriam agreed to go with him. Cukurs told her to climb in the boot of his olive-green Cadillac and wait for him. The next time he opened the boot, Miriam found herself at Lidoni, the Cukurs family farmhouse, deep in the countryside.

Miriam lived out the war at Lidoni, a spacious home located outside the small village of Bukaiši. At first, Cukurs and his wife Milda kept her hidden away from their children, bringing food to her room in secret. It was a large house, a point of pride for the family, a spoil of Cukurs's pre-war prestige. Still, they couldn't hide Miriam for ever. When this initial arrangement became untenable, they introduced Miriam to the children as Mara, their new English and German teacher. Only the housekeeper, a woman named Ludmila, knew her real identity. Miriam became part of the family, the children's tutor. A 1942 photograph shows her crouching down on the grass and cradling Cukurs's son, Herberts Cukurs Jr, in her arms. A bow tops her cascade of light curls. She smiles for the camera.

Towards the end of 1944, with the Soviet army approaching, Cukurs moved his family to Liepāja, and Miriam and Ludmila soon joined them there. He procured a fake passport for Miriam that bore his last name, stamped twice with the seal of the Reich. As 'Marija Cukurs', Miriam travelled on to Berlin with the family, posing as their eldest daughter. Cukurs wore his SS uniform on the journey, she recalled. Sheltering Miriam in this way was no small feat. 'Even for a collaborationist it was a risk,' writes the Brazilian historian Bruno Léal, author of the first definitive account of Cukurs's time in South America. 'If he was caught, not only Miriam, but Cukurs and his family could face very severe punishment.' In Berlin, Cukurs went to work at an aircraft factory, where he also secured a job for Miriam. When the Soviet army began to approach the city, they fled further west and hid in a forest near Kassel. From there, they piled into the Cadillac and headed towards France, stopping only once they had reached Marseilles. In a photograph from the journey, Miriam stands next to the Cadillac cradling Herberts Jr in her arms, flanked by members of the family.

From the port of Marseilles it would be possible for them to buy passage to South America on one of the many ships carrying Europeans away from their destroyed cities and towards the boulevards of Buenos Aires, São Paulo and Rio de Janeiro. Cukurs started selling paddle-boat trips from Marseilles in order to save up funds. He sold off his family's belongings one by one. Miriam checked in with the local office of HICEM, a Jewish immigration agency, which specialised in preparing refugees for relocation abroad. She gave the agency her real name, and they helped her secure a first-class ticket to board the *Cabo de Buena Esperanza*, bound for Rio de Janeiro. The Cukurs family travelled below deck. The seas were full of ships carrying refugees from Europe – victims, perpetrators, bystanders, opportunists – from east to west, north to south. Upon arrival, they would sign their names into the port register – name, birthdate, port of embarkation. Some would take the opportunity to reinvent themselves – some for fear of prosecution, some for the simple want of a new life. Cukurs did not bother with these deceptions. When he and his family – and Miriam – arrived in Rio, they spent their first night all together, camping on the beach.

All this time, Miriam claims not to have known of Cukurs's position in the Kommando, not to have heard about the burning of the Great Choral Synagogue in Riga, or of any of his misdeeds. But in Brazil, things were different. Miriam went to live with a Jewish family and continued to visit the Cukurs family regularly. Slowly, she began to get wind of accusations against her famous benefactor. Cukurs was too well known to hide, and besides, he didn't think he had to. He told a journalist that he chose Brazil as a place to settle because it had more than 300 aerodromes. Perhaps he hoped to pick up his career as a pilot where he had left off, to reclaim his fame and good fortune. He started by creating another small tourism business, once again selling paddle-boat trips and seaplane rides at the Rodrigo de Freitas lagoon. He couldn't stop himself from courting the press, from selling his new venture. In March 1949, the paper *A Manhã* ran a flattering profile of him under the headline 'From the bellicose skies of Europe to the calm waters of the lagoon'. 'Herberts Cukurs, an aviator and shipbuilder, has adventure in his blood', it reads. 'He fought against the Russians, travelled half the world, and ended up in Brazil.' By then, Cukurs and his wife Milda had successfully applied for Brazilian naturalisation, and business was going well enough for them to make do. Maybe, by then, they had an inkling of the storm brewing on their horizon. Perhaps they had noticed that a small army of Jewish refugees was surveilling the lagoon, collecting testimonies and photographs, building their case.

On 24 June 1950, *O Cruzeiro*, one of the largest Brazilian tabloids, ran what would be one of the last complimentary profiles of Cukurs, perhaps the last piece in which words like 'butcher', 'criminal' and 'murderer' were nowhere to be seen. Written by the journalist João Martins, the piece framed the Cukurs story as a triumphant tale: 'This is the story of a man who had to rebuild his entire existence at the age of forty-six, with his whole family, in a strange land, with a strange language, habits and climate ... When everything seems lost, humankind can find enough energy and capacity to look ahead, forget the past, and rebuild your own destiny. Instead of discouragement and regrets, willpower and work. This is the hallmark of humanity.'

In Rio as in Riga, with coverage came recognition. Latvian survivors recognised Cukurs's face in the newspapers, in streets and shops in town, and knew what he had done. One day, soon after arriving in Brazil, Cukurs had sold his Leica camera to a man who just happened to be friendly with Wolf Vipmans, the president of the Aid Society for Lithuanian and Latvian Jews. Vipmans then wrote to his cousin, a film producer and Latvian survivor named Gustav Joffe, who confirmed that Cukurs was a 'war criminal'.[4] The Jewish community began to organise, petitioning that Cukurs be extradited and tried, made to account for his sins. In London, Michelson had received photos of Cukurs at work in the lagoon. In one, he leans over the prow of a small boat, his face obscured. '*Das ist Herberts Cukurs!*' the sender writes above the frame. In another, he sits in the pilot's seat wearing an aviator cap, the calm waters of the lagoon rippling above his head.

On 30 June 1950, just a week after the *O Cruzeiro* report, the Jewish Federation of Rio de Janeiro held a press conference and invited all the major news outlets to attend. The purpose of the conference was to declare 'what then seemed unbelievable', the historian Bruno Leal writes. That 'the owner of the paddle boats in the Rodrigo de Freitas lagoon was, contrary to the reports of the Rio papers, a Nazi war criminal responsible for the death of about 30,000 Jews during the Nazi occupation of Latvia. His crimes, according to the organisation, also included the burning of the largest synagogue in Latvia, with Jews inside it, in addition to the drowning and execution of children, women and the elderly, among others.'

The press conference was a last resort. The Jewish community had spent years trying to push anyone who would listen to do something about Cukurs. 'This movement was characterised by caution, discretion, and above all, secrecy,' Leal explains. They feared that Cukurs was a flight risk, literally – they did not want him to hear of their plans and fly himself to safety. In the late 1940s, a Federation member named Moses Hoff had approached the Soviet ambassador to Brazil to raise the question of Cukurs's extradition. The independent nation of Latvia had by that time ceased to exist, and Soviet authorities were busy identifying and punishing those who had collaborated with the Germans and contributed to fascist crimes. The 'little Nuremberg' in Riga had been followed by a series of similar tribunals and executions throughout the newly reclaimed Soviet territory. Those who had escaped prosecution – the ones with information, with needed skills – were absorbed into Soviet security organs, others into British ones.[5] Still others successfully drifted away into obscurity, some just for a few decades, some for the rest of their lives.

The Soviet ambassador dismissed the Jewish community's extradition request. Shortly afterwards, on 20 October 1947, Cold War tensions led Brazil to sever diplomatic relations with the USSR, eliminating the possibility of further discussions. The Brazilian government was the Jewish community's next best hope. The Jewish Federation formed a 'special investigation commission' led by Israel Scolnicov, which would have two goals: to alert the Brazilian public about Cukurs's past and to pressure the government to expel him from the country.

Following the revelations, the story shifted from one extreme to another. The Brazilian press surged with reports and accusations against Cukurs. One paper called him 'one of the biggest criminals of the Second World War'; another 'chief commander of the Nazi occupation forces'; and yet another 'a fugitive from the Nuremberg tribunal'. Protestors outside his paddle-boat business demanded his expulsion. Editorials suggested that the fact that Cukurs had been granted safe passage to Brazil was part of a much larger problem, and accused the Brazilian authorities of colluding with former Nazis to bring a 'wave of undesirable elements' to their shores. Cukurs, for his part, gave interviews denying the allegations. In one photo from this period, he appears wearing a neat suit and tie and thick, black-framed glasses. He holds a book in his hands, a list of names. A newspaper caption explains that it is a list of criminals indicted at Nuremberg. Cukurs is attempting to prove his innocence by showing that his name is not among the accused.[6]

In late July came news of another trial. It was a 'simulated trial', nothing more than a play. It would be held by a new entity called the 'United Committee', an alliance of fourteen Brazilian Jewish organisations. It would be akin to a moot court, with a judge, jury and court clerk. Both the prosecution and defence would consist of three lawyers. The point of the 'simulation', the committee said, was to raise awareness of anti-Semitism in Brazil and to alert the public about the 'concentration of war criminals' in the country.

On 12 August 1950, this mock court convened in a downtown Rio auditorium. It was an imitation of justice, a theatre piece. The organisers hoped that life would imitate art, that their performance would be a mere prelude to the real thing. The prosecution listed all the heinous crimes attributed to Cukurs, and to Nazism writ large. The defence, for its part, pleaded insanity on behalf of their absent client. The jury delivered a unanimous verdict: Cukurs, they ruled, was a 'convict' who should be expelled from the country; his presence in Brazil was an 'outrage', an affront to the Jewish community and to all their dead relatives.

Two days later, Miriam Kaicners would be summoned to provide her statement to the Jewish Federation. She would never speak to Cukurs or his family again. She lived out the rest of her life in Brazil, married and had children. To her dying day, she would tell them almost nothing about how she had survived.

10

The Crime Complex

Despite the best efforts of the Committee Men, the Brazilians do not pursue the Cukurs case, and the Germans do not pursue Arājs. The whole Riga ghetto case had been handed over to West German prosecutors, with much hard-won information, including some of the defendants themselves, lost along the way. From a seat at the Wiener Library in London, I read reports of how this long heartbreak unfolded.

In January 1950, Michelson sends one of his trusted allies, Joseph Berman, a survivor of the Riga ghetto, to present himself to the Hamburg regional court. A prosecutor meets him there, and Berman asks him about the status of the Riga ghetto case: 'I tried to find out from him something about the people released by the British authorities, whether any material was handed over, whether he had any documents, how much of the evidence had been lost which was sent from London and other parts of the world during the past few years, and in general, I tried to put the jigsaw puzzle together by asking him what had happened to this case,' Berman wrote in his report. '(I was terribly depressed, and that night I went straight to bed.)' But the prosecutor does ask him to do one thing while he is in town: the SS *Unterstrumführer* Rudolf Reese, who served in the Riga ghetto, is in his custody. Would Berman go to the prison to identify him?

In fact, Berman is asked to identify not just Reese but nine men from the Riga Gestapo. He goes up to each one and says their names. 'I could not believe that this was at last really happening; that it had been possible to outlive the Nazi tortures and to help to bring them to justice,' he writes in his report to the committee. Berman told Michelson that after the war he had come to envy the dead, to regret that he was alive. But just for that fleeting moment, he was certain that the dead would have wanted to be standing there with him. The next day, he returned to the prison to participate in an interrogation of Reese. He conducted his conversations with the accused 'without any feeling of revenge,' he writes. 'I was willing to forgive even murder if they told the whole true story to the world of what they had done and what had taken place during the German occupation of the Baltic States.'

> To the utter amazement of all present in the room Reese asked to speak to me privately. Dr. Voigt [the prosecutor] was a bit shocked, as this had never happened before, but he immediately consented. Not being able to find a room for us, and Reese not being allowed to leave without the Police Officer, they all left the room and left us two alone.
>
> I went over to Reese and he started to embrace me and to cry bitterly. Then he told me how he used to watch on certain days where the other Gestapo officers were, so that the Jews could leave for Sweden.
>
> I repeated what I had said to him before during the morning that I am willing to defend him in front of the whole world no matter what the consequences may be to me, if he confesses to everything he was involved in.

Reese begged to be released. He said he wanted Berman to be his lifelong friend. He promised to 'confess from A to Z' if only it meant that he would get out alive. But when the prosecutor returned to the room, he decided that Reese was too broken down to be deposed, and the police officer accompanying them wanted to go to lunch. So they adjourned.

When they reconvened, the accused asked, once again, to speak privately with his accuser. 'Immediately they had all left and I had closed the large double padded doors Reese knelt in front of me for about 2 minutes and started embracing me and crying bitterly and asking me to help him,' Berman writes. 'I told him again that he should confess to everything, implicating himself and everybody else, and I would help him.' The Nazi got down on his knees and begged for mercy.

When the prosecutor again re-entered the room, Reese and Berman were seated next to each other, 'practically on top' of each other, Berman writes. 'Our hands were clasped together for most of the time, as I had to stop him from crying. We sometimes even smoked the same cigarette.' Reese begins to confess. Upon their final meeting, Berman handed him a few bars of chocolate and some cigarettes. But he did not grant him forgiveness. How could he? He did not yet know the full scope of what had to be forgiven. 'I had said that I would do everything in my power to help him and defend him in court, if he spoke the whole truth from A to Z,' Berman wrote to Michelson. The trouble, he worried, was that he would never know if or when Reese had confessed to all of his sins: 'How would I know when it is "Z"?'[1] How do you know when you've reached the end of a story?

It would be nearly a decade before the West Germans would finally decide to take these cases seriously, which required figuring out a system for cataloguing the 'whole truth from A to Z'. It would take the form of an index. Today, the index lives in the south-western German town of Ludwigsburg, locked behind a vault door in the basement of an eighteenth-century tower. It is guarded like the rarest of treasures, yet it looks just like an ordinary archive, consisting of rows and rows of metal filing cabinets painted a single shade of beige. Only one copy of its contents exists, stored on microfilm at an undisclosed location. The drawers are labelled alphabetically: Behr-Bern, Horz-z, Zat-Zil. Some are organised by category: 'Luftwaffe', 'Marine', 'Ordnungspolizei', 'Einsatzgruppen im übr. Europa'. It is an index of names – more than 1.7 million of them, each one logged on a green or yellow index card, many of them handwritten: 4,252 military units, 27,858 place names.[2] There are perpetrators – members of every branch

and every rank of every Nazi organisation; there are victims –
those who survived to testify in some form; and there are those
who might be called bystanders – people who watched a calamity
unfold and later spoke of what they saw. Their names mingle
together, in alphabetical order, in what is the most comprehensive
directory of Nazi personnel and their crimes and of post-war
attempts to bring them to justice.

The building where they are held, an austere former prison
set back from the road, is easy to miss. Give someone on the
street in Ludwigsburg its name and address – *Zentrale Stelle
der Landesjustizverwaltungen zur Aufklärung nationalsozialistischer
Verbrechen*, the Central Office of the State Justice Ministries for the
Investigation of National Socialist Crimes – and you are likely to
receive a strange look and a shrug. 'It's a bit of a riddle for Germans,
this tiny, modest little office, with only a few people coming and
going,' the historian Annette Weinke told me. Most people have no
idea that it exists, and yet it is the epicentre of post-war justice, the
place where almost all Nazi prosecutions begin and end.

The first index cards were logged in 1958, the year the Central
Office opened. A prosecutor named Erwin Schüle was its first
director – the index was his invention. Earlier that year, Schüle
had led the prosecution in the Ulm Einsatzgruppen trial, a
landmark case that forever altered the German approach to
war crimes prosecutions, a case that exploded 'like a bomb'
on the public psyche, as another German historian put it.
Schüle had been a late addition to the case, taking over as lead
prosecutor a year into the investigation, when it looked like it
wasn't going anywhere fast.[3] At the time, there was only one
defendant: Bernhard Fischer-Schweder, the former police chief
of Memel, a seaside city on the Lithuanian coast (now Klaipeda).
Fischer-Schweder had joined an SS unit, *Einsatzkommando Tilsit*,
and led the executions of hundreds of Lithuanian Jews. After the
war, he attempted to erase his past: he changed his name and
birthdate and successfully secured an 'exoneration certificate',
colloquially referred to as a 'Clorox card', from a denazification
court.[4] In 1953, he applied to join the German civil service, and

through a series of small frauds his application was accepted; a
former SS officer thus became the head of a displaced persons'
camp in the city of Ulm.

Almost immediately, questions about Fischer-Schweder's past
arose, and his SS membership was discovered. Officials quietly
asked him to resign from his post, fearing a public relations
nightmare. Fischer-Schweder fought against his firing, claiming
to be a victim of the Nazi regime, not an accomplice. The papers
quickly caught wind of this 'interesting labor court trial',[5] and the
Ulm district attorney's office opened a criminal investigation into
his past. It didn't take long for the two lead investigators to uncover
horrifying allegations about Fischer-Schweder and identify some
of his murderous colleagues, many of whom had also fled to
Germany; Jewish survivors came forward to testify to his unit's
crimes. But the investigators quickly ran up against the limitations
of German law, which required the prosecution to establish that
Fischer-Schweder had initiated the shootings himself, not on the
orders of others, in order to arraign him for first-degree murder.
The testimonies they collected conflicted too much to indicate the
precise date, time and location of the executions. Meanwhile, their
bosses were losing interest in the case, and in Nazi prosecutions in
general. After a year of investigations, 'the two men were isolated
and burdened with the near insurmountable task of reproducing
whole cloth the mechanisms of the Holocaust during early 1941 in
Lithuania,' according to the historian Patrick Tobin. '[T]he events
in question were extraordinarily complex, with overlapping chains
of command and various units involved in the massacres. As a
result, the investigators had found many witnesses but gathered
little concrete evidence. With limited resources at their disposal,
they had few other choices than to focus on perpetrator testimony,
and, even then, they needed to rely on other departments to
conduct interrogations. The investigators had done the best they
could do with the hand they had been dealt, but they had been
dealt a very bad hand.'

Enter Schüle. He was not an ideal candidate for the job, as a
former Nazi Party member and Wehrmacht soldier. He had been

appointed as a public prosecutor shortly after his release from a Soviet POW camp in 1950, and approached the question of Nazi prosecutions with zeal. He ordered the detectives to expand the scope of the investigation and 'interrogate individuals involved at all levels of the Third Reich' in order to get a better idea of how the Holocaust unfolded along the German–Lithuanian border.[6] They consulted historians, archivists and Jewish survivor organisations. Schüle was determined to uncover what he called the 'crime complex' of Memel – the entire constellation of actors and actions that allowed mass executions to take place. This approach allowed them to draw nine more men into the fold. At the resulting trial in April 1958, all ten men were convicted.

The idea of a 'crime complex' was a novel legal concept. It treated entire swathes of the Nazi administration as criminal organisations and presumed the complicity of everyone involved, including secretaries and radio operators and cooks. It required investigators to begin with a place, or a name, or a date, and comb through vast amounts of information to fill in the blanks: who had been killed, and how, and by whom? How many 'Aktions' were there, and on whose orders? How many Nazi personnel had been involved? Were they still alive and in Germany? If they were able to answer all these questions with certainty, then they could initiate criminal proceedings.

The Ulm trial was the first time that SS men had been tried by the new laws of the Federal Republic. When the Basic Law of the Federal Republic of Germany was ratified in May 1949, it included a twenty-year statute of limitations for murder and a fifteen-year statute for manslaughter; that made 1960 and 1965 the respective deadlines for the prosecution of Nazi crimes. Schüle and his team were running out of time even before they got started. The Ulm trial was meant to expose the arbitrary nature of post-war prosecutions that until then had proceeded 'without a system, unplanned, by chance,' as Erich Nellmann, attorney-general for Baden-Württemberg, argued in a 1958 op-ed in the *Stuttgarter Zeitung*. Nellman claimed that it was unfair that some Nazis had been prosecuted, but not all.

To date prosecutions occur purely by chance. One person has the bad luck to be charged, the other not. Indeed there are thousands of unprosecuted crimes. So if everything really has been done to find the perpetrators, then we need to accept that. The worst and most extensive crimes have been prosecuted, but not all. Those convicted know that many other criminals roam free. For those convicted and those that go free, this inequality is an injustice.'7

Three months after the ten Ulm defendants were sentenced, the Central Office opened its doors. It was supposed to be a temporary outfit, a stopgap measure meant to demonstrate that West Germany was taking denazification seriously. Schüle got right to work. It was a race against the clock. With only a handful of investigators under his direction, he began building the index and connecting the dots between different perpetrators, witnesses, locations. In the first six months, his team opened 208 new cases, each one a 'crime complex' of its own. Their work was at once a product of the Nuremberg proceedings and a refutation of their logic. Where the Nuremberg IMT had focused on the individual crimes of senior Nazis, the Central Office cast a wide net, looking at the entire network of criminality. The IMT had operated according to a hodgepodge of Allied laws; the Central Office operated under German law alone. In some sense, the Central Office emerged as a 'counter-project against Nuremberg', as Annette Weinke told me. 'It offered a way for the German people to "take the past into our own hands", to try its own population with its own criminal code.'

In his closing statement at the Ulm trial, Schüle described how one witness had upbraided his detectives when they contacted him, asking for answers: 'Why are you digging up these old things?' the witness said. 'This witness thus posed a question which has doubtless also been posed to you by your friends, namely, "Even if such atrocities were committed, why must we – the Germans – inflict wounds on ourselves by making a display of our own shame for all the world to see after seventeen years?" ' Schüle told the courtroom.

'And why must we once again rip open wounds that have barely healed since 1945?' For Schüle and his colleagues, the point was to establish the rule of law, Rechtsstaat, in Germany, to ensure that the laws that had already been applied to some perpetrators would be applied to all of them. They sought to ensure that their nation's past would not undermine its future.

Schüle thought he would be the first and last director of the Central Office. Today, in the eighteenth-century gatehouse next to the old prison building in Ludwigsburg, a workstation from the early days of the operation is encased in glass. Stacks of files line the walls; the desk is littered with books, paper and stamps; a binder lies open to a page full of portraits of notable Nazi officers; one wall displays an organisational chart of the Nazi hierarchy; on another, leather belts used to bind thousands of pages of evidence hang from mounted pegs.

These days, boxes rather than belts are used to store files from the few cases that see the inside of a courtroom. Six men have thus far succeeded Schüle as director of the Central Office. The current head of office, Thomas Will, is likely to be the last, as the Central Office is slated to operate only until 2025. Every day until then, its prosecutors add cards to the index and amend existing ones, they pore over lists of names from Nazi staff files and emigration registers, they consult the same organisational charts. They are adding texture to the narrative of the Holocaust, slowly filling in the outstanding gaps. Nearly eight decades after the Holocaust, Central Office prosecutors still refer to concentration camps and killing sites as crime scenes whose killers remain at large. 'This is a giant cold case operation – looking at crimes that happened a long time ago, with only the sketchiest information about who the perpetrators might be,' the historian Devin Pendas told me. Every year, Central Office prosecutors identify about thirty perpetrators living in Germany and send their cases to regional district attorneys for further action.

Jens Rommel, a good-humoured former criminal prosecutor who sports frameless glasses and a goatee, led the office until February 2020. In 2017, I visited him in Ludwigsburg on an assignment for the *Guardian*.[8] Oskar Gröning, a former SS guard at Auschwitz, had recently been sentenced to a four-year prison term, a direct result of Rommel's work. The trial, and the spectacle of a nonagenarian in the dock, had attracted international press attention. Like all the cases that Rommel and his team had helped reach the courts, it was dubbed 'the last Nazi trial', a moniker laden with equal parts hope and dread.

I was in Ludwigsburg to find out what else Rommel and his prosecutors were working on, to observe their investigative procedures. He told me that he never thought he would end up leading the Central Office, that in some ways it was a world away from the homicides he was used to investigating, while in others it was exactly the same. 'It's the same book, the same law, the same task when it comes to murder cases, but the work is completely different,' Rommel explained. 'Out there, with current cases, you interact with police, searching the house, making arrests, checking bank accounts, you have a SWAT team. Here, we have paper. So it's a completely different way of working,' he said. 'There are crimes behind these words, but there's no blood here.'

Schüle's innovations – treating the Third Reich as one large 'crime complex', and using ordinary German law to prosecute mass murder – had over the course of five decades proven to be both a blessing and curse. He irrevocably widened the net of Nazi criminality, ensuring that hundreds of men and women who aided and abetted the Third Reich would have to account for their misdeeds before a judge and jury. But he also ensured that the laws by which these people would be tried would always be inadequate for the scale and nature of their crimes.

'It's a legal and moral question,' Rommel told me. 'Who's responsible in the chain of command? What does he have to do in the chain of command to be a perpetrator? Is it sufficient to be at Auschwitz? It's a question of personal guilt and responsibility. We try to work with our legal tools, but they are not made for mass crimes organized by the state, they are made for a single person having committed a single crime,' he said. 'It's very difficult to find adequate rules, because we have just one law. It's the same definition of murder, whether you [kill while] robbing a bank, or kill your husband because you're annoyed – the same definition is applied to mass killings organized by the state.'

He had accepted that, in his current position, 'success is not a daily experience'. It was nearly impossible to find living perpetrators, and those whom they did find often died during the many years it took to investigate and then prosecute their cases. But it was still important to try. As far as Rommel was concerned, the Holocaust would cease to be an open crime scene only when the last perpetrator was dead. Until then, the men and women of the Central Office would continue to fulfil their imperative, impossible mandate: to treat the past not as history, but as crime.

I asked Rommel if he would show me the index. Past an entrance guard, down a small set of stairs, through the vault door, and there we were. There were a few records, in particular, that I wanted to see. I asked Rommel for Adolf Eichmann's entry first: ten index cards, stacked together in a clear plastic sachet. On the first card, his name, birthdate, and his position in the SS: head of Jewish Affairs. The address had been left blank – at the time the card was filed, Eichmann's whereabouts were still unconfirmed. Only later, after his kidnapping, trial, and execution, did someone take a pen to his record and draw a small blue cross next to his name to signal that he was dead.

The next file I asked for was Cukurs's. Rommel extracted it from its cabinet – the first card listed his name, address, position: Herbert Cukurs, Hauptmann a.D. Address: 'Avenida Epiasio, Pessoa 574, Ap.3, Rio de Janeiro, Brasil.' It noted that he might also be located via the Latvian Legation of Brazil. On the reverse side, a record of his fate: 'The embassy of the Federal Republic of Germany in Montevideo wrote that Cukurs was murdered. Estimated time of death: 23.2.65.'

The last card I asked to see was my grandfather's. One of Rommel's investigators, Manuela Zeller, told me that the first thing the lawyers do upon arriving for their postings at the Central Office was look up their own grandparents, so I didn't think it would be such a strange request. I didn't say anything about who Boris was or what happened to him, and his record did not have much to divulge. The card was almost blank, containing only the most basic facts of his life. Born in Rybinsk, Russia, in 1918; served in Latvia; died in 1949. Next to his name, another small hand-drawn cross.

11

Mr Pearlman's Non-Fiction

On 21 July 1960, Erwin Schüle and two of his colleagues arrived at the National Archives records depository in Alexandria, Virginia. Two months earlier, on 23 May, Israeli prime minister David Ben-Gurion had announced that Adolf Eichmann, Hitler's former head of Jewish Affairs, the man who made the death trains run, had been kidnapped from his home outside Buenos Aires and flown to Israel, where he was now awaiting trial. The intervening months had seen a flurry of activity in the CIA archives, with emissaries descending upon the Second World War Division records depository en masse.

'Remarkably, in ten workdays during two weeks they culled the Eichmann records from among literally tons of captured German language records, processed them through all the micro copying, declassification clearances, and legal requirements of the Departments of Justice and State, and completed transfer to Israel by June 15,' the former US Army officer Robert Wolfe, who was in charge of microfilming war crimes records at the time, writes in his account of this period. When Schüle and his team arrived in July, Wolfe acted as their research assistant, helping them sort through and collect CIA records regarding Eichmann and 400 other Nazis. 'All 400 had already been indicted as war criminals by the Federal Republic of Germany to forestall inhibiting their prosecution by the expiration of a long-standing German 20-year statute of limitations,' Wolfe recalls in an undated government memo. 'Also in July 1960, I provided Israeli investigators the same information about Eichmann that [I] furnished to Dr. Schüle.'[1]

Eichmann had been living with his wife and children in a nondescript house in the city of San Fernando, just north of Buenos Aires, when they found him. It was Fritz Bauer, a German Jewish district attorney, Holocaust survivor and crusading pursuer of Nazi prosecutions, who first received word from Jewish contacts in Buenos Aires that the Eichmanns were living there. Bauer was able to confirm that the SS *Obersturmbannführer* was living under the alias 'Ricardo Klement' and working at a Mercedes factory. This was in 1957, before the Central Office was established, before the Ulm trial took its turn. Concerned that West German authorities would not pursue the case, Bauer took his intelligence to the Israelis instead.

In Israel, Bauer met Haim Cohn, legal adviser to the government, and Isser Harel, the director of Mossad. Harel quickly dispatched one of his agents, a man named Zvi Aharoni, to Buenos Aires to confirm Eichmann's whereabouts. When Aharoni returned with positive results – the first photographs of Eichmann in Argentina, taken with a concealed camera – Harel went to see David Ben-Gurion. Ben-Gurion told him one thing: there had to be a trial, and the trial had to be in Israel. The prime minister wanted Eichmann to be apprehended and punished for his crimes, but, above all, he wanted a trial, and he wanted his country to be the one to hold it.[2]

It seemed to be a personal matter to the prime minister; not only to avenge the annihilation of the Jewish people, but to marshal the performative power of a trial towards the consecration of his new state. 'The trial is the important thing, not the penalty,' Ben-Gurion told the American *Saturday Review*.[3] 'It was of fundamental importance to Ben-Gurion to demonstrate in this way that the Jews, too, now had a strong state, not least of all because the trial suggested that the Jews should not expect to be protected by others; that they could only rely on Israel,' the legal scholar Yosal Rogat writes in his 1961 pamphlet on the proceedings. The prime minister, Rogat writes, 'made it perfectly clear that he believed that only an Israeli court could have tried Eichmann, and that he did not want (would not have allowed?) any other court to do so. For Israel to have handed Eichmann over to another court would have been like saying "we are like an ordinary state"; Israel wanted to make exactly the opposite point.'

But to try Eichmann, first they had to catch him. Harel selected eleven agents, ten men and one woman, from Shin Bet, Israel's counter-intelligence and security agency, and Mossad, its intelligence agency, for the job. They would travel to Buenos Aires on different routes and under various pretences – as tourists, diplomats, businessmen – kidnap him, and transport him to Israel alive and in one piece. Aharoni would lead the team; an agent named Yaakov Meidad would handle the logistics; and a doctor would accompany them, because someone had to sedate the captive for the return journey.[4] It was a simple mission, really: grab and go.[5] The agents staked out the Eichmann residence and learned the details of their target's regimented daily routine. He returned from work every night at the same hour, walking a short distance between the bus stop and his home. On 11 May, he returned from the Mercedes factory later than usual. Harel's agents were waiting on the street, pretending to fiddle with their cars: one of them got Eichmann's attention and quickly wrestled him to the ground. 'No drugs, no ropes, no handcuffs were used, and Eichmann immediately recognized that this was professional work, as no unnecessary force had been applied; he was not hurt,' Hannah Arendt wrote of the incident. He was blindfolded, bundled into the back seat and driven to one of the safe houses. The agents asked him to identify himself and told him that if he moved he would be shot.[6] '*Ich füge mich meinem Schicksal*,' Eichmann allegedly responded. *I accept my fate*.[7]

On 23 May 1960, Ben-Gurion announced Eichmann's arrival in the country in a short, triumphant address before the Knesset. 'A short time ago, Israeli security services found one of the greatest of the Nazi war criminals, Adolf Eichmann,' he told the lawmakers. 'Eichmann is already under arrest in Israel and will shortly be placed on trial in Israel under the terms of the law for the trial of Nazis and their collaborators.'

The problem was that the involvement of the security forces was not meant to be publicly known. Admitting state involvement also meant admitting that Israel deliberately and brazenly violated Argentinian sovereignty, acting in breach of international law. The attorney general attempted to spin Ben-Gurion's statement, claiming that the security services had merely located Eichmann. The kidnapping, they insinuated, had been left up to anonymous others.

In an effort to distance itself from the spectacle of the forced extradition, the government is said to have turned to the literary world for assistance. One of the first tellings of the Eichmann kidnapping was a fictionalised account, though it was presented as fact. The author, a former information service officer named Moshe Pearlman, titled his work *The Capture of Adolf Eichmann*.[8] In it, he claims that Eichmann's kidnappers were merely a team of childhood friends named Yigal, Dov and Gad, all in their 'late twenties', who had become close friends as 'youthful pioneers' on a 'cooperative farm village in a desert outpost in southern Israel'. They had arrived in Buenos Aires to kidnap Eichmann as a kind of reunion tour. 'This book is in no way an official publication,' Pearlman writes in his author's note. He had retired from official government service eight months prior to devote himself to writing; he assured readers that 'this book thus contains no information which I acquired in my capacity as a civil servant'.

Pearlman does not go so far as to claim that the three young pioneers worked completely alone. They were in close contact with a 'group' in Israel, which, he explains, was a 'body of men who had been engaged in other activities during the previous years'.[9] There were conferences in Israel, cables between the pioneers in Buenos Aires and their colleagues back home. In a chapter titled the 'Ghost of Nuremberg', Pearlman describes how Eichmann's name was spoken into the trial record at the IMT, how his crimes came hurtling to the attention of the Allied powers. 'Suddenly, it was a name on everyone's lips, an unknown, revealed by the central spotlight as the star player in a stark tragedy, a symbol of the awesome crimes this international tribunal had been convened to judge,' he writes. 'If the ghost of Hitler hovered over Nuremberg as the trial opened, it was now joined by another ghost – the ghost of Adolf Eichmann. For all thought that Eichmann was dead.'[10] In the same chapter, Pearlman copies out the testimony of Hermann Graebe, the Ukrainian engineer whose chilling eyewitness account had informed Sir Hartley Shawcross's closing speech at Nuremberg.[11]

Everyone knew what really happened in Buenos Aires: 'No doubt, however, exists about the identity of the captors,' Arendt writes in her trial report. Yet Pearlman's account had needlessly introduced a hint of fictionality to the Eichmann saga. Where does the fiction begin and end, in this story? Are its tentacles sunk too far in to be properly extracted?

Arendt, too, could not resist resorting, even fleetingly, to speculation in her own trial report. For a brief and revealing moment, she contemplates an alternative scenario, a counterfactual: why hadn't the agents just 'killed him right then and there, in the streets of Buenos Aires'? Why bother with all the trouble of a kidnapping when the final verdict was preordained? The same thought had occurred to many contemporary commentators, for it seemed to offer a more expedient path to justice. 'The notion was not without merit, because the facts of the case were beyond dispute,' Arendt writes. '[B]ut those who proposed it forgot that he who takes the law into his own hands will render a service to justice only if he is willing to transform the situation in such a way that the law can again operate and his act can, at least posthumously, be validated.' Vengeance could not come at the cost of justice. For that reason and that reason alone, Eichmann had to be kept alive. Later, after the verdict had been read and Eichmann had been sentenced to death by hanging, Arendt was so disappointed with the language – but not the sentencing – of the final ruling that, in the epilogue to *Eichmann in Jerusalem*, she launches into a strange and dreamlike monologue in which she casts herself into the role of judge and delivers her own death sentence.[12] '[J]ust as you supported and carried out a policy of not wanting to share the earth with the Jewish people and the people of a number of other nations,' she wrote, 'We find that no one, that is, no member of the human race, can be expected to want to share this earth with you. This is the reason, and the only reason, you must hang.'[13]

The Beit Ha'am, the 'House of the People', a cultural centre in Jerusalem, was chosen as the location for the trial. Outfitted with a capacious, spare auditorium, it was one of the only spaces large enough to accommodate the many witnesses, survivors and spectators who would come to observe the proceedings. The trial would take place in a renovated theatre, the judges' dais positioned where there would normally have been a stage or screen.

It wasn't just the trial chamber that the government had to renovate for this new purpose; it also had to re-envision its own laws. In 1950, the Knesset had adopted the 'Nazi and Nazi Collaborators Punishment Law', allowing Israeli courts to sit in judgement of those who contributed to the Nazi regime. But it had not yet been enforced by way of a trial. Putting the law into action required additional considerations regarding the presentation and admissibility of evidence, the use of witness testimony and the general scope of the proceedings. 'The law that Israel applied to Eichmann itself authorized special rulings about evidence: "the court may deviate from the customary rules of evidence if the court believes that it is necessary for a proper and just trial",' Rogat observes.[14] The court invoked the Nuremberg proceedings as a precedent: '[T]he Eichmann trial, then, was in actual fact no more, but also no less, than the last of the numerous Successor trials which followed the Nuremberg Trials,' Arendt writes. Eichmann's defence counsel, Robert Servatius, had defended several Nazis at Nuremberg. The only difference between those proceedings and this one, Arendt explained, was that in Jerusalem the Jewish people would for the first time sit in judgement of one of their own executioners.[15]

The trial was a spectacle in every sense of the word, a striking public display of grief, mourning, terror and mystification. The judges in their billowing black robes, their judicial dress 'infused with a primitive kind of alchemical power,' Rogat writes. The defendant seated in his bullet-proof glass box, flanked by his guards. The theatre was packed; on some days, spectators lined up around the block for a chance to partake in the proceedings. A special police unit, 'Bureau 06', had prepared the evidence: 1,600 documents on the Nazi programme to annihilate the Jewish people, many of them bearing Eichmann's signature. One hundred and eight survivors took the stand.[16] They swore on the Hebrew Bible, they listed the names of the dead. One witness, a forty-five-year-old man named Yehiel Dinoor, a Polish writer who went by the pen name 'K-Zetnik', began by telling the judges a stirring kind of tale:

> This is a chronicle from the planet of Auschwitz. I was there for about two years. Time was different there from what it is here on earth. Every split second ran on a different cycle of time. And the inhabitants of the planet had no names. They had neither parents nor children. They did not dress as we dress here. They were not born there nor did anyone give birth. Even their breathing was regulated by the laws of another nature. They did not live, nor did they die, in accordance with the laws of this world. Their names were the numbers ...

Dinoor was his chosen name, meaning 'residue from the fire'. When the judges tried to interrupt his monologue, he fainted and collapsed to the floor.[17]

Another day, a short, bald and somewhat slouching witness took the stand. His name was Eliezar Karstadt. He appeared before the judges wearing a white button-down shirt, a pen tucked into his breast pocket, dark pleated trousers and a wristwatch. He was forty-seven years old, a survivor of four concentration camps. Born in a small Latvian town called Talsen (now Talsi), in the Courland region, Karstadt spent three years interned in the Riga ghetto, and then in Kaiserwald concentration camp, on the outskirts of the city. In Jerusalem, the presiding judge peppered him with questions in German: 'How many Jews were there in Riga when the Germans came?' 'Forty thousand,' Karstadt answered. There had been one hundred thousand Jews in Latvia altogether, he reported. 'So how many survived?' 'I believe eight hundred,' Karstadt answered. 'Of all the Jews of Latvia?' 'Yes.'[18] There was a gasp in the courtroom.[19]

Karstadt spoke of the horrific conditions of the ghetto and the camps, of how he witnessed Jews from all over Germany arrive in Riga. In the ghetto, Jews lived in hometown clusters: deportees from Hanover in one building, from Leipzig in another. Early on, when the ghetto had held only Latvians, the internees had been killed in batches, over the course of a series of murderous 'Aktions'. One day, a third of the men were taken out and shot. Then there was another 'Aktion', and then another, targeting craftsmen. 'This "aktion", like all the other "aktions" in the small towns, was not conducted only by Germans, for they gave the right of conducting them to a certain group of Letts,' Karstadt told the judges. 'Their leader is living at present in Brazil. His name is Herberts Cukurs. I saw myself how on Tuesday, 9 December, he shot women and children in the ghetto. He claims now – just as do all those who took part in the "aktions" against Jews – that he had never been in the ghetto, had never murdered a Jew, but had always helped Jews.'

On 11 December 1961, eight months after the trial began, the court issued its judgement. Eichmann was convicted on all fifteen counts of his original indictment, with the notable exception of the crime of conspiracy. The first four counts convicted him of committing crimes 'against the Jewish people', 'that is, crimes against Jews *with the intent to destroy the people*,' Arendt clarifies. The next seven counts dealt with his crimes against humanity, for murdering and persecuting Jews, gypsies, for seizing and destroying entire towns. 'All crimes enumerated under Counts 1 through 12 carried the death penalty,' Arendt writes. The final three counts convicted him of membership in criminal organisations: the SS, the SD and the Gestapo.[20] On 15 December, Eichmann was sentenced to death by hanging.

At the prison where Eichmann was being held, the guards drew lots to see who would perform the execution. The lot fell upon a man named Shalom Nagar. 'We brought the rope from the third floor, we put it over his head, and I went into where the table was. I pressed the button, the flaps opened, and he fell,' he says in a documentary about his life.[21]

The sight of Eichmann's dead body haunted him. 'I've been scared ever since,' he tells the filmmakers. 'I had nightmares for a year because of him. After that, I became religious, I started wearing a kippah, praying, putting on tefillin, keeping Shabbat. I kept at it, and I felt better.' He became a kosher butcher. He comforted himself with the thought that he had carried out God's will: 'It's the greatest commandment there is: "Wipe out the memory of Amalek."' Amalek, Israel's eternal enemy. In Deuteronomy, God commands the Jewish people to 'blot out the remembrance of Amalek from under heaven; you shalt not forget it'.[22] Here, remembering and forgetting, destroying and preserving, appear as two sides of the same coin, two pathways towards justice.

12

Shangrilá

Some events mark moments when the world shifts from one version of itself to another, ripples in the uneven flow of historical time. The detritus they generate – photographs, receipts, certificates, letters – is transfigured into residue of the past, source material for the historian of the future. Sometimes these events pass relatively unnoticed; some flicker across newspaper headlines, buried deep inside the print edition; others are consigned to obscurity immediately after they occur. But each one alters the relation between past, present and future. Each one leaves sediments. The historian Reinhart Koselleck argued that history takes place in the space between expectation and experience, between hope and memory. To study history, then, is to reckon with the great disparity between the world as it has been and the world as we might like it to be. It is to devote one's life to the study of events that extend and explode the reach of the past upon the present, that alter the relation between individuals and their families, communities, nations and laws.

The murder in Shangrilá on 23 February 1965 was one such event. It was a cascade of events, really, the actual killing just one dramatic link in a long and twisted chain.

What is there to say of the execution itself? Cukurs's death doesn't matter except for what it signifies, except for the long chain of conspiracy and revisionism it has wrought. His manner of death marked him as unique, entitled to a spectacular end. It would have been better to let him live out the rest of his life from a cell, to have condemned him to obscurity and unquestioned criminality rather than awarding him the prize of martyrdom, and with it the prize of an arguable, uncertain, mutating story. From the moment he joined the Kommando, he was a dead man. Mossad called him 'The Deceased' well before he was murdered.[1] And yet his death gave him life. It allowed him to join the unfortunate order of Eastern Europe's 'uncommonly lively' dead bodies, denizens of what the anthropologist Katherine Verdery has dubbed the realm of post-socialist 'corpse politics'. In the former socialist world, Verdery explains, 'The *axis mundi* has shifted; whole fields of the past await the plowshare of revisionist pens, as well as the tears of those whose dead lie there insufficiently mourned.'[2] In this case, a small army of revisionist pens were indeed lying in wait, biding their time until the moment came to take up the cause of this bloody, battered corpse. They would reanimate it and make him speak again, not just in the pages of conspiracist novels and web forums, but also in court. His murder was their greatest gift.

Anyway, this is how it went.

Herberts Cukurs buys a gun. He followed the news from Jerusalem: he read of Eichmann's kidnapping, trial and hanging, and he feared the same fate awaited him. In June 1960, a month after Eichmann's abduction, he wrote to Brazilian authorities requesting permission to carry a weapon for self-defence, which was duly granted. 'Brazil did not want the repetition of an "Eichmann" incident on its territory,' Marcelo Silva writes in his account of the murder. 'That would be intolerable.'[3] The kidnapping had been a national humiliation, in addition to a flagrant violation of territorial sovereignty. Cukurs was armed, suspicious and defensive, but he was also vain and somewhat desperate. His pre-war fame had been, by this time, extinguished and eclipsed by his wartime sins. Like many other Nazis, he had fled to Brazil looking to escape the trials, literal and metaphorical, which would have overtaken him had he stayed in Europe. He also, no doubt, hoped to rebuild his reputation. He did not flee from press coverage. Perhaps he even derived a perverse pleasure in seeing his name and photograph return to the papers, no matter the cause. A Latvian emigré paper, *Latvija Amerikā*, reported on his tenuous status in November 1960: 'KOMINTERN TRIES TO ARRANGE FOR A LATVIAN EICHMANN: Brazilian bodyguards stand watch day and night.'[4]

There are varied accounts of how and why the Israelis decided to kill him – if such an overt decision was ever really made. The records have never been released. The only official account takes the form of a memoir written by the lead assassin, with the help of the former Mossad agent and journalist Gad Shimron. It is titled *The Execution of the Hangman of Riga: The Only Execution of a Nazi War Crimial by the Mossad*.[5] The author is identified only by his operational pseudonym, Anton Kuenzle, not his real name, Yaakov Meidad. The story it tells proceeds roughly as follows: a meeting of the Israeli intelligence agencies is called in late 1964. The subject is the hunt for Nazis around the world. A list of possible assassination targets is circulated among the attendees. One of them is Herberts Cukurs. The very sight of the name makes one of the participants – Major General Aharon Yariv, head of military intelligence, formerly Aharon Rabinovich, of Moscow – collapse. It turns out that Cukurs murdered his relatives. According to the journalist Ronen Bergman, the then head of Mossad, Meir Amit, was close to Yariv and, seeing the emotional disturbance the mere mention of Cukurs caused him, decided then and there that Cukurs would be their next target.[6] He then asked the prime minister for permission to proceed with the mission, which was granted, and began to assemble his team.

Meidad, who had handled the logistics for the Eichmann operation, was selected to lead this new mission. Born in 1919 in Breslau, Germany (now Wrocław, Poland), he emigrated to Palestine alone in 1934. Both his parents were murdered in concentration camps. He was the first Jew among the new settlers of Palestine to volunteer to fight with the British Army in the Second World War.[7] In 1948, when the Israeli Defence Forces were created, Meidad joined as an artillery officer. In 1955, he became a covert operative for Israeli intelligence. His first mission: go undercover in North Africa, help the Jewish community there defend themselves and set up secret lines of emigration to Israel. He didn't cut a particularly striking figure: 'Walking down the street of almost any Western capital, he would not stand out as a dashing James Bond character. With thinning hair and a slight paunch, he looks just like thousands of other citizens going about their daily business,' the Israeli intelligence scholar Shlomo Shpiro writes in his introduction to Meidad's memoir.[8] His unremarkable appearance was one of his greatest strengths.

On 1 September 1964, Meidad writes that he was summoned to a meeting with his handler in Paris, at a rented apartment on the Avenue de Versailles. He is given a new identity and a new mission: he would pose as an Austrian businessman named Anton Kuenzle, he would travel to São Paulo, where the Cukurs family had moved,[9] to befriend his target and persuade him to leave Brazil. Then he would kill him. According to Meidad, his handler offered him a long and perhaps improbable – yet nevertheless revealing – disquisition on the urgency of this mission, underscoring the approaching expiration of the West German statute of limitations for murders committed during the war, and the need for Israel to act to prevent the expiration from occurring.

> The German elite is filled with people from all walks of life who would prefer to erase from their curriculum vitae the answer to 'Where were you and what did you do in the years between 1933 to 1945?' The supporters of the implementation of the statute of limitations have plenty of arguments for why legal proceedings against the Nazis should be halted. They find it convenient, for instance, to use a formal argument, namely that the statute of limitations, which was enacted as a law in Germany in 1871, should apply not only to ordinary murders and crimes; it should also apply to such crimes as genocide and the Nazi horrors.[10]

The handler takes a sip of coffee and continues. He explains that, at that moment in Bonn, politicians were considering proposals to extend the statute of limitations for another ten years, to 1975, or to push forward the date from which the expiry is counted, from 1945 to 1949, when the Federal Republic was founded. Neither would be acceptable to the Israelis. The former seemed unlikely to pass, but the latter might. 'This proposal has some chance of being accepted as a compromise solution, and therein lies the danger. All it really means is that the criminals who have not been apprehended yet will only be able to crawl out of their hiding holes in September 1969, rather than in 1965,' he explains. '[T]hose who have a vested interest in forgetting the past and in implementing the Statute of Limitations on Nazi war crimes can be found not only in Germany.' Putting a lid on the events of the war had broad political and popular support. The Eichmann trial had raised awareness of the nature of the Holocaust, but the 'strong impact' of its televised victim testimonies had been 'losing its effect'. His voice rising, he goes on: 'It's been only 20 years since the release of the survivors of the death camps, and we owe it to them, and to the 6 million who did not survive and are unable to avenge themselves – we must thwart this shameful process of the Statute of Limitations.'[11]

The speech, as relayed in Meidad's pseudonymous memoir of the mission, is overly dramatic, almost maudlin. It is hard to imagine the handler, described as a former paramilitary soldier and high-ranking IDF officer named Yaakov, speaking in these terms. The memoir cannot be blindly regarded as a trustworthy document – just as it had initially sought to cover up the truth of the Eichmann kidnapping with a semi-fictionalised account, the Israeli government seems to have followed the same playbook here. But the very fact of the memoir's existence and the stories it contains tell us much about how Israel wanted the world to perceive the Cukurs assassination, and just how much was at stake. Framed in this manner, the murder becomes an event that explicitly extended the reach of the past upon the future, and the future upon the present; it was a manifestly illegal act that aimed to expand the parameters of legality.

They killed him, supposedly, because he wasn't that important, because time was running out. 'One question hanging over the Cukurs mission is why Cukurs was killed and not kidnapped like Eichmann,' Shpiro writes in his introduction to the memoir.

He offers three reasons: 'First, the small Mossad was unable to invest such extensive resources', given rising tensions at home. The approaching expiration of the German statute of limitations 'precluded the extensive operational requirements of a kidnapping operation'. But most of all, Shpiro writes, 'the nature of the Nazi criminal himself was different. Eichmann was a bureaucrat, a manager on a grand scale of the Holocaust, often described as a "desk murderer".' Eichmann had 'inside knowledge' that needed to be publicly aired 'for preserving the historical legacy of the Holocaust', whose trial therefore carried 'unique historical value'. Cukurs, meanwhile, was nothing more than a 'low-level, sadistic killer, whose crimes were characterized by their brutal violence and sheer inhumanity. The horrific nature of the crimes seemed to justify a violent punishment.'[12]

It is a striking explanation, a thicket of contradictions. The Cukurs operation was in many ways a more intricate mission than the Eichmann one, though it is true that it required half as many operatives – six agents to eleven, respectively. Meidad spent months travelling to and from Brazil, ingratiating himself with his target, posing as a successful businessman, asking Cukurs to invest in his invented real estate projects. He could have been exposed at any point. There was extreme risk and considerable expense involved, though it is true that the end result saved Israel the immense cost of a trial. The second defence, regarding the German statute of limitations, is a curious one. The approaching expiration of the statute of limitations would have little to no bearing on Cukurs's fate. Nothing precluded Israel or the Soviet Union from trying him in their courts. And by the time the Cukurs operation was approved, West German prosecutors were already pushing for the abolition of the statute of limitations, but on completely different grounds: in 1964, the West German government issued an international appeal for evidence against potential suspects, and German prosecutors were granted access to the Polish archive of Nazi crimes for the first time. 'What they found convinced them that there was not enough time before the 8 May 1965 deadline to sift through the material fast enough to effect interruptions in the statute's tolling period in the majority of the newly discovered Nazi murder cases,' the political scientist Robert Monson writes.[13] If the Cukurs operation had any bearing on the decision to extend and, eventually, abolish the statute of limitations, it would be as a footnote or curiosity, by no means a primary cause.

The third and final explanation, on the nature of the criminality at issue, is particularly knotted. While its basic premise is grounded in fact – Cukurs was a lower-ranking SS man who directly participated in mass murder while Eichmann, a lieutenant colonel, orchestrated many millions of deaths from his office – it is hard to understand how one could claim that no historical value, much less testimonial evidence, could be derived from Cukurs's trial, or to argue that none of his surviving victims would have welcomed the opportunity to confront him in court. To suggest that Cukurs's crimes were somehow more horrific than Eichmann's is to engage in a grotesque comparison, to weigh the deaths of thousands against that of millions, to ask which kind of killing weighs more heavily upon the scale of human sin. Did Eichmann not deserve a violent punishment? Is that not precisely what he received, what his hangman sacrificed his sanity to deliver? Is there not some sense in which sparing Cukurs the embarrassment of a trial and awarding him a quick and spectacular death might also be a form of clemency, a gruesome kind of gift?

From September 1964 to February 1965, Meidad worked his target. He appealed to his ego, he proposed a business partnership, he made Cukurs feel like someone again. He even met the Cukurs family and ate in their home. In October, he met Cukurs in Montevideo to scout for investment properties, and the two men made plans to meet there again in the new year.[14] In January, Meidad returned to Paris to confer with his handler and the other operatives assigned to the mission, maintaining his correspondence with Cukurs. They hatched a plan for the execution, they practised and trained. 'We were all aware that we were going to take the life of a man, but none of us had any doubt that this was the just punishment for the sadistic criminal, Herberts Cukurs,' Meidad writes in his memoir. They heard that their colleague, the Israeli spy Eli Cohen, had been uncovered in Damascus, that he was being tortured and interrogated. They went over the plan again.[15] Meidad arranged to meet Cukurs in the transit lounge of São Paulo airport on 28 January. They would travel on to Montevideo together.

Cukurs arrives at the airport with his film camera, a Kodachrome 16mm, and his gun. He points the camera at Meidad as he disembarks. The film strips would later appear in the pages of a Brazilian tabloid, salacious artefacts of the assassination. Six partial, blurred frames capture a scene on the tarmac. A Lufthansa bus sits parked to the right of the camera's gaze, and a small procession of passengers appear to be making their way on board. The fanned edges of a palm tree dance across the top of the frame. As the camera approaches a distant staircase, three men come into focus. They face the camera – their dark ties draw their bodies barely into focus – one raises his arm as if in greeting, or perhaps to block his face from the lens.

In Montevideo, Meidad books Cukurs a room at the Hotel Victoria Plaza, a grand high-rise on Plaza Independencia. They check in and go for a drive, ostensibly to look at potential real-estate acquisitions. Meidad heads towards Shangrilá; he tells Cukurs he wants his opinion on a property. He pulls up in front of the house on Calle Colombia. Cukurs follows Meidad out of the car and towards the entrance. Three of Meidad's colleagues are positioned inside, the others keep watch down the street. 'The original plan had been to overpower Cukurs, but not to kill him instantly,' Meidad explains. 'We had planned on a very brief court martial, in which we intended to read the charges to him, in the name of the thirty thousand Jews from Riga and Latvia – children, women, the elderly and men – who had been murdered by him over twenty years ago.'

It did not go quite so simply. Cukurs fought back. 'His attempt to reach for his gun shortened the proceedings,' Meidad writes. 'One of us put a gun to Cukurs' head, and pulled the trigger twice. The silencer and the noise of our struggle completely swallowed the sound of the shots. It was Tuesday, 23 February 1965, 12:30 p.m.'[16]

The agents take Cukurs's passport and his gun, an Italian Beretta. One of them had purchased a trunk in town and brought it to the property. They deposit the body inside the trunk and crown it with a folder containing Sir Hartley Shawcross's closing speech at Nuremberg, which someone, apparently, had thought to secure in advance. Then they wash the blood off their bodies and depart Shangrilá, driving back towards the city along the contours of the sea.

13

Past as Prelude

At first there was silence. The corpse rotted; the assassins escaped. In Buenos Aires, the agents reconvene at a café for a champagne toast to their success. Only once all the operatives are safely across the Atlantic do they alert the press. An agent calls the offices of German news agencies to say that 'a Nazi criminal had been liquidated in Montevideo by "Those Who Will Never Forget" as revenge for the horrors committed by the Nazis against the Jews of Europe,' Meidad writes. 'We all waited with bated breath for the story to break out in the press and on the radio.'

The news agencies ignored the message, so the assassins decided to put 'everything in writing,' according to Meidad. They sent telegrams with the details, beginning with the word 'VERDICT'. In his memoir, Meidad claims that this 'verdict' had been typed up in advance, that they had planned to deposit it with the body all along, after the 'brief court martial' that never came to pass. In reality, the telegram was sent weeks after the sentence had been meted out. It informed the journalists whose body it was, what he had done and where he could be found. Then the journalists informed the Uruguayan police.

When Police Commissioner Alejandro Otero arrived at the property, he noted that the house sat on a road with unfettered access to the sea. He learned that an Israeli commercial ship, the *Har Rimon*, had been anchored nearby. His men documented the crime scene, they opened the trunk and photographed the battered body and the pool of blood that had seeped out from the trunk's burlap seams. For the rest of his life, Otero would maintain that it was supposed to be a kidnapping, that there were holes drilled into the trunk, that a man locked inside would still have been able to breathe.

The papers finally pick up the story. In New York, Washington, Berlin, Munich, Frankfurt, Tel Aviv, Riga, Moscow and Paris, news of Cukurs's fate goes to press. Interpol issues a warrant for the arrest of Anton Kuenzle, Meidad's alter ego, and one of his colleagues. The assassination of Herberts Cukurs briefly becomes a subject of international attention. Some journalists quickly conclude that the assassination was an act of 'Jewish vengeance', while others, like the infamous muckraking *Washington Post* correspondent Jack Anderson, wonder if that was too simple an explanation, if perhaps Cukurs has been murdered in a 'double-cross plot' aimed at protecting the locations of higher profile Nazi officials like the Auschwitz doctor Josef Mengele, who was still hiding in South America.[1] The Brazilian tabloids print images of Cukurs in life and in death; they speculate about the identity of 'Those Who Will Never Forget'.[2] Jewish businesses and organisations in Montevideo, including the Israeli embassy, receive threats of death and destruction.

The Cukurs family gives Otero permission to cremate the body. Gunnars Cukurs, the eldest son, travels to Montevideo to collect the remains. When he returns to São Paulo with the urn, his mother asks him to open it so that she can look inside. 'Soon, she fell prey to a nervous breakdown that required medical attention,' Silva writes in his account of the murder. 'Among the remains were artificial teeth that did not belong to her husband.'[3] Otero had supervised the cremation himself. 'But the ashes and dental pieces that appeared in the urn are part of the mystery,' Silva writes. He suggests that they should be attributed either to human error or to the greed of the crematorium workers, who were sometimes known to claim golden tooth caps for themselves. Still, this small detail fuelled the engine of conspiracy. The Cukurs family came to believe that their paterfamilias could not have died in the manner that

'Those Who Will Never Forget' claimed. He was an innocent man, they maintained. He did not deserve such a fate.

There was a strangeness to the whole spectacle, the slightest suggestion that something, somewhere, had gone wrong. An abundance of evidence and a dearth of conclusions, a profusion of holes in the plot. For decades, Israel maintained a stance of public ignorance. Meidad's memoir was first published in Hebrew in 1997; it appeared in German in 1998 and in English in 2004. He died in June 2012. His role in the Eichmann operation is celebrated as his greatest achievement.

In 2021, I got in touch with Shlomo Shpiro, the intelligence scholar who wrote the introduction to Meidad's memoir. Twenty years had already elapsed since he had worked on the book; he told me he would have to take some time to look back through his files, but he was happy to talk. He had a genial and gregarious demeanour; he asked me about my background, which I had by then learned to distil into a few bullet points: I told him that both of my parents are from Riga, that my mother is Jewish and my father is not, and that in the process of learning about my own family story I had been researching the Cukurs case. When I initially asked him about the assassination, he redirected the conversation. 'Let's leave the killing aside for now,' he said. 'It's less interesting than the rest.'

He told me that he had edited the English manuscript of the book, just as he had edited a previous account of the Eichmann kidnapping called *The House on Garibaldi Street*. He had met and spoken with Meidad many times. I asked him, again, what he thought of the assassination, why Mossad went after Cukurs in particular, why, of all the Nazis on the run at the time, it was he who had been chosen. He responded with a question: 'You told me your mother is Jewish. Do you *feel* Jewish?' And once again I responded with a rehearsed set of bullet points: I told him I had grown up living only with my mother, who had sent me to Jewish day school and paid for my Bat Mitzvah lessons. I told him that I had never felt any other way. He nodded. 'I ask because, the Cukurs story, it's kind of a universal story, but it's also a very Jewish story,' he said. 'It's a lot simpler than a lot of people think. There

wasn't a huge discussion, "*Who are we going to kill tomorrow?*" '
he explained. 'It sounds very banal, but there weren't many other
Nazi criminals on the Mossad list at the time.' Cukurs was killed
because Mossad knew where he was, and because they were given
information about his crimes. That was that.

Shpiro told me that, as far as he understood, 'there was never any
question of kidnapping him'. The agents had orders, and they had
to execute them. If they ended up extending the German statute of
limitations in the process, well, that was icing on the cake. At the
time, catching Nazis was not an institutional priority for Mossad.
Israel was a new and fragile state, with war brewing on all sides.
When the Six-Day War broke out, in June 1967, whatever Nazi-
catching operations that had been on the table had to be dropped.
('Think about the CIA on 10 September 2001,' Shpiro said.) He
told me about a case I hadn't heard of involving the Auschwitz
'doctor' Horst Schumann, whom Mossad had located in Sudan
and later Ghana in the mid-1960s. 'Mossad discovered him, sent
in a team of people. What were they going to do, kill him in the
jungle, or bring him to trial?' Instead of killing him, the Israelis
pressured the Ghanaians to extradite Schumann to West Germany
in 1966. Every day during the trial proceedings, Shpiro told me,
Schumann was allowed to drive himself home in his Mercedes. He
was found guilty of murdering 30,000 Jews and was released from
prison after two years served because of a medical condition. He
lived for eleven peaceful years after that.

'There was a lot of bitterness after the Schumann trial,' Shpiro
told me. 'A trial is always better than an assassination, but that was
a red line in the sand. People believed that justice would be done
in West Germany, but it ended in an absurdly lenient sentence,
a travesty of justice. After the Schumann debacle, people at the
Mossad said, "forget it". It was a kind of closure for the Israelis.'
But the Schumann case did not explain why Cukurs was killed –
Schumann was extradited in 1966, Cukurs killed in 1965.

There were no breathing holes in the trunk that bore the body.[4]
The Cukurs operation was almost certainly meant to end in
murder, one way or another. But it was not meant to unfold as it

did. The Eichmann and Cukurs cases shared a great many things in common. The latter was launched on the coat-tails of the former, involved many of the same characters and followed a somewhat similar script. One cannot read of how Major General Aharon Yariv fainted at the very sight of Cukurs's name without thinking of how Yehiel Dinoor's, or K-Zetnik's, body tumbled to the ground at the Beit Ha'am. Dinoor was a reluctant but critical witness, one of the few who had personally encountered Eichmann at Auschwitz. He had spent the intervening years writing novels about the camps, 'consumed by the search for the word that will express the look in the eyes of those who headed toward the crematorium', as he put it in his memoir. He tried to tell the prosecutors that he wasn't up to the task. 'I said: Sir, describing Auschwitz is beyond me!'[5] They did not believe him, and so when he took his place on the witness stand he quickly ended up in the hospital ward. He gave his testimony to the judges, but they could not – or would not – hear him. Maurice Blanchot wrote of this phenomenon: when the survivor speaks, his words may be unintelligible, unformed, or illogical; but reliably, 'here and there a correct note sounded, like a cry from behind the mask, revealing someone who eternally asked for help without being able to indicate where he was'.[6]

Perhaps, seeing Yariv faint in front of his colleagues in Israeli intelligence, Amit decided that his agents would serve as witnesses, judges and executioners all at once. The 'very brief court martial' to which Meidad refers in his memoir, the legal proceeding which never came to pass, overcome as it was by the physical force of the accused, would have been a trial in miniature, conducted at warp speed. The very mention of it is an invitation to speculation. Why did Meidad include this detail in his memoir? Mossad had by then engaged in targeted killings that did not waste time with such formalities. Why attempt to bother with them here? Where did the excerpt of Shawcross's speech come from? Why did the assassins rip out those pages, in particular? Where do the fictions begin and end? When do you know when a story has travelled all the way from 'A to Z'?

In his preface to Meidad's memoir, Amit writes that the Cukurs assassination is unique in the history of his intelligence service.

'Eichmann was not the only one,' Amit writes. 'We have before us a fascinating book, based on real facts – a classic case of truth being stranger than fiction.' But it is, in reality, far more complex than that. In the story of this assassination, fact commingles with fiction, vengeance with justice, memory with oblivion. It was an act committed as a kind of final judgement, an attempt to lend some finality to the future, to rid the earth of a man who had long ago forfeited his right to cohabitate with humanity. The murder was supposedly conducted in order to close the case of Herberts Cukurs so that others might be opened – so that the statute of limitations would remain in suspension, so that thousands of others might be arraigned. Their extralegal act was meant to finalise the narrative of his life and fate; when they closed the lid on the trunk, the assassins thought they were also putting a lid over his story. They did not stop to consider the possibility that their operation might have the exact opposite effect.

In Jewish tradition, law and literature have a dialectic relation, inflecting and following upon one another. Where the law fails, parables point the way. Where stories are silent, law speaks. In this way, literature and law produce and revise one another. 'The two are one in their beginning and their end,' wrote Haim Bialik. The assassination of Herbert Cukurs marks the moment when law gives way to literature. It may have been intended as a final word on the subject, but it was only the beginning.

PART II

This
Is the best of all possible worlds
Tanks in the streets
Tanks at our feet
Tanks in our heads
Tanks in our hearts.

Ivars Lindbergs, '1968'[1]

They built on rock.
They didn't trust the bog's will-o'-the-wisps,
betrayed the bog.
They didn't allow the past to rule over the obvious,
They knew for sure: there is no god.
Have to get by with the Russian rod.

Uldis Bērziņš, 'In Defense of Informers'[2]

14

Aron Kodesh

There is only one synagogue left in Riga. There are EU flags, minimalist coffee shops, Bentleys, banks. A weekly ferry from Stockholm deposits a small army of Scandinavian consumers. Latvia is no longer 'Eastern European' but, rather, 'Baltic', or, even better, 'Nordic'. The country is emptying out, day by day. Its beaches bereft of beachgoers, its villages bereft of villagers. The taxi drivers prefer to speak Russian, the young baristas prefer Latvian or English. Foreigners come for stag nights, for architectural tours, for Jewish heritage tours, for neoconservative foreign policy junkets. Hipsters fly in from London to feel the flavour of communism, to breathe in the cold air of the new Europe. Writers, artists and dissidents fly in from Moscow, looking to find a more accommodating home and hoping they will not be unwelcome. If Latvia makes it into the foreign press, it is usually because of a money-laundering scheme, or the spectre of Russian invasion, or the yearly SS memorial parade. March the 16th – Remembrance Day of the Latvian Legionnaires. The Latvian Legion, a division of fighters that was subsumed into the Waffen SS.[1] Every year, the old men march. Some carry canes, some carry Latvian flags, their burgundy and white stripes billowing in the wind. They lay flowers at the Freedom Monument in the centre of Riga, they are surrounded by press and police. The veterans die, but the march continues. In 2009, five years after Latvia formally joined the European Union, police detained a Russian counter-protestor, who, watching the legionnaires march by, cried out, 'Hitler kaputt!' They did not detain the legionnaires.[2]

On a tourist blog I once read that there is no building in Riga whose mouth is not drawn in pain. A casual utterance, a light observation from a foreign eye, recorded in a foreign tongue. But it is true: to gaze up at its famous Jugendstil facades is to encounter a world resplendent in agony, terror, decadence and loss. The buildings are covered in statues of angels, medusas, sphinxes, gods. Six Valkyries top the house at 2a Alberta Street, Isaiah Berlin's childhood home. They stare down upon the street; they decide who lives and dies.

The Jugendstil style, grotesque in its excesses, is limited to a few blocks, but the pain is everywhere. The whole city – the whole country – is an archive of losses. Lost empire, lost nation, lost revolution, lost wars. An index of 'memorial places' compiled by the University of Latvia leaves few factories, highways, or forests untouched. A fish processing plant, a bend in the road, an old school. Here, Jews were killed by Germans or by local Latvian 'self-defenders'.[3] In the 1960s, the Soviets put up the first memorials, wooden signs, stone obelisks and statues at the killing fields and concentration camps, honoring the murdered as Soviet citizens, not as Jews. In the village of Bauska, once called Boisk, where my grandmother's summerhouse still stands, where my sister spent the summer days of her childhood, they put up a small monument in the Old Jewish Cemetery, inscribed: 'Eternal glory to deceased heroes for liberating our motherland in 1944–1945'. Later, it is replaced with a bronze plaque honouring the 'Victims of Fascists' Terror'.[4] In the 1990s, the bronze plaque is stolen and likely used as scrap metal. In 2004 it is replaced with a granite plaque funded by the Council of Jewish Communities of Latvia, with Latvian, Russian and Hebrew script. In 2012, on the other side of the river, a monument dedicated 'to the defenders of Bauska against the second Soviet occupation' is unveiled. Below the dedication is a quote from Kārlis Ulmanis, the interwar authoritarian ruler: 'Latvija jabut Latviesu Valstij', 'Latvia should be a Latvian state'.

The new millennium brought on a rush of memorialisation. The Soviet collapse meant that the Baltics turned westward and welcomed the belated arrival of the neoliberal 'memory boom', and with it what historian Nikolay Koposov calls the 'Holocaust-and-heritage paradigm', the liberal democratic 'culture of memory'.[5]

In 2001, a memorial is unveiled at Biķernieki Forest, the site of fifty-five mass graves, the final resting place of Jews from Latvia, Germany, Austria and Czechoslovakia. The memorial is financed by the Austrian and German governments. In 2002, another memorial, designed by the same artist and financed by Latvia, Israel, the US, Germany and private donors, is unveiled at the site of the Rumbula massacres. In 2004, a stone bearing a Star of David and a message engraved in three languages is erected on the grounds of the Salaspils concentration camp, financed by a donation from a survivor. It reads: 'To honour the dead and as a warning to the living. In memory of the Jews deported from Germany, Austria, and Czechia, who from December 1941 to June 1942 died from hunger, cold, and inhumanity and have found eternal rest in the Salaspils forest.' Every year on 4 July, the national Commemoration Day of Genocide Against the Jews, dignitaries dutifully shuffle towards the killing fields, towards the ruins of the Great Choral Synagogue. They lay wreaths, they make promises, they half-heartedly call for all of the complicit to be held to account.

Around this time, the US began sending its 'Special Envoys to Monitor and Combat Anti-Semitism' to the region, to see what progress was being made, to see if all of those absolutions were being sufficiently embraced. In 2016, I was invited to sit in on a meeting between the then Special Envoy and a group of Latvian historians and primary school teachers. They lamented the fact that they did not have enough Holocaust stories to share with their students. There was no Latvian Anne Frank, no popular, paradigmatic victim tale. The stories that did exist had been written in Russian and were unintelligible to young Latvian schoolchildren. The first Latvian translation of a survivor's diary had just been released earlier that year. Would there be others?

*

In theory, the sudden embrace of the past inaugurated an era of acknowledgement, awareness, education and repentance. In practice, it meant that the performance of penitence became a proxy for Europeanness.[6] Not long after the commemorative plaques enumerating national sins went up, so too did the blue flags with their perfect circles of yellow stars. Latvia became a European country, a NATO member. It sent soldiers, doctors and nurses to serve in the American wars in Iraq and Afghanistan. The currency changed: the Lat became the euro, though for two weeks in 2014 both currencies were in circulation.[7] Tourism grew and so did the tourist shops, which sell amber, linen and liquor. Also available for purchase are textiles and jewellery engraved with ancient Latvian symbols, pagan signs for the sun, water, earth and fire. They are simple runic designs, solid lines crossed and hooked. One of them is called the Thunder Cross, or Swastika. It adorns rings, bracelets, amulets, mittens and belts.[8] It is a cliché to make note of this, I know. They were pagan symbols before they were Nazi ones. But does it matter?

The 'memory boom' was not unidirectional. In Latvia and throughout Europe, it marked a chaotic explosion of conflicting narratives, the acceleration and contestation of memory politics. It became fashionable, in the academy, in the courts, in the streets, to engage in the new 'memory wars', to vie for ownership over the categories of victim, survivor, defender, hero.

It was in 2005, at the height of this chaotic era, that a small art exhibition opened in the depressed former imperial naval port of Karosta. Located on the south-western shore of Latvia and formally part of the city of Liepāja, Karosta was once the base of the Soviet Baltic Fleet, a closed city accessible only to military personnel. Today, some of the Soviet sailors and their families remain, though the empire they served is no more. The neighbourhood has emptied out, the streets fallen into disrepair, the old fortresses are slowly being cannibalised by the sea. A new nation has emerged all around them, a nation which they do not recognise and where they do not feel welcome, for they are living reminders of an uncomfortable past. 'It's a sad place, but it's an important one,' Sanita Jemberga, an investigative journalist, tells me over coffee at Liepāja's renowned boulangerie. 'You have to understand. Here, it's like World War II happened yesterday.'

The exhibition, entitled 'Presumption of Innocence', was unveiled in February 2005 at a now-defunct cultural centre called K@2, founded by a Swedish artist named Carl Biorsmark who hoped to turn the decaying city into an artistic hub. Biorsmark was inspired to create the exhibition after coming across a translation of Yaakov Meidad's memoir in the window of a Latvian bookshop. 'You see such a book in a window, and you want to know what's inside,' he said in a radio interview. 'I became very fascinated ... I went, in Riga, to museums and archives, I asked about this story, and wherever I went, they said, "Shh ... don't speak about this."' But he kept going. He found the Meidad account to be rather one-sided and began investigating the Cukurs case himself. Working with the filmmaker Kristine Briede, he flew to The Gambia to retrace Cukurs's historic flight, and to Brazil, to interview his descendants and sort through the archives. They produced a fifty-two-minute film documenting these journeys, which would anchor the exhibit, and which was also titled 'Presumption of Innocence'.

The exhibition consisted of three rooms: one detailing Cukurs's inter-war aviation career, one full of testimonies for and against him and one with photographs from his encounters with Meidad in South America. The point, according to Biorsmark and his collaborators, was to suggest 'that a person is not considered to be guilty if the court has not recognized him as such'.[9] 'This is what artists have to do – stay in the middle and raise question marks,' Biorsmark told journalist Aaron Eglitis.[10] The exhibition enjoyed the tacit support of a Member of Parliament who, a few weeks prior, had been kicked out of his party for suggesting that Latvian Jews stop 'acting like they did in 1940 when they welcomed the enemies of Latvia'.[11,12]

On the fourth day of the exhibition, Biorsmark received a telephone call from the Latvian Prosecutor General's office. At first he thought it was a joke. On the other end of the line, a man explained: 'As we understand, you have very serious material, so if it is possible, we would like to come and have a look at the exhibition.' Biorsmark said they could come whenever they wanted. 'The next day comes a red bus with four people from the prosecutor's office. They walk into the gallery, click click click – they treat it like an investigation – spending hours.' What was presented as 'art' would be read as evidence.

A few days later, the curators received a letter from the prosecutor's office, asking them to scan the documents on display. The Prosecutor General was going to reopen a criminal investigation into Herberts Cukurs. 'There was such a case – it was never closed,' Biorsmark explained, 'but it was kind of a sleeping case.' 'They are still working on it. They are doing the same thing that we did – they are going to Yad Vashem, they are going to the archives in Moscow, and everywhere, the doors are closed.'[13]

The exhibition was just the start. A number of revisionist projects would follow. There were more documentaries, books and articles about the great injustice visited upon the national hero and therefore upon the nation. The artists and authors track down the survivors. They ask them for interviews, they try to recruit them to their cause. They ask them to refute what they know, what they saw with their own eyes, what they testified to in signed affidavits, over and over again.

*

Am I getting ahead of myself, letting the story run out from underneath me? Maybe this is what revisionism does – it makes those who try to slow it down and retrace its steps stumble over their words, lose the plot. It can be difficult to keep pace with the velocity of elision, erasure.

I began this chapter by saying that there is only one synagogue left in Riga. There are two prayer houses and two Jewish museums, but there is only one synagogue. There used to be four. When it was completed in 1905, the Peitav Shul was furnished with warm wooden floors and colourful Moorish columns. Its location, in the heart of the medieval old city, is what spared it from destruction. It was too close to other buildings to risk burning down, so the Nazis and their local sympathisers turned it into stables instead.

The priest from the church next door, Gustav Shaurums, is said
to have hidden the synagogue's Torah scrolls in a cabinet in the
eastern wall of the building, where they were discovered intact
after the war. In 1944, as evacuees and exiles filtered back into
the city, a list of survivors was posted on the synagogue doors.
Thirteen names in all. The returnees sought them out, they
asked if the survivors knew what had happened to disappeared
families and friends. 'More often than not, they received only a
downward glance and a monosyllabic "yes" or "no" in response
to their questions,' the childhood survivor Musya Glants writes
in her memoir.[14] The synagogue survived bombings in 1995 and
1998; the culprits were never apprehended.[15] Today, its interior is
a pale pastel blue, its columns decorated with green, red and blue
zigzags and topped with golden palm capitals, the Bima made
from a screen of latticed marble. A security guard is permanently
stationed outside. When I walked inside one Friday morning, the
man on duty chased me through the doors.

Rabbi Kalev Krelin, who led the congregation at the time, greeted
me with a nod and waved the guard away. As he led me into the
synagogue, he said hello to the few members of the congregation
who are coming to say their morning prayers. We sat on a wooden
pew in the back of the cavernous room and he explained that he
had recently moved to Riga from Brooklyn, that he considered his
current posting to be a difficult one. He gestured to the inscription
arching over the aron kodesh, the Torah ark: 'Blessed be the Lord,
who has not given us as prey to their teeth.' 'Nowhere else will
you see an inscription like this,' Krelin said. 'They tend to be more
positive.' As he led me downstairs to a smaller, more intimate prayer
room, I asked him what he thought of how Latvia had addressed
its complicity in the Holocaust – I was going to visit the ruins
of the Great Choral Synagogue after our meeting and wondered
what he made of it. 'In Lithuania, they say they had nothing to do
with it. Here, they don't even do that, they just don't talk about
it,' he said. He had heard of Cukurs, of course. 'Because Mossad
assassinated him, they use that as proof of his innocence.' On a
bookshelf, Krelin rifled through decrepit prayer books and ledgers

documenting Jewish life throughout the twentieth century – some were from Riga, others were from rural Jewish communities, now extinct, that no longer had anywhere to keep them. He wanted to show me one book in particular. Its leather binding was punctured by a bullet hole.

15

Before the Law

Once I discovered the criminal investigation into Cukurs, I began closely following its development. In 2015, the newspaper *Delfi* reported that the Israeli government had not responded to the prosecutor's repeated requests for information. 'The criminal investigation is ongoing,' the article stated. 'Criminal law stipulates that a person who has participated in genocide is not barred from criminal liability.'[1] I wondered what 'criminal liability' would look like for a corpse. I went over my correspondence with the prosecutor: in his letter enumerating the potential legal outcomes of the case, he wrote,

> Theoretically, this case could continue to exonerate a
> deceased person – Herberts Cukurs[–] under Chapter 56
> of the Criminal Procedure Law, 'Criminal Proceedings in
> Cases Regarding the Exoneration of a Deceased Person' …
> '[I]f the prosecutor decides to continue the proceedings for
> the exoneration of the deceased person, the final adjudication
> of the issue for the exoneration of Herberts Cukurs according
> to Sections 613–616 of the Criminal Procedure Law may reach
> the court …'[2]

I looked up the relevant clauses in the criminal code: Sections 613 and 614 codified how cases involving deceased persons should proceed, enabling the court to schedule hearings and summonses.

Section 615 set the rules for how a criminal investigation should be concluded: the corpse would either be exonerated or non-exonerated, placeholding words for 'innocent' or 'guilty'. Section 616 laid out the procedure for appealing these decisions.[3] All these rules would soon become central to the story, but at the time I just stared at them confusedly, bemused by the legal jargon.

I emailed the press secretary requesting an in-person meeting with the prosecutor, and began planning another trip to Riga. We agreed on a time, early one morning on a mild day in early June 2017. When the day came, I walked the two kilometres from my apartment to the Prosecutor General's understated art nouveau building in the centre of the city.

The meeting lasted no more than an hour. I was not allowed to record, so instead I took furious notes as the prosecutor spoke. One of his colleagues sat beside him, patiently translating our exchange from Latvian to English and back again. He asked me again if I had any pertinent information, and I realised that he would probably not have agreed to the meeting had I not had a personal connection to the case. He seemed to be speaking to me as an interested party, not as a journalist, despite the fact that I had identified myself as both. I tried to approach our appointment matter-of-factly; I just needed to understand what was going on. Ever since I had learned about the proceedings, my mind had been on fire. Just as Cukurs's assassination had been a direct result of the Eichmann kidnapping, so I could not think of this case as anything but a curious continuation of the celebrated proceedings in Jerusalem, a ghostly successor to that 'world trial'. Eichmann had ensured that the cattle trucks took millions to their deaths; that they arrived promptly at the camps. Cukurs had chauffeured the murderers to the killing sites, even if it cannot be proved that he ever pulled the trigger himself. Both of them had contributed to the infrastructure of mass murder. The Eichmann trial had taken place under the glare of a thousand cameras, under the watchful eyes of a global press corps. This proceeding was taking place slowly and quietly, virtually unknown to all except to its stakeholders, its immense import almost completely masked.

The prosecutor explained that he had inherited the case, No. 12812000506, from his predecessors, that it had been reopened in 2005 – as a result of the art exhibition – but that the seed for it had been planted nearly a decade prior. In 1996, five years after Latvia regained its independence, Cukurs's daughter, Antinea Dolores Rizzotto, had filed an application for his formal rehabilitation. In the decades following the collapse of the Soviet Union, hundreds of people would file these requests in the hope of clearing their own names or that of their relatives, colleagues, friends. It was also a way of reclaiming family property that had been confiscated under Soviet rule. Her application was probably stacked in a file with hundreds of others, its handlers unaware of where it would lead. This was the 'sleeping case' to which Biorsmark had referred.

'Rehabilitation' was a Soviet legal invention, a product of the thaw of the 1950s and 1960s. It was a radical new policy when it was first instituted, in 1953, by Nikita Khrushchev, then the newly installed First Secretary of the Communist Party of the Soviet Union. It enabled any Soviet citizen, dead or alive, who had been convicted of a counter-revolutionary crime in the previous decades to petition the state to have their records expunged and their names formally cleared. It was a formal legal procedure overseen by the state prosecutor's office, a bureaucratic avenue for securing forgiveness and paltry restitution. Over the course of Khrushchev's eleven-year tenure as Soviet premier, 900,000 people, living and dead, underwent this process. 'The Soviet government did not generally solicit cases for posthumous rehabilitation,' the historian Samuel Casper writes in his dissertation on the subject. 'The onus lay with relatives, friends, and occasionally erstwhile colleagues to initiate the review of convictions by filing an appeal with the Procuracy (the state prosecutor's office), which was authorized to reopen criminal cases. This arrangement required persons who had already suffered tremendous loss at the hands of the regime to resubmit themselves and their loved ones to state scrutiny; that many were willing, if not eager, to do so speaks to the benefits promised by rehabilitation beyond the symbolic restoration of individuals' good names.'[4]

The petitioners would be investigated, interviewed and judged all over again. In return, if things went well, they (or their corpses) would receive permission to rejoin the Party in good standing, any record of their crimes expunged. 'They receive deeds in which it is presumably written that they are rehabilitated, that they were not enemies,' the novelist Daša Drndić writes. They are assured 'that their country now loves them, and some also received badges. Except that not one of them is still alive.'[5]

The collapse of the Soviet Union gave 'rehabilitation' a new meaning. The legal procedure was kept largely intact by the newly independent former Soviet states, but expanded to accommodate a new category of applicant: not only those who had been repressed and condemned by Soviet authorities, but also those who had been accused of collaborating with them. If, during the Soviet period, rehabilitation was a formal mechanism of reinstating Party members and reclaiming bodies for the communist cause, in the 1990s and 2000s rehabilitation came to play a similar role for the newly reconstituted nation. Those whose applications were approved could reclaim their good names and proudly proclaim that they were card-carrying patriots, that they had never betrayed their people. They could rejoin the Latvian national community, itself newly restored.

Posthumous rehabilitation, Casper explains, was a curious, vaguely sacral and deeply political process. Adam Hochschild has described posthumous rehabilitation as 'a kind of sainthood for martyrs', but, as Casper points out, its primary purpose was political rather than spiritual. It created a mechanism through which the Soviet leadership could more deftly navigate the novel political considerations of the post-Stalinist period. 'Khrushchev and his cohorts were adept at invoking the posthumously rehabilitated in moments of political extremis, but at no point did they transform their erstwhile comrades into objects of any sort of regular reverence,' Casper writes. 'The kind of afterlife that posthumous rehabilitation promised in the 1950s and 1960s was therefore one predicated on the ability of past actors to help mediate present-day struggles, rather than the notion of an eternal reward for faithful, yet repressed Communists.'[6] Much the same would be true of its post-Soviet uses. After 1991, rehabilitation became a means of formally separating the nation's democratic future from its communist past.

For those unfamiliar with these kinds of proceedings, posthumous legal cases might at first seem to be almost blasphemous, precisely the kinds of spectacles that sophisticated legal systems are supposed to prevent. Most Western legal codes, after all, include some version of this universal rule: per mortem extinguitur omne crimen. Death extinguishes every crime.

This is the kind of rule that legal scholars call a 'legal fiction' – a legal statement, like 'the constitution is the will of the people', or 'judges simply declare and never make the law' – which is only aspirationally true.[7] These fictions make up the scaffolding of law. 'The influence of the fiction extends to every department of the jurists's activities,' the legal scholar Lon L. Fuller writes in his unforgettable book on the subject. 'Fictions are, to a certain extent, simply the growing pains of the language of the law.'[8] This particular fiction has been operative since ancient times.

In ancient Athens, if a man were found guilty of treason, tyranny, or a similarly egregious crime, he and his whole family would be permanently cast out of the city. Their homes would be razed, the graves of their ancestors exhumed, their bones thrown over the city walls. Their neighbours and acquaintances would never again invoke their names and would proceed as if the family had never lived among them, indeed as if they had never lived at all. Death did not protect traitors from this fate. Corpses, too, could be tried for treason.[9] Their bones would be removed and expelled, as would those of their kin. In 897, Pope Stephen VI exhumed the corpse of one of his predecessors, Pope Formosus. The corpse was clad in papal robes and put on trial, found guilty, stripped and dismembered and thrown into the Tiber. In seventeenth- and eighteenth-century France and its colonies, les procès des cadavres allowed for the trial and public sentencing of the dead. 'Some criminals, because of the "enormity" of their crime, had to be "accused and condemned after their death and the punishment executed on the corpse against their memory",' writes the French legal scholar Serge Dauchy.[10] The bodies of suicides, heretics and rebels were exhumed, tried and dragged around the city streets.[11] These were thought to be educative communal events, as one jurist argued, 'absolutely necessary for the public interest to make an example of the dead, for the survivors and for those who are not delinquent, so that the prosecution and execution of the corpses and their memories, who are no longer capable of having feelings, serve as examples for those who still do'.[12] They tried the dead to teach the living. Was the Cukurs case any different?

Cukurs could not be formally rehabilitated because he had never been repressed by Soviet authorities. But he could be investigated – and then cleared – of criminal offences. In his case, the distinction between rehabilitation and posthumous exoneration was merely procedural. The prosecutor explained that the case was akin to a pre-trial proceeding. It was a near impossibility that the case would go to trial, given the fact that there were almost no living witnesses, and given the fact that the subject had been dead for fifty years. He explained that it would be terminated 'on non-exonerating or exonerating grounds'. Cukurs would be exonerated – that is, deemed not guilty, non-culpable – if there was insufficient evidence to prove that he participated in mass murder. It was important, the prosecutor told me, 'to clarify these issues.' When he had inherited the case from his predecessors, it 'contained the opinions of historians, but no records of investigations in Brazil, Uruguay, or Israel'. Without authoritative documents, he could not make a ruling. He had sent out requests, received some information and hoped more was forthcoming. He had interviewed Cukurs's daughter the previous year, and the Cukurs family had already submitted all the relevant documents in their possession. The family was militating for his exoneration. 'They say he was not guilty and that he was never sentenced in any country,' the prosecutor explained.

That Cukurs had definitively belonged to the Arājs Kommando was not enough to confirm his complicity. 'It is impossible to convict anyone just for belonging to a group in Nazi-occupied Latvia,' the prosecutor told me. 'It must be proven that he gave orders to kill or shoot, or personally participated.' There were documents from Germany that suggested Cukurs was present during the killings, but the prosecutor had questions regarding their reliability: 'On the basis of these documents, we cannot convict.'

In Germany, where the notion of a 'crime complex' continues to govern Nazi prosecutions, the very fact of Cukurs's membership in the Kommando would have been more than enough for the Central Office to open an investigation and pass along his case file for prosecution – but only if he was still alive. (The office does not process cases against the dead.) The degree to which Cukurs was or was not complicit in the Holocaust is not an open question, if you ask the lawyers in Ludwigsburg. In Latvia, where the national criminal code holds that establishing, leading, or participating in the activities of a criminal organisation is a punishable offence, the threshold for 'participation' remains up for debate. There is no precedent for this kind of case, no well-oiled judicial system for punishing and prosecuting mass criminality, no case law on how to conduct an investigation into an assassinated man. 'The world often presents cases no mind could anticipate, in circumstances no one could wholly foresee,' writes the legal scholar James Boyd White. 'The most important message is the one the judge performs, not the one he states.'[13]

During our conversation, the prosecutor seemed to be performing his own indifference to the outcome of this strange investigation. He had nodded glumly, almost despairingly, towards the thick stack of evidence he had collected. He was still waiting for certain nations, including Israel and Brazil, to respond to his requests for information. I asked him if the testimony of Jewish survivors was included in his files. He nodded, explaining that while the testimonies had been submitted as evidence, they may not be formally admissible.

I got the feeling that he could not wait for the case to be over and to be free of this particular crime scene. He probably hoped that it would be a simple matter, despite its potentially explosive political implications: when the time was right, he would simply write up his decision, send it to the relevant parties and that would be that.

I asked him when he thought that might be. He said maybe later that year, but he could not say for sure. He was close to making a decision, though it seemed he had already formulated one in his mind.

In the meantime, he reiterated the recommendation he had emailed me, encouraging me to read a historical novel that had recently come out about Cukurs. I might learn something about my grandfather in its pages, he said.

16

The Plot

So I went looking for the novel, for the story within this story, the plot within the plot. From the prosecutor's office, I headed for a bookshop in the old city.

I have already described how I found the novel *You Will Never Kill Him* propped up on the new releases shelf, the feeling of vertigo that the discovery induced, a feeling that never quite went away. I had difficulty situating myself in relation to the past and present; I tried to remind myself of my own coordinates in time.

You can understand how it quickly became confusing: from the scant facts of my grandfather's life, the novelist had woven a fictional story. From this story, the prosecutor seemed to have learned something about Cukurs. And from the prosecutor, I had been sent back to the novel (and the novelist) to look for facts and sources. It was a closed loop: I had to find my own way out.

The author, Armands Puče, made his name as a sports journalist in Riga. He has written several biographies of Latvian athletes and is a regular commentator on Latvian television. The story of Herberts Cukurs and my grandfather is a diversion from his regular repertoire, yet it is written in the breezy, triumphant mode of the sportscaster, the hero cast in a familiar, uncomplicated mode. True to the genre of the spy novel, the events of world history, the deaths of millions – the birth of the Latvian nation, the Bolshevik Revolution, the world wars – are described like twists and turns in a sporting contest. The Cukurs operation is depicted as a 'chess gambit', a risky move in a global tournament of wits.

As I flipped through its pages, I could not help but feel that I was approaching this whole subject from an irrecoverable depth of naivety – I was an outsider looking in, at once too close to and too far removed from the story to see it straight. A large part of the shock of that moment came from the realisation that *someone else* had spent enough time researching Boris to try to tell his story. Had he seen something that I had missed? How much did I not know? Puče had excavated my grandfather from his missing grave and reanimated him as a fictional personality, a compromised character in a story of conspiracy. Why? What was Boris doing in his story?

Before I had read the novel, before I knew the depths of its distortions, I wrote to Puče and asked him for an interview. We arranged to meet at a chain coffee shop in downtown Riga. It was winter – he arrived wearing a jacket and a scarf. There wasn't much small talk. 'I know who you are,' he told me. 'Your grandfather is a character. His story is about what happens when you play a double game, what kind of person you might be.' Cukurs didn't die the way Mossad says he did, Puče told me: 'He tricked them.' There was a glint in his eye, and he smiled slightly as he spoke – a conspiratorial demeanour that, by then, I had become well acquainted with. 'It's like fiction, it's like literature, but it's ninety per cent based on facts,' he said of his novel. '*You will never kill him* – I don't mean Cukurs, I mean this country. You're never going to kill us. This land isn't just territory between east and west, between Russia and the West – no, for us this is *our* land, and we should tell the next generation how this happens. It takes time. In ten or twenty years more, people will accept him,' he said, speaking of Cukurs. 'My generation is starting to ask questions. Why are we just sitting in a corner? Who is responsible for these accusations, especially if there is no evidence or witnesses?'[1]

When we parted, he gave me a copy of the novel, inscribed 'Linda!'

I kept the copy he gave me and sent another one to my mother in Boston. I started taking Latvian classes so I could eventually read it myself, while my mother – always too kind, too generous with her time – began combing through it, taking detailed notes along the way. At first, she tried reading it at night before bed, but its contents were too gruesome, its subtext too hateful for her to fall asleep. She would come across a particularly anti-Semitic passage – about Jewish control over the Latvian economy, or about the Protocols of the Elders of Zion, or about secret troves of Jewish gold – and have to put the book down (and then call me to air her frustration). As I familiarised myself with the special consonants and sounds of the Latvian language – rife with hard *k*s and flat diphthongs – I began slowly making my own way through the text.

You Will Never Kill Him is a braided narrative, with alternating chapters telling the stories of my grandfather and Cukurs until their trajectories finally, fatally intersect.[2] Cukurs's story begins in the military port of Karosta. Young Cukurs, fifteen years old in 1915, watches German ships launching shells at the shore. Though thousands of Latvians fled their country during the First World War, the Cukurs family are depicted as proud patriots, true Latvians who stood their ground. Four years later, Cukurs brings home the Bolshevik proclamation. He is tempted to follow his friends to Russia, to join in the revolution, but at the last minute he changes his mind. The hero remains unblemished by Bolshevism. Crisis averted.

The first glimpse the reader gets of my grandfather is not of my grandfather at all, but of his fictional alter ego. In Puče's imagination, the story of Boris Kinstler begins in the summer of 1918 at a Moscow apartment building directly across from the new headquarters of the Cheka, the Bolshevik secret police.[3] The protagonist of this story is a young Latvian man named Juris Spakovskis, who comes from a poor family whose members are all either dead or imprisoned. Spakovskis soon winds up in jail, too, and befriends a Bolshevik prisoner in his cell. A 1917 amnesty sets them free, and Spakovskis sets off with his new friend for Moscow.

At a poetry reading, Spakovskis meets a well-dressed gentleman who appears to be British but speaks perfect Latvian. He says his name is Jēkabs Peterss – he is the deputy chief of Lenin's secret police, one of the founders of the Cheka. The two men hit it off and they meet up a handful of times. Spakovskis needs money and Peters seems to have some. Soon, Peterss invites Spakovskis to his office; he offers him a job and a new name. 'I'll give you new documents, and you will go to Germany,' Peters tells him.

'Why Germany?' Spakovskis asks.

'From this point on, your name will be Boris Kinstlers. You are fleeing from Bolshevik atrocities and are seeking political asylum in Germany.' The most direct route to Germany was through Latvia. In Riga, 'Boris Kinstlers' would be born.

In Riga, Kinstlers is assigned a Soviet handler who trains him to blend in with Latvian society. When the Second World War breaks out, he is told to infiltrate Nazi organisations in Riga. In the Arājs Kommando, he is told to instigate local violence against Jews, to create the ghetto, and, in the ghetto, to create a brothel for German soldiers.

Meanwhile, Cukurs's star has risen. He can do no wrong in the world of the novel. He laments the annexation of Czechoslovakia, he turns down an invitation to work with Soviet aircraft designers, he saves Russian prisoners of war and Jews alike. He joins Arājs's Kommando only because one day he is called to the police prefecture and held at gunpoint, suspected of being a Soviet collaborator. Arājs appears, intervenes and saves his life.

At no point in the novel is Cukurs implicated in murder. Puče includes a long and detailed description of the killings at Rumbula, but disregard this and denies local involvement: 'The Germans bring their own shooters; they do not trust Latvians with this important mission,' he writes. Only in one scene does Cukurs appear at the killing site, and only because Arājs asks Cukurs to chauffeur him and Kinstlers there. When they arrive, Cukurs nobly refuses to get out of the car. He leaves the Kommando shortly afterwards.

When the war ends, Cukurs flees and Boris becomes Spakovskis again. He interrogates Arājs Kommando members for the Soviet NKVD, the successor agency to the Cheka, and is soon given a new mission: return Cukurs to Riga. Not because the Soviets wanted him to stand trial for war crimes, but because he is suspected of having smuggled 'Jewish gold' out of Riga, and the Soviets want it back.

In 1949, Kinstlers is given a new identity, along with a mass of other agents, as a 'precautionary measure'. In the NKVD building, he and his colleagues brainstorm how to get Cukurs extradited from Brazil. The most expedient method, they decide, is to 'find' evidence of Cukurs's war crimes. Kinstlers is told to embellish and fabricate testimonies from Jewish survivors, then sell them to the media. His boss tells him to 'bring in the Jews' – to cooperate with Mossad – to see the mission through. 'Why is the Cukurs case so important to the communists? Because he symbolizes the success story of the independent Latvia,' Puče writes. He stood for a nation that had ceased to exist.

The novel brazenly undermines the status of survivor testimony – it suggests that it was not Edward Alperovitch who laboriously collected, transcribed and telegrammed survivor testimonies, but, rather, my grandfather who found and fabricated them. It also entertains the possibility that Cukurs was supposed to have been brought home alive. This idea is, in fact, its operating premise: just as Eichmann had been kidnapped and spirited across the Atlantic Ocean to stand trial, the same fate, it suggests, had been planned for Cukurs. In the saga of Herberts Cukurs, the Soviet Union sought its own spectacular kidnapping. But it was not justice the Soviets were after – it was Jewish gold. A stereotypically anti-Semitic suggestion, printed in black and white and propped up on the bookseller's shelf.

You Will Never Kill Him is the product of a virulent strain of nationalism that is a far cry from the romantic nationalism that Herder identified in Latvian peasant songs. In Puče's imagination, my grandfather is the worst kind of spy – a foreign agent, a mole, a murderer, a traitor, a communist – a man with no scruples and no country. Cukurs is made to represent Mother Latvia, both man and nation principled and pure. The former is martyred for the sake of the latter, but neither carries the stench of sin. My grandfather enters into the story, then, as a convenient vessel for all that is unholy.

But what is known about Boris's life is enough to condemn him; there is no need to resort to fiction. Puče takes indisputable facts – Jēkabs Peterss was indeed one of the founders of the Cheka, and Latvians did occupy a number of high positions in Lenin's security services – and weaves them into inventions and rumours. He makes use of historical documents and survivor testimonies while simultaneously invalidating them. The novel is a ballad of a revanchist nation, an exercise in denial. Remember the author's impassioned explanation of his project: '*Why are we just sitting in a corner? Who is responsible for these accusations, especially if there is no evidence or witnesses?*'

The thing is, it is easy not to find any evidence or witnesses when you yourself have undermined them, omitted them, hidden them away.

17

Forgotten Trials

In the summer of 1973, a former member of the Arājs Kommando living in Ludwigsburg, Germany, receives a set of letters in the mail. His name is Jānis Eduard Zirnis – a strange man, well known to West German authorities for his somewhat exaggerated commitment to tracking down Latvian war criminals, a commitment that, up until that moment, has yet to produce any actual leads. For seven months, from March to October 1942, Zirnis had served under Arājs's command. 'According to his own account, his ejection from the unit was the direct result of his refusal to follow an order to participate in a mass shooting,' the historian Richards Plavnieks writes in his definitive account of Arājs's pursuit and trial. After leaving the Kommando, Zirnis spent several months in German custody, where he is said to have been tortured. One friend of his told German authorities that he had been 'broken in the chambers of the SD', despite having once been a member of the SD himself.

After the war, Zirnis settled in Ludwigsburg, not far from the *Zentralstelle*, where he was repeatedly interviewed by West German police and prosecutors. But he had never once supplied the authorities with valid or new information. When an 'annoyed investigator' from the Central Office was sent to interview him in 1964, the investigator reported that Zirnis's 'affectation of mysteriousness could easily be seen through. He hardly knows anything about the crimes.'[1] In other words, he was a crank, an armchair investigator peddling useless information, a man consumed by conspiracy.

Then came these letters. Both were written by the same source, whose identity Zirnis refused to disclose to the authorities. And both letters contained the same information: Viktors Arājs has been killed by Soviet agents in West Germany. One of the letters, later obtained by the German police, read as follows:

> First I would like to disclose to you that the SD chief, Sturmbannführer Viktors Arājs was executed by Soviet security officers in the area of Nordrhein-Westfalia on 19 January 1973.

The other reads:

> One need have no more fear of the mass murderer, Viktors Arājs. He was in South America for a long time, but came back to West Germany under a false name, and as an English agent. But the English got fed up with him and gave us a tip. On 19 January 1973, he was executed by our Special Team. No one will ever find him. He certainly wasn't the first, and he won't be the last. Our list of war criminals is long. We have also actually brought some back to Riga.[2]

Zirnis told a German acquaintance of his about the letters' contents, and the acquaintance promptly alerted the police. It was illegal in West Germany to be made aware of a crime and not report it; his friend was trying to be a good citizen. Zirnis was taken in for questioning. He divulged the letters, but hid their source.[3]

The allegations about Arājs's murder meant that police were obligated to investigate the tip. By the 1960s, German investigators working out of the Central Office's old prison building had identified three major crime complexes pertaining to the Holocaust in Latvia. The first and largest was the 'Riga-Komplex', whose defendants were being prosecuted in Hamburg; the second complex addressed crimes in Liepāja, Ventspils and Jelgava, and was being prosecuted in Hanover; the third, the 'Dünaburg-Komplex' (or Daugavpils-Komplex) was being tried in Dortmund.[4] The investigation into Viktors Arājs's alleged murder was assigned to the Hamburg court, which was given jurisdiction over Arājs's crimes because he was an 'accomplice of Hitler, Himmler, and Jeckeln', Plavnieks explains. 'In the sense of the West German Criminal Code, because the crimes had been ordered from Germany, Germany was also the scene of the crime – and hence the crimes could be tried in Germany.'[5]

First, they checked the morgues, where they did not find the body they were looking for. A forty-year-old Hamburg public prosecutor named Lothar Klemm was put in charge of overseeing the investigation. He unearthed old depositions from British investigations into Arājs's crimes, and starting poring over them for clues.

In one old deposition, Klemm comes across the following sentence: 'It has been said that Arājs supposedly lived under his wife's maiden name in Frankfurt after the war.' Underneath it, the detective who took the deposition left a note explaining that the husband's information could not be found in the records of the federal registration office. 'I have refrained from making further inquiries about the husband,' the detective wrote. Klemm put an exclamation mark in red ink next to this remark.[6]

It did not take Klemm long to find him. Arājs had spent the last twenty years living a quiet life under his wife's maiden name, working at a printing press and living in a small attic apartment in Frankfurt. He had false papers and a travel pass issued by the Latvian Legation in London. He had socialised with the Latvian community in West Germany, taking care to avoid those who showed any hint of recognition. His wife had stopped speaking to him years ago, and he had taken a West German mistress, 'the ill-starred and anonymous Ms. Irmtraud Oedgingen, ten years his junior,' Plavnieks writes. 'Ill-starred for having had the cosmic misfortune of falling in love with a Holocaust perpetrator and anonymous because no statements from her are known to exist, as far as this author is aware, making her unknowable to history.'[7]

On 10 July 1975, Viktors Arājs the mastermind of the murderous Kommando, is confronted and detained. He is taken to prison and read the warrant for his arrest. He stands accused of taking part in 'riots against the Jewish population in the course of which at least 400 Jews were slain, tortured to death, thrown in burning synagogues, or were shot in the area surrounding Riga by Latvian Sonderkommandos' under his command; of leading a Kommando that in 'July/August 1941 took part in the shooting of at least 10,000 Jews over the course of multiple mass shooting actions in the area surrounding Riga'; of participating in the liquidation of the Riga ghetto and killing no fewer than 24,000 Latvian Jews and 1,000 German Jews in Rumbula Forest; of shooting six Jews in the Riga ghetto; and of ordering his subordinates to shoot Jewish people in the vicinity of Riga.

He is interrogated until after midnight at the prison, refusing to reveal anything about his past:

> Arājs's last words to his interrogators late that night were: 'This stuff, which was just read out to me, I don't believe it, this is fantasy. I don't believe any of it, I'm sorry, I can't help you. I have nothing to do with this business. I am who I am, and not this Arājs person.' The interrogation was concluded at 01.30.[8]

He confessed the next day. He was locked up in a Hamburg prison while the prosecution readied its case. There, he was quite comfortably appointed: 'Through his lawyers, Arājs requested and received from the Court, with the assent of the prison administrators who had their security considerations: a radio, a television, a travel-sized typewriter, and a chess set. Arājs was observed to play chess almost daily with various fellow inmates. In addition, Arājs requested and received a daily subscription to Frankfurt's conservative daily newspaper of record, the *Frankfurter Allgemeine Zeitung*,' Plavnieks reports.[9]

Klemm and his team of prosecutors embarked upon an international search for evidence and witnesses. In Haifa, Frida Michelson, who survived the massacre at the Rumula Forest, sat for multiple depositions, telling them how she played dead and

Boris (second row, center) in a wedding party, Riga, April 26, 1942.

Herberts Cukurs poses for a photograph on May 04, 1934. *Atpūta* Newspaper, Issue 496.

The "Latvian Lindbergh," his small nation's "aviator hero," on the landing field.

SAL, 1986 Fund, Description 1, Case 45285, Volume 8, page 104. Latvian National Archive

A group photograph of the Arājs Kommando, 1942. Arājs sits in the first row, labeled number three; Rudolph Lange, commander of the SS and SD in Latvia, sits next to him, labeled number four. The man who may be Boris is labeled number eight.

Hamburg State Archive, 213-12 Staatsanwaltschaft Landgericht – Nationalsozialistische Gewaltverbrechen (NSG), Nr. 0044 Band 015

A group portrait at the Führerschule der Sicherheitspolizei und des SD Berlin. Charlottenburg, the Führer School for Security Police and the SD, Autumn 1942. Arājs sits in the first row, second from left. Boris stands in the top row, center.

Miriam Kaicners working on Cukurs's farm in the Latvian countryside, 1943.

Edward Anders in Munich, 1949.

A German report on the mass murders of Jews on the territory of the occupied Soviet Union. The map was submitted as evidence for the International Military Tribunal at Nuremberg and the trial of Viktors Arājs.

Miriam (far right) with Cukurs's daughters Milda and Antinea on board their ship bound for Brazil, 1946.

Boris and Biruta waiting to sign their marriage contract, 1949.

Paul Semenoff's father, Sasha, (then known as Abram Shapiro) playing the violin in Riga in 1940.

Sasha later in life, playing the violin with President Bill Clinton in Las Vegas.

Surveillance photograph of Cukurs in Brazil, date unknown.

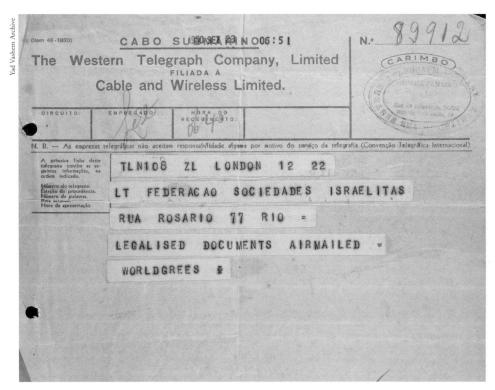

Herman Michelson's telegram to the Federation of Brazilian Jews informing them that legalized copies of survivor testimonies were en route to Rio de Janeiro, September 1950.

achado já em decomposição, num baú, numa casa vazia. Uma carta, evidentemente apócrifa, chegou a São Paulo dois dias depois da morte de Çukurs.

A clipping from the Brazilian tabloid *OCruzeiro*'s report on Cukurs's murder, April 3, 1965.

Yaakov Meidad as Anton Kuenzle.

An undated photograph
of Boris, probably 1949.

A Latvian newspaper
reports on the assassination.

H. Cukurs nogalināts pēc ievilināšanas slazdos pārvešanai uz Izraēlu

allowed herself to be buried under a pile of shoes, how she heard
Latvian men speaking about how efficiently organised the mass
murder had been. Her testimony, and that of about a quarter of
the 130 individuals in the witness pool, ended up being completely
excluded from the indictment, largely due to the old age and
infirmity of the deposed. Well aware that the Soviets had been
documenting Nazi crimes committed on their territories since the
early days of the war, Klemm approached Soviet authorities for
help with his case, and they willingly obliged. He and his team
travelled to Moscow and Riga to collect documentary evidence and
take witness depositions – witnesses were denied travel visas so the
court had to come to them. They sat in Soviet courtrooms and
listened to their stories.

In Riga, a survivor named Ella Medalje is deposed a half-dozen
times. She was a newlywed when the Germans arrived. A photograph
from her wedding day, in 1939, shows her cradling a bouquet of
flowers and tilting her head gently towards her husband, Pinchas.
She is a beautiful bride, twenty-six years old, her hair neatly coiffed,
her lips coloured, smiling.

Her husband was arrested within days of the German invasion.
Ella was first sent to work in the Jewish hospital, and then
arrested and detained at the headquarters of the Kommando.
Remember: they turned the basement into a prison. Like Michelson,
she was then sent to the Riga ghetto, and, on 8 December 1941, she
was transported to the Rumbula Forest to be killed. She survived
only because, after feeling the barrel of a pistol at her back, she
screamed: 'Let me go! Don't you realise, I am not a Jew!' The soldier
looked at her, mumbled unintelligibly, and told her to go and talk
to the leaders of the massacre. This is when she came face to face
with Arajs. 'His face was like that of a disfigured animal, his bestial
lips twisted in a grin, he moved from one group to another, terribly
drunk from vodka and mad with blood. I was sobbing, I burst
out and cried: "I am not a Jew!" I was feverish. Arājs, unfazed,
yelled: "Here there are only Jews. Today, Jewish blood must flow!" '
Her life was spared just long enough for her to plead her case,
convince them she wasn't lying and secure a new set of false papers.

In her 1966 memoir, which was translated into German for the purposes of the trial, Medalje writes that Arājs's words would echo in her mind for the rest of her life.[10]

She will provide some of the strongest evidence against Arājs. After the war, she toured what was once the Riga ghetto with Soviet investigators. She showed them where she was detained, she described how she watched Cukurs drunkenly parading through its streets, his pistol drawn. In a 1960 interrogation with Soviet authorities, she describes seeing Latvian men, including Cukurs and Arājs, returning from the killing field covered in bloodstains and carrying shovels.

The Soviets supply Klemm's team with ample documentary evidence, including Medalje's descriptions. The West Germans regard these documents with excessive suspicion, but forensic analysis later proves they are authentic.[11] A KGB inspection report dated 16 February 1976 and filed in relation to Arājs's ongoing prosecution lists all the men known to have worked under his command. It begins by listing forty-one men whose names turned up in the evidence against him; number thirty-six is Cukurs, who is described as a battalion commander. About thirty men are listed whose fates and locations are unknown. And then, at the bottom, in the middle of a list of men whose death certificates had been reissued and sent to the Council of Ministers of the USSR, there is my grandfather's name. Two KGB investigators sign at the bottom.[12]

The investigation turns up more clues, among them a photograph of Arājs and his men posing for a commemorative photograph in Berlin in the autumn of 1942. They have been sent there for training at the Führerschule der Sicherheitspolizei und des SD Berlin-Charlottenburg, the Führer School for Security Police and the SD. Arājs, seated second from right in the first row, wears a suit and frowns at the camera. The photograph is a strange echo of the blurred image of the Arājs Kommando in Riga, only in this one there is no mistaking the identity of the man in the dead centre of the top row. The photograph is ruthlessly clear. His terribly large forehead, his sharp, angular face. He has dressed up for the occasion, with his silly pocket handkerchief and striped tie. My grandfather stares straight ahead.

The final indictment against Arājs did not mince words. 'The "Sonderkommando Arājs" became synonymous with the unheard of cruel participation of National Socialist and right-extremist Latvian groups in the murder of the Jews,' it reads. 'The history of National Socialism and of the state measures of Jewish persecution by totalitarian system of rule HITLER's are generally known and are facts known to the court. They require no proof.' It includes a brief history of Latvia, and a detailed account of how Arājs came to lead the Latvian Auxiliary Police. 'Through the end of 1942, the extermination of the Jews in the Latvian area was the particular task of the ARĀJS units ... These Latvians fanatically hated Jews and Communists and exploited every opportunity in order to inflict terrible vigilante justice on their opponents.'[13] It continues: 'For the entire period charged by the prosecution from July 1941 through February 1942, he exercised complete command authority over the Kommandos of the Latvian Security Police within the framework of the directives issued to him by the security police.'[14] Arājs was personally responsible for participating in shootings in Liepāja, Rumbula, Biķernieki and Riga in which over 30,000 Jewish men, women and children were murdered. 'His disrespect for the right to life of Jewish persons is also demonstrated by the fact that he, during the ghetto action, killed Jews who could not run fast enough or who had held themselves concealed in their houses out of fear,' reads one of the final pages. 'The accused's motives in the on-going extermination of human life are according to the prevailing moral view generally despicable and are at the lowest moral point.'[15]

On 7 July 1977, exactly two years after he was arrested, the Arājs trial opens at the District Court of Hamburg. The defence attorney, Georg Bürger, had spent the last two decades defending Nazis on trial, and, like most Nazi prosecutions, these proceedings would hardly prove expedient.[16] Medalje's testimony, for instance, would not be read into the record until 14 February 1979, and the final verdict would not be issued until 21 December 1979, four and a half years after Arājs's Frankfurt arrest. Even then, Nazi prosecutions were thought to be almost comically belated, primarily performative ordeals. A December 1978 article in *Der Spiegel* laments that the dozen or so cases ongoing at the time, including the Arājs trial, no longer attracted the interest of the public or the press. 'On average twice a week, the prisoner on remand is brought before a jury in Room 139 of the Hamburg courthouse and confronted with his SS past. Three lawyers and a doctor offer support to the Latvian Viktor Arājs 68, who, after having had a heart attack while in custody, actively follows the trial from a wheelchair for a maximum of two hours at a time, including a cigarette break,' it begins. (The defence deliberately tried to make Arājs appear frail and sickly, arguing that he was too feeble to stand trial or serve a prison sentence.)

Few outside the courtroom seemed to care about what was being aired inside. 'The monotony of horror no longer makes headlines,' *Der Spiegel* argues. It dubbed the ongoing trials '*Vergessene Prozesse*' – Forgotten Trials – not even three decades after the war, when many of the survivors and perpetrators were still very much alive. It was becoming increasingly difficult, the magazine reported, to get witnesses living abroad to testify to their experiences. The psychological stress could prove too great. And in addition to psychological burdens, some had also encountered physical ones: the magazine reported that a witness in an ongoing Nazi trial in Aschaffenburg, in northern Bavaria, had recently provided two contradictory statements to the court. On the first day of his appearance, he unequivocally condemned the accused. When he returned to court the next day, he withdrew his statement. What happened in between? After his first court appearance, he was followed back to his hotel by two men. In his room, he found that someone had left him a message ordering him to take back his accusations. Otherwise, the messenger told him, he would encounter a fate 'worse than Auschwitz'.[17]

Arājs read the *Spiegel* article from his cell in the Frankfurt prison and took it upon himself to write a letter to the editors, which was later obtained by the Hamburg court (the magazine refrained from publishing it):

Re: Correction to your report 'War Crimes – War Graves' in
Der Spiegel Issue 52, Page 55.

As a *Spiegel* reader of many years, I was very pleased with
your coverage of the so-called war criminals. Allow me to
quote briefly from my correction. Thirty years ago I was
acquitted by an English War Crimes Tribunal because the
so-called witnesses could no longer truly remember. [Yet]
[t]oday – after 30 years – they can. Doesn't the unavoidable
question pose itself, that this is happening only because of
the pressure of certain press and media? Just to correct the
record: you identify me as SS-Man and *Obersturmbannführer*
[SS Lieutenant Colonel]. Neither of these corresponds to the
facts. As a Latvian citizen, I could never become a member of
the SS or Waffen-SS. My membership was in the Volunteer
Latvian Legion, where, shortly before the end of the war, I was
promoted to *Sturmbannführer* [SS Major]. Through the general
negative press reportage about me, I get an ever stronger feeling
that I am the object of a public spectacle, not the subject of
jurisprudence, as it truly should be.[18]

The letter was a bare-faced attempt to clear his name at a time
when the facts he was contesting were far beyond dispute. 'The lies
in this letter represent an extremely clumsy and squalid self-serving
manoeuvre desperately or perhaps naively conceived as an appeal
to the press, and thereby to the public at large, for sympathy,'
Plavnieks writes.[19] Arājs was ultimately sentenced to life in prison
for the deaths of 13,000 people. The court had been unable to
determine his direct involvement in the shootings in the Riga ghetto,
or whether he acted on his own accord when he shot thousands of
Jews in the Biķernieki Forest. All it was able to ascertain beyond
a reasonable doubt was that Arājs had personally participated in
the second day of the massacre at Rumbula, when Ella Medalje
pleaded for her life, when 13,000 people were murdered. The court
did not claim that the number represented a complete tally of his
victims. But the available evidence implicating him in thousands of
other murders did not meet the court's standard of juridical proof.

Remember that his arrest warrant charged him with more than 36,000 murders, and yet he was convicted for 13,000. There is a chasm between these numbers, a great and terrible void. Anyone even passingly familiar with legal systems might shrug at this disparity. But I stare at these figures, bewildered and confused. The difference between these two numbers – between what law reads as hearsay and what it consecrates as fact – is in many ways the reason I am writing this book. The verdict does not suggest that the 23,000 additional murders did not happen, not so directly. It simply cannot prove that they occurred, not in that forum, not in that court.

This evidentiary 'issue' would be a continuing problem in Nazi prosecutions. One egregious example is the 1999 trial of Andrei Sawoniuk, a seventy-eight-year-old former member of the Belarusian Auxiliary Police, in which the judge refused to admit the defendant's SS registration form as evidence because the man who signed it could not be called up to testify to its authenticity. 'Standards of proof are often rather different in law and in history, and historians may find it difficult to argue that their conclusions put any matter with which they deal "beyond reasonable doubt", as is required in the criminal law before a conviction can be reached,' the historian Richard J. Evans writes. 'The law frequently cannot take for granted what in history would count as common knowledge. In convicting a killer, the law does not need to prove that he committed a thousand murders if it can prove he committed a hundred. Thus the carefully defined and circumscribed purposes of a trial often fail to satisfy the wider remit of history.'[20]

Arājs was imprisoned for a total of thirteen and a half years. He died in January 1988 of heart failure. 'This means that Arājs was jailed for about one year per 1,000 murders of which he was convicted,' Plavnieks writes. '[T]o say nothing of the greater number of murders in which the participation of Arājs is certain but which were considered by the Court as juridically unproven.'[21]

A legal historian once told me that the relation between law and history is like that of two sprinters in a relay race. Law hands the baton to history, to literature, to make up for its flagging stride, its many omissions and gaps. 'Unlike law, history's content is remainders, whether people, things, or events,'[22] writes the legal scholar Christopher Tomlins. The work of history is to collect the detritus of law, to piece together all the things that law cannot metabolise – things that evade judgement, that do not testify to easily categorisable facts. But what happens when the historians cease to be able to do their jobs because the law insists upon intervening? What happens when it becomes clear that after this supposedly final transfer, that the race is not yet over? That law and its emissaries have picked it back up and start to run? They may be wildly underprepared for the task at hand, ill-equipped to keep pace with history – sometimes the lawyers even run in the opposite direction, undoing the progress the historians have made – but yet they keep running, their pace flagging more and more, until finally they seem to be limping towards a moving finish line. Will they know when they have reached it? Or will they just keep running until they tire, until their legs give out beneath them?

18

Agent Stories

In the 1990s, a particular genre of rumour began to spread in Riga. This was the 'agent' story, a kind of story that sought to ferret out those who had collaborated with the Soviet organs, to name names, to bring them to account. The Soviet Union officially collapsed in December 1991, six months after I was born. I never have to wonder how many years it has been since this monumental event: I am exactly as old as the Soviet Union is dead. For those who lived through it, its demise was unimaginable yet anticipated, inexplicable yet hyper-explained. Everyone had a theory, everyone wanted to claim authority over the fickle hand of fate. It wasn't just the nation of the USSR that had vanished – it was also the Soviet conception of history and time, of achievement, happiness, success and selfhood. The immediate post-Soviet environment was one in which there 'was a surfeit of descriptions and diagnoses of social change; there were numerous equally comprehensive and plausible yet apparently mutually exclusive conceptions of the same events', according to the anthropologist Caroline Humphrey. This 'diagnostic oversaturation, together with the collapse of Cold War certainties,' she writes, led to the emergence of a certain kind of paranoia, a suspicion of everyone and everything, a belief that 'nothing is done by chance', that the whole truth can be rooted out, discovered, possessed.[1]

For the first time it was possible for individuals to look inside the archives of the KGB and its predecessors and partners; lists of former collaborators began to circulate, and neighbours began swapping stories about what they discovered. Powerful myths about the nature of collaboration began to emerge: that only those who were 'morally deficient, who can now be blamed',[2] collaborated; that 'everyone had a secret file; that justice amounts to assigning blame; that agents had committed more wicked transgressions than party officials; and that informants were victims themselves'.[3] There was a furied interest in identifying the agents of the former regime, and for good reason. Latvia, like other newly independent nations, wanted a clean start. Latvians wanted to celebrate their own heroes for the first time in over seventy years, and to punish their former oppressors. The trouble was that these categories were hardly clear cut; as Václav Havel put it, 'the fundamental lines of conflict run right through each person'.[4] These lines were thick, tangled, knotted. They would not be easily unravelled.

But the rumours had long been swirling. The collapse just meant that, all of a sudden, there was some hope that the truth would come to light. 'The suspicion was always there – nobody ever believed anybody during Soviet times,' my mother tells me, when I ask her about this era. 'Yes, it is true that almost everyone had a file. Yes, the agents were everywhere. Yes, the informants were victims themselves. I can tell you all this.' She doesn't like my 'academic' approach to understanding the conditions of her own life. She doesn't like being made to feel like a specimen.

The truth is that she had always lived among rumours. They were a fact of life – she breathed them in along with Riga's salty sea air. She hadn't known that she was Jewish, until one day someone called her an evreyka, a Jew, in the courtyard, and she went upstairs to ask her parents what that meant. The family religion was communism; the rest my mother would have to intuit.

There were plenty of clues: the Yiddish her father sometimes spoke at home, the accent and intonation of her grandfather Lev, who had married into a family with a long rabbinic line, the fact that her family ate matzoh around Passover, the odd sense of kinship they shared with the other Russian-speaking families in the neighbourhood. On Simchat Torah, a joyous holiday that marks the days when one year's reading of the Torah is complete and a new cycle can begin, she and the other Jewish students stood outside the synagogue and watched the celebrants dancing and singing. They knew they were being watched, that their presence would be reported. 'I came with some friends and didn't stay long,' she told me. 'I was aware that there were people among us who were stukachi, informers. They were Jewish students who looked just like us but were required to report to the KGB.'

Her parents were both from Ukraine, Mikhail from Belaya Cerkov, a small town outside Kyiv, and Esther from the eastern city of Kharkov, both from old Jewish families. Mikhail, or Misha, was the grandfather I grew up with, the one who would join us for holidays and anniversaries. He was a force to be reckoned with, strong, stubborn and elegant, with a booming voice and a deliberate manner. He loved to dance and sing. He never spoke of his past.

He wrote his memoirs by hand when he was eighty-three years old, living in a Russian retirement community in San Diego. When he was born in 1922, his given name was Moshe, or Moses. He became 'Mikhail' later, a preliminary erasure of his past, a concession to Soviet assimilation. He fought with the Soviet Army's 53rd Artillery Regiment during the war. He was a communications expert, tasked with running radio lines between the trenches on the Western Front, and later between regiments defending Moscow. He was a reliable Party man; in his memoirs, he writes that he worked 'part time' as the sledovatel of his division, which in English merely means 'investigator' but in the Soviet context means far more. To be the sledovatel meant that he was reporting to the security services, to the NKVD, during the war.

My grandfather writes of his early childhood memories, of how his own grandfather Benjamin would come to visit his parents, how he would watch him wrapping tefillin and donning tallit in the morning. They spoke Yiddish at home and with their extended family – Benjamin had four children, three of whom survived the war. The one who did not was named Klara. She and her husband and their two children settled in Kyiv. My grandfather writes about what happened to them only obliquely: 'Oni ushli v Babiy Yar.' They went away to Babi Yar, to the place where the Holocaust 'began'. My grandfather writes this as if they calmly relocated to a faraway city. We know from the historical records, films and photographs that it was an orderly procession, that the Jews of Kyiv were told to assemble at a designated corner in the city, that they believed they were being sent on a long journey, that they were being paraded on their way to the train station. Though it was September 1941, the end of summer, they packed warm clothes and put on their boots. Then they marched to their deaths, suitcases in tow.

It was not one of our protagonists who orchestrated the massacre at Babi Yar, but their boss's boss's boss, 'a real sadist', the SS Obergruppenführer Friedrich Jeckeln.[5] His orders ushered Klara, her husband, their child and over 33,000 others to their deaths: he directed German soldiers to line them up in front of Kyiv's famous ravine, its plunging slope perfectly fitted to their purpose. (Their older daughter survived because she had been sent away to live with relatives before the war and was evacuated with them to Kazakhstan.) Jeckeln had forty-five police battalions under his command, and an assistant whose title was 'Chief of Staff in Charge of Counteracting Gangs and Jews'. Jeckeln was the head of police in Ukraine, and he did such a good job there, with his special methods for murder, that he was soon transferred to Riga to repeat his successes. In September 1941 he oversaw the killings in Kyiv in Kyiv, and by November he was in Riga, ordering the Arājs Kommando and their colleagues to do the same.

Rumours proliferated among Jews during the Nazi occupation, and the subsequent Soviet re-occupation only furthered their spread. The war created a 'rumor culture', writes the Holocaust historian Amos Goldberg, in which Jews shared whispers of developments from abroad, of possibilities of escape. These rumours afforded them the slightest illusion of control. 'Rumors are not random: they are a means of public interpretation of an enigmatic reality. They expose deep social and cultural emotions such as anger, fear, and hope,' Goldberg explains. 'The rumor's hermeneutic is thus to seek to decipher the chaotic and murderous reality in a hopeful and comforting manner.'[6] This 'rumor culture' continued into the decades after the war, when no one spoke of what happened in the forests and ravines of Babi Yar, or at Rumbula, or at Biķernieki. Those who survived held a few clandestine memorials, and these, too, were monitored by the secret police.

In the 1960s, a few murmurs arose in the form of literature, in the words and poems of Anatoli Kuznetsov and Yevgeny Yevtushenko. Kuznetsov had grown up near the Babi Yar ravine, he had heard the shootings: 'We could only hear bursts of machine-gun fire at various intervals: ta-ta-ta, ta-ta … For two long years I could hear them, day after day, and even now they still ring in my ears,' he writes. When the fences came down and the Germans were gone, Kuznetsov and a friend went back to the ravine, back to the stream where they had played as children. 'The riverbed was of good, coarse sand, but now for some reason or other the sand was mixed with little white stones,' he writes. 'I bent down and picked one of them up to look at it more closely. It was a small piece of bone, about as big as a fingernail, and it was charred on one side and white on the other. The stream was washing these pieces of bone out of somewhere and carrying them down with it. From this we concluded that the place where the Jews, Russians, Ukrainians, and people of other nationalities had been shot was somewhere higher up.'[7]

In Riga, my mother read these accounts. That is how she learned what exactly had happened during the war, and why it was a small miracle that anyone survived. She went to school with other Russian-speaking children, some of whom were Latvian Jews, sons and daughters of the lucky few who had been hidden away by righteous gentiles, or who had fought with the famous 43rd Latvian Rifle Guards Battalion of the Soviet army. The others, like her own family, had moved to Riga after the war, their families mostly intact, having spent the war in the eastern evacuation zones.

Some of her schoolteachers were survivors themselves, but no one knew for sure. The survivors, they were silent. They had not yet been glorified, honoured, beatified. They simply went about their lives as best they could. Only decades later did my mother find out that the school principal, Nina Dmitrievna Alieva, was an inmate in Salaspils concentration camp.[8] Only later did she learn of rumours that their strict chorus teacher had climbed out of a ditch in Rumbula.

It is not for me to try to approximate what life was like in Riga during these post-war decades. What I know has come to me largely from the anecdotes my parents relay, off-hand remarks from our conversations. My mother and father had very different experiences in these years: my father dogged by constant rumours about Boris, haunted by the occasional encounter with someone who recognised his last name, cognisant of the fact that his country was under occupation. My mother was learning slowly about what had happened during the war. She declined to join the Communist Party, and because of that, and because of her Jewishness, she was penalised. She was excluded from a student exchange abroad, and later denied a place at her university's graduate programme. No one particularly wanted them to marry.

One story she relays tells me all I need to know: after she married my father, he once brought home a book that he wanted to show her. He had seen it on the bookshelf at a friend's house. He brought it back to warn her, to let her know that the prejudices of the war were still present, even if they had become less overt. The book was a compendium of anti-Semitic stereotypes, complete with vicious illustrated caricatures. My mother looked through it and tried to forget its contents. To this day, she regrets she didn't burn it.

My parents left Riga in 1988, when my older sister was nine years old. They were the first of our family to leave – the rest of my mother's family would soon follow. Officially, they left because they were a Jewish household – they claimed that they wanted to reunite with family in Israel. Really, they just wanted to cross the border. It did not matter so much what came next. First they flew to Vienna, and on from there to the poor southern suburbs of Rome, where they began the process of petitioning for asylum in the US. They sought what they thought would be a better, freer life, rid of the constrictions of Soviet communism. It took me decades to understand that they were also fleeing history.

As they settled in the United States, Riga began to open up. Western tourists arrived, witnesses of all kinds emerged. In a 1992 documentary about her life, *A Child for Hitler*, Jeckeln's daughter tours the Riga auditorium where her father was sentenced to death. Peter Krupnikov, who served as the translator during the trial and who had by then become a prominent historian, leads her around the space. 'The tribunal was there and the prosecution was on the left,' he tells her, gesturing towards the stage. He shows her where her father sat during the proceedings.

'How would you describe his character?' Jeckeln's daughter asks.

'He was a very clear-thinking man, a competent man, and one sensed a certain charm,' Krupnikov answers. 'Other than that, he was a totally cold-blooded man, a man who had ordered people to death, and now that he faced his own, showed no fear.'

'When I read about the trial, I saw that he never tried to hide his guilt, he really admitted everything,' the daughter says.

'Look. When you kill one or two people, you're likely to get the death sentence,' Krupnikov answers. 'If you've killed thousands and thousands of people, it's a foregone conclusion.'

'The death sentence?' she asks.

'*Ja*,' the historian responds.

'What about the verdict?'

'You have to remember, the room was full of witnesses. When the death sentence by hanging was pronounced, they clapped for minutes on end.'

'How did Jeckeln react?'

'Absolutely nothing.'

'Nothing at all?'

'What reaction do you expect?'

By this point in their exchange, the daughter is crying. She wipes away her tears, she glances at the stage. 'Can I say, all my life I've been convinced that there is no collective guilt, and no guilt from one generation to another,' Krupnikov tells her. 'That is why when I was asked to talk to you, it was no problem for me. One thing does not exclude the other. A man can be cultured – which Jeckeln wasn't – and still behave in this way. This is very tragic, but neither culture nor education nor artistic leanings can exclude it.'[9]

The rumours about Boris followed my parents to America. Stories appeared in émigré newspapers, in the online comment sections of the Latvian papers. After settling in California, my father began collecting these records and books, highlighting and circling the relevant columns of text. In two books by a Latvian émigré, he reads that his father was an NKVD officer charged with killing Latvian partisans. The author accuses Boris of killing his brother, a partisan who spent the war fighting Soviet troops and hiding among thick pine forests.[10] In the émigré paper *Latvija Amerika*, an article titled 'New discoveries about Cheka agents' appeared on 5 February 1994. New records revealed that there were 'at least four NKVD agents in the Arājs unit' during the Second World War, it reported. 'The highest of them, it seems, was Ltn. Boris Kinstler, who was one of the first Arājs men to receive a war cross for the killing of Jews. Maybe someone is interested in what happened next?'

19

The Cosmochemist

Stories, like graves, come with their own caretakers – people who keep track of who lies where, when they were laid to rest, which family members showed up for the funeral. They maintain the plots, keep them consistent, well-groomed, accessible and uncontested.

For the past eighty years, the caretakers of the Holocaust story have been the survivors themselves. Men and women who miraculously escaped their own certain deaths. The ones who are still alive were young people, barely more than children, during the war. They are the final authorities on matters of memory. And so long as they are still able to speak, we ask them to tell us what they saw. The closer they come to their own deaths, the more we ask of them, the more we are overcome by the 'terrible desire', as Maurice Blanchot put it, to pose questions, to record answers.[1] We turn survivors into the spokespeople of disaster; we look to them for confirmations, reminders, warnings of what has been and what might be.

As an émigré in America, Edward Alperovitch, one of Michelson's 'Committee Men', became one of these caretakers, both literally and metaphorically. He changed his last name to Anders and soon became an award-winning cosmochemist, devoting his professional life to studying the chemical makeup of asteroids, moons and stars. He won prizes for his research, which helped win him tenure at the University of Chicago. In retirement, he turned his attention to another unexplored field: he used his own savings to make an inventory of names of Liepāja Jews, to memorialise precisely who had been killed, to make visitors to the shore where they were murdered have to stop and confront their names. He began managing book and memorial projects on two continents; he commissioned a geospatial firm to identify exactly where the mass graves lie. Over the dunes of Šķēde, he erected a small series of plaques, in Latvian, Russian and English, honouring those who lay beneath the sand. 'We honor the memory of our relatives and all other victims who lie here, united in death,' the memorial reads. He used much of his free time, and his free income, trying to trace how exactly the Holocaust had been perpetrated in his hometown, who the perpetrators were and what became of them. Tracing the movement of SS battalions, he told me, was not so different from cosmochemistry: 'It's just like studying meteorites. They don't come with a tag saying what part of the sky they fell from,' he told me. 'So you have to infer a lot of things from indirect clues.'

I came across him almost by pure chance. In the spring of 2018, a colleague asked me if I knew Anders. My colleague had seen a documentary, on Netflix, called *Einsatzgruppen: Nazi Death Squads*. In one episode, Anders is interviewed about the Liepāja massacres of December 1941, known as the Šķēde Aktion. He holds photographs of the Aktion in his hands – infamous photographs because of the naked brutality they depict, the undressed young women crouching and trying to preserve their modesty while their murderers look on – he shuffles from one image to another, he names the individuals they depict, all of them in their final minutes of life.

The photographs were taken by an SS man and then secretly copied and stowed away by a Jewish electrician, David Siwzon, who had been called into the SS man's office for some repairs. Siwzon buried the copies in a metal box behind a stable. He survived the war, and so did the photographs: they ended up in the State Archive in Moscow, and were discovered and printed in 1959. Several of these photographs appear in Yaakov Meidad's memoir about the Cukurs assassination, as pictorial evidence of the Arājs Kommando's gruesome crimes. It was true, the Arājs Kommando was there. They came, shot and left. In 1964, the SS man who took the photographs is given a subpoena and called to testify at the trial of one of his colleagues: 'One day I noticed that a commando called Arays [Arājs] was in the city and that clothing was falling out of the commando's trucks, driven by the Latvians,' he said. 'I learned that they were goods belonging to Jews who had been shot.'[2]

My colleague, a scholar of history and photography, wanted to ask Anders about the Šķēde photographs – how they were taken, how he came to know so much about them, how they were reproduced and circulated. I wanted to ask him about the Cukurs case. So together, one sunny spring day, we drove to meet Anders at his retirement home south of San Francisco. He was ninety-three years old. Over lunch in the first-floor restaurant, he began to tell us his life story.

Anders spoke in a quiet, raspy voice, almost a whisper. His muted tone is deceptive – he has an exacting memory, and in his memoirs he writes about the Holocaust in much the same manner, mobilising mathematical logic to articulate the most irrational and inexplicable of crimes. In a section of his memoir called 'Tallying up Latvian Conduct', he attempts to calculate precisely how many Latvians actually wanted to expose Jews in hiding and lead them to their deaths. It is as if he wants to find the precise, mathematical ratio of good and evil:

Let N be the average number of people (neighbors, grocers, market vendors, mailmen, etc.) able to detect suspicious activity in the rescuer's apartment. Given that $1/11$ of the rescuers were betrayed, the fraction of informers, t, in the population is $1/11N$. If $N=1$, then $t=1/11=9\%$; if $N=2$, $t=1/22=5\%$; if $N=3$, $t=1/33=3\%$. Under the crowded conditions and limited privacy of wartime Latvia, N almost certainly was greater than 2, corresponding to less than 5% *murderous* anti-Semites.[3]

I suppose you could call this an even-handed approach to a fraught history. Anders took care to underscore that for every anti-Semite who volunteered to murder his friends and neighbours, there were others who had helped hide and protect the Jews of Latvia.

He told us that he had spent the better part of the last year corresponding with another man from his hometown of Liepāja, a Latvian man who seemed to need to share his memories of the war. 'He said he had kept clean hands, but that he knew a young man who had joined a self-defence unit,' Anders began. One day, the young man casually told Anders's correspondent, 'I shot Jews.' Anders relayed this anecdote calmly, explaining that 'they got one or two litres of vodka for that sort of work. This man wasn't the least bit troubled.'

Anders had heard of the Cukurs case, of course. But at first he did not let on exactly *how much* he knew, how long he had been involved. 'Some people think that he was the worst of the scum who deserved to be killed, and others think that he saved several Jews, which would be a clever manoeuvre by somebody who had murdered a lot and decided to save a few to testify for him,' he told us. The horrific stories about Cukurs seemed to him to 'not just be an invention', he said. 'There are usually some embellishments in such stories, but it's hard to see how somebody like Cukurs could keep his hands clean when he worked. Of course, not everybody in the Arājs Kommando became a murderer, but they tried to recruit people who were willing to shoot, people who had no great qualms.'

Anders told me that years ago he had been asked by a prominent Latvian historian to testify on behalf of Cukurs in the prosecutor's investigation. He refused. 'I was not convinced,' he told me. The historian had sent him Cukurs's 1945 account of the war, the one he typed up when he took Miriam and his family to Cassis. 'If you read it carefully, you realise the man knew too much ... He was at least knee-deep in guilt.' During our first conversation, he had mentioned that he spent the immediate post-war years collecting survivor testimonies for use in war crimes trials, but I had not thought to probe him on this detail. I did not yet realise how intimately involved he had been in collecting the evidence against Cukurs. I had not yet seen the reams of correspondence with his signatures.

After that first meeting, Anders did everything he could to support my work. I received packages from him in the mail with copies of his books and survivor memoirs, and a CD with the extra footage from the *Einsatzgruppen* documentary. Via email, he sent me zip files of documents – postcards of historic Liepāja, but also records of his war crimes work, his testimony at Nuremberg, his correspondence with historians, survivors and revisionists. In one email he tells me that the revisionists tried to recruit him to their cause. 'A Latvian apologist couple tried for a while to get me to exonerate Cukurs,' Anders wrote. 'I declined, the woman blew her stack, the man held his temper. I have our correspondence.'

I asked to read their exchanges, and soon another pair of zip files arrived in my email: Anders had archived and compiled all his email exchanges with this 'apologist couple', as well as all his emails on the subject of Cukurs. Before I read through his correspondence, I thought I had a solid grip on what the revisionist renaissance in Latvia had looked like – I thought I understood how the ugly underside of the neoliberal 'memory boom' had emerged. Amid the great rush to revisit and rewrite the past, not everyone had agreed on what stories should be told, which sources should be trusted, which histories unearthed. 'Europe' was a mutating concept; so were the pasts and futures it would bring. As I read through Anders's emails, I saw how he had tried to engage with the revisionists, seriously and methodically pointing out the holes and falsehoods in their arguments. He did this out of a sense of scientific honour, I suppose. And because, as he later told me, 'I have a low tolerance for injustice, in any country. It upsets me. This means I have a low threshold for action.'

I mentioned earlier that the art exhibition in Karosta was just the beginning of the revisionist renaissance. Over the course of a few short years, a number of books and films emerged that claimed to tell the true story of Herberts Cukurs. In 2010, National Geographic adapted Yaakov Meidad's memoir into a television documentary, part of a series called *Nazi Hunters*.[4] The episode restages Meidad's arrival in Montevideo, and even features an interview with the man himself, his face hidden behind sunglasses and a black fedora. He is identified by his pseudonym: ' "Anton Kuenzle": Former Mossad Spy'. He recounts how he was presented with the assignment at a meeting with his handler in Paris: 'He told me that Cukurs was living in Brazil. He told me that Cukurs was responsible for the extermination of 30,000 Latvian Jews,' Meidad says. 'Thinking of my parents, who both died in the Holocaust, I agreed immediately.'

A year later came a counter-documentary, filmed, directed and starring a well-known Latvian ultra-nationalist. Between 2010 and 2015, a number of similar projects emerged. In a right-wing newspaper, Herberts Cukurs Jr 'tells the true story about his father' to a local journalist. The narrative he offers is predictable, familiar: his father was pressured into joining the Arājs Kommando, he had no other choice. He never shot a single Jew. The testimonies against him are exaggerations, fakes. Cukurs had been persecuted while he was alive, and now it was up to his family to fight back against the 'fairy tales'. 'If we could pay enough to print the truth about Herberts Cukurs in all the major newspapers, that would be great,' he tells the journalist. 'But we don't have that kind of money.'[5]

Sympathetic minds came to the Cukurs family's aid. In 2010, a Latvian writer named Baiba Šāberte published a non-fiction book, *Let Me Speak!*, featuring interviews with the Cukurs family. The title was a reference to Cukurs's purported last words, the book an effort to give the murdered man the final word on his own fate. A colleague, a Latvian academic, emails me about this book: am I aware that there are a couple of pages dedicated to Boris? 'It is a less of a sham than I expected,' she writes. 'A bit too lyrical and messy to be taken fully seriously, but also based upon publications by historians and journalists.' The author argues that Mossad should have gone after my grandfather instead of Cukurs, that the only reason they weren't interested in him was because he was KGB. The book notes that there are multiple versions of Boris's death: either he committed suicide, was killed by Estonian partisans, or disappeared into a new life. It mentions that he was seen 'after his death' in Poland and Germany.

Through an intermediary, Šāberte contacted Anders in 2010, wanting to gain his endorsement for her full-throated defence of

Cukurs. She had heard that he was an exacting, precise person. She thought that he could be recruited to the revisionist cause. The intermediary was a Latvian émigré businessman, a man who once served as the nation's honorary consul in Chicago.[6] The intermediary told Anders that he had become 'involved in the Cukurs issue' after seeing the National Geographic documentary, an 'inflammatory film' that portrayed Latvians as 'conspiratory criminals'.

At first, Anders is unfailingly polite to the revisionists. He, too, wants to defend Latvians against unfounded claims; he is trying to honour the few who played their part in rescuing their Jewish neighbours from the slaughter. He addresses the intermediary in much the same way a professor might address an unthinking student: 'You are not a historian but neither am I,' one of Anders's first emails begins. 'Trained as a chemist, I have spent my professional life studying meteorites and moon rocks, which have led me into astronomy and earth sciences in addition to physics and chemistry. None of these subjects in themselves are relevant to historic studies of Latvia, except that as a scientist I have acquired certain habits of thought (skepticism, reliance on evidence rather than opinions and beliefs, quantitative thinking, etc.) that are also the norm in history and – more importantly – in law. I do hope that we will be able to develop a fruitful dialogue if we listen to each other and find common rules and common ground.'

Anders spends hours on his reply, picking apart the revisionist claims, one by one, linking to historical sources that back up his counter-arguments. 'I sense that you are in denial about the Commando and the murders committed by it,' he writes. 'After spending several hours on your letter and my reply, I am much less optimistic about prospects of a dialogue than I was at the start of my reply. You are very uncritical in your selection of evidence: many of the arguments are implausible, unconfirmed, or even known to be false.' He warns the intermediary that if he continues down this road, denying and refusing to acknowledge reality, he will only further harm the reputation of the nation that he claims to hold dear.

In another email, he continues to try to engage with these revisionists, to refute their claims and refuse recruitment to their cause. 'It is undeniable that the Arājs Commando killed 26,000 Latvian Jews as well as German Jews, Byelorussian Jews, and Byelorussian partisans, for a total of 60,000,' Anders writes.

Cukurs was deputy commander of the Commando, ergo, Cukurs shared guilt for these mass murders, even if every single witness accusing Cukurs of individual murders was a liar. That is the elephant in the room, and it is pointless to ignore it while chasing mosquitoes. Moreover, by the rules of logic one cannot prove a negative, such as that Cukurs NEVER killed a Jew. No matter how eloquently Ms. Šāberte defends Cukurs, at this late date the only thing she would need to refute are the two points above. Does she?[7]

With that final word, he politely asks to be removed from their mailing list, and shortly thereafter their correspondence comes to an end.

The Musical

In March 2014 comes the most egregious of these revisionist efforts, a stunt almost too absurd to document.

It took the form of a musical. The brainchild of a young producer named Juris Millers, the show was called nothing less than *Cukurs, Herberts Cukurs*. It was a deliberately provocative title that cast Cukurs as Latvia's homegrown James Bond. In the ensuing months, it would ignite a firestorm.

From the start, Millers insisted that the musical was not a rehabilitative project. He was not interested in framing Cukurs as guilty or innocent. His only agenda, he claimed, was to bring Cukurs's story to the public's attention. 'Through this production, we are not his advocates, nor his judges: that work has to be done by an international tribunal,' he said in a TV interview at the premier. 'Society is divided on his story: one half absolutely believes that he participated in the Holocaust, that he is guilty of murder. The other half believes that he only saved Jews during World War II. These are all facts – we tried to show them in one musical, in one court, on the stage.'[1]

The motives behind his production were not purely artistic: the musical was slated to debut in Liepāja, where Millers had invested in extensive renovations to the city's theatre and hoped to fill that year's calendar with as many hits as possible. He had come across the name 'Herberts Cukurs' in a magazine article about Cukurs's career as a star aviator, which also mentioned his affiliation with the Arājs Kommando. Millers's interest was piqued. In Herberts Cukurs's life story he smelled a bestseller, which he described as Latvia's very own 'Indiana Jones'.[2]

After discovering his subject, Millers began doing his homework. Time was tight: he needed to research and write the script in just two months in order to ensure that the play was ready in time. For source material, he relied largely on two books: *You Will Never Kill Him* and *Let Me Speak!* The title page of both books noted that they received funding from a group called the 'Herberts Cukurs Memorial Fund'. The same entity had provided evidence to the prosecutor's office. The other members of the production – the composer, lyricist and actors – read these books as well, and consulted the revisionist documentary published on YouTube. They did not appear to have consulted the wide array of scholarly histories about the Holocaust in Latvia.

On Latvian and Russian-language talk shows, guests debated whether the musical should exist at all. One public media station polled its viewers: 'Do we need a musical about Herberts Cukurs?' Two-thirds of respondents answered in the affirmative.[3] Local Russian-language newspapers expressed outrage over the musical's purported glorification of a Nazi collaborator. These early responses prompted the show's lyricist, Andra Manfelde, to quit the production because, as she told the press, she hadn't known about the accusations against Cukurs when she signed on to the project. She allowed that he might not be guilty of participating in genocide, but she did not want to offend those who believed otherwise. Millers sued her for breach of contract, and their public dispute only further fanned the flames of controversy that accompanied the musical's impending debut. Manfelde accused him of 'raising hatred among nations, insulting the victims' and promoting Nazism.[4]

On 11 October 2014, *Cukurs, Herberts Cukurs* opened at the Liepāja Theatre. Millers wore a tuxedo for the occasion; protestors who had purchased tickets showed up in concentration camp stripes and were not allowed to take their seats. The demonstration had been organised by a group called 'Russian Dawn', which aims to protect the rights of Russians in Latvia. On the steps at the outside entrance, they had deposited baby dolls covered in fake blood and taped with yellow Stars of David, a reference to the allegation that Cukurs had thrown Jewish infants into the air and shot them.

Inside, the theatre was only half full. Before the curtain rose, Millers took the stage. He invited the attendees to fill in the front rows, left empty, he said, because 'many who planned to come today have decided not to' due to political pressure. He repeated his one-liner about the project: 'We are not Herberts Cukurs' advocates and we are not his judges ... I hope this performance will make you think.' From the audience, the journalist Mike Colliers observed that Millers was right on that point: '[N]o one could watch this show without pondering what it is they are witnessing,' he writes in his review. 'But the show itself asks few serious questions and suggests no answers at all other than a heavy implication that Herberts Cukurs was a good guy who saved rather than killed Jews.'⁵

The first act opened to reveal Cukurs as a little boy, dreaming of flying one day and playing with his toy plane. The audience watches as he grows into a tall, handsome and capable young man, attracting the attention of young women, learning to build his own planes and slowly rising in the aviation world. The adult Cukurs is played by a charismatic young actor with an impressive tenor voice. The music in the first act is light and joyful, depicting inter-war independent Latvia as little more than a series of carefree flamencos, a nation coming into its own. Cukurs's only worry is preparing for his ambitious trip to The Gambia. He secures financing for the endeavour from a Jewish businessman with the surname Shapiro and from the Latvian ambassador to France. His triumphant arrival in The Gambia is briefly depicted in a scene in which he is received by a Gambian matriarch, played by a Latvian actress in blackface.

The second act is marked by what Colliers describes as 'doom laden and disharmonic' melodies. Cukurs's fortunes begin to turn, though seemingly through no fault of his own. The Year of Horror begins in Latvia, and soon the Germans arrive. Through all this,

'Herberts Cukurs is an almost entirely passive figure. Things happen to him, first good, then bad,' Colliers writes. 'When they are good he is happy. When they are bad he is sad. He has the emotional range of Pinocchio, without the added depth of a trick nose.' The Latvian ambassador reappears in his story, first as an NKVD agent, then as an SS man. In both uniforms, he forces Cukurs to sign a contract, the contents of which are left unclear, and the helpless young protagonist obliges.

The Holocaust is only referenced obliquely, in two abbreviated and confused scenes: in the first, Cukurs and his wife Milda are escorted to their new apartment in the city centre, which belongs to the Shapiro family. Abram Shapiro and his little son are still inside, the father is crying because he knows they are about to be sent to the ghetto. He begs Cukurs to spare his son's life, and then runs offstage, fleeing from an SS man who calls 'Halt, Jude!' after him. The sound of a gunshot follows his exit. The implication, Colliers writes, is that Shapiro was shot for running away from the SS, not because he was Jewish, and 'not because it was all part of the genocidal master plan'.

A later scene, set when the war is over, shows people gossiping about Cukurs's wartime activities. Some say he collaborated with the Nazis, while others say he worked to undermine them, saving the few Jews that he could, like Shapiro's young son. This is the only scene in which his direct culpability is hinted at. In the final scene, the rumours start to close in on the hero. The lights on the stage are dimmed and the cast slowly encircles him, chanting 'Killer!' as they close in. Out of this accusatory circle, the hero emerges once more, bathed in triumphant light. 'Let my name be written in the heavens!' he sings, wearing his military uniform. 'Am I a hero or a victim?'

The first performance in Liepāja received a standing ovation. Roughly half the audience rose to praise the cast, while the rest, Colliers reports, looked 'like the audience at the end of *Springtime for Hitler*, completely slack-jawed and incredulous'. The musical was performed ten times in 2014. Each time, some version of this macabre scene would replay, half of the theatre rising to applaud the rehabilitated hero, half of the audience aghast at what they had just seen. The lead actor was delighted by the standing ovations: 'I am happy that Latvians stand for savējie,' he told a local journalist.[6] For savējie– for one of their own.

Springtime for Hitler was a joke, the comedic creation of a Hollywood studio, portrayed in *The Producers* as both spoof and satire. The Latvian musical was indeed uncannily like *Springtime for Hitler*, complete with gratuitous chorus lines and choreographed dance numbers. 'Those who had seen the show almost universally interpreted it as an attempt to glorify Cukurs and absolve him of responsibility for any crimes against Jews,' the scholar Maija Spurina writes in her study of the production. 'While Latvian media mostly avoided the broader topic of the Holocaust and collaborationism, a number of articles in the Russian media used the show to criticise military patriotism and encourage humanism.'[7] The musical was like *Springtime for Hitler* in almost every way – saccharine, cloying, disturbing – except it was not satire. It was dead serious.

Millers knew exactly what he was doing. He needed a hit, so he had created a scandal. To the press, and to his audiences, he said he was not interested in advocating for Cukurs nor judging him. He claimed not to have picked a 'side', to have created a neutral presentation of his life story. In staging the musical, his hope was 'to start an international discussion' about Cukurs's fate, one that could instigate a 'judicial process for Herberts Cukurs,' he told one television talk-show host. The fact that there had never been an international trial, the fact that no 'international court made any kind of decision, a final decision', about Cukurs's complicity, was to him a curiosity, and an opening.[8] He did not want to sit back and let half of the country decry Cukurs as a murderer, when in fact he had also been a national hero.

The musical was, by Millers's metrics, a great success. It did indeed prompt an 'international discussion' over Cukurs's fate: Russian outlets decried the musical, Anglo-American news services tacitly ridiculed it, while Latvian journalists tried to tread carefully around the subject, neither accusing nor alienating their readers. The Israeli and Russian embassies issued statements condemning the musical, as did the Latvian foreign minister. 'Being a member of the Arājs Kommando is not worth singing about,' he wrote. 'Let those who attend the performance appraise the production for themselves; however, the position of the government is that this is not in good taste.'[9] As in his glory days, Cukurs's name once again regularly graced the national papers. Meanwhile, the Prosecutor General's office slowly continued to investigate the case.

Cukurs, Herberts Cukurs thus joined the growing compendium of cultural artefacts that cast Cukurs in a favourable light, that sought to absolve both him and his nation from any allegations of complicity. 'The diversity of cultural forms – an exhibition, two books, and a TV movie – created the illusion of an abundance of information,' Spurina writes.[10] Each of these artefacts mingled fact and fiction to create an alternative history of the Latvian nation. The lies they spun began with the truth, and this gave them both frightening potency and popular appeal. These narratives slowly began to change what people knew of Cukurs, and what they understood about the Holocaust.

The Latvian Council of Jewish Communities responded to the premiere with a public letter titled 'Herbert Cukurs's Second Entrance' outlining all of the available evidence of Cukurs's crimes.[11] 'Does Latvia really want to see its future generations raised to view Cukurs as a hero?' the authors asked. They invited the public to come and read the evidence files for themselves, but received 'zero interest.'

Not long after the musical closed, I met with a historian named Didzis Bērziņš who teaches Holocaust history at the University of Latvia. I asked him what he thought of the renewed attention to Cukurs's story. 'It's very dangerous,' he said. The recent wave of nationalistic reclamations of Cukurs's story, he believed, had successfully shifted public opinion in some sectors of Latvian society. 'The question,' he said, 'is would Cukurs still be condemned?'

21

The Body of the Crime

I was asleep when the prosecutor's decision arrived, three hours past midnight and seventy-seven years after the events in question. A gmail notication illuminated my iPhone screen, its packaging innocuous, so dramatically at odds with the news that I suspected it contained.

The prosecutor's office had sent me the file via secure electronic transfer. 'DECISION: Re: Termination of Criminal Procedure', it began.[1] Over thirty-five dense pages, the prosecutor described the whole trajectory of Cukurs's life, from birth to death to afterlife. Just like everyone else, the prosecutor had his own version of the story to tell. He reiterated the origins and rationale behind the case, explaining that because Cukurs was suspected of having participated in 'campaigns of mass extermination of Jewish civilians in Latvian territory during World War II,' and therefore to have violated the criminal code, his office had been required to investigate. I scrolled to the final page to read the wording of the decision: 'There is no evidence that Mr. Cukurs wanted to or did carry out acts that qualify as genocide – that he had taken any action to destroy, in whole or in part, Jewish civilians,' the prosecutor concludes. '*Even quite the opposite – information has been obtained in the matter that he had assisted several Jewish civilians, risking his own safety and that of his family, including also hiding them in his house.*' Cukurs could not be accused of any violations of the criminal code, the decision stated. 'Thus, these criminal proceedings against

H. Cukurs should be terminated, as his activities as clarified in the matter are not among the criminal offences provided in Section 71 of the Criminal Law.'

In a textbook for young lawyers, James Boyd White argues that judicial opinions should be read in the same way that one reads poems and novels. Both literature and law, he explains, tell stories of a given place and time, and both are ultimately creative and constitutive acts. The prosecutor's decision was a compendium of stories, bits and pieces of police interrogations and witness statements collected over the past eighty years, handed down from Soviet, Brazilian and German prosecutors to Latvian ones, sent from archives in Hamburg, Ludwigsburg, Montevideo, São Paulo and Moscow to Riga. The document enumerated and acknowledged the 'totality of testimonies', to use Marc Nichanian's damning phrase. It stated quite clearly and repeatedly that none of them would matter.

I searched the document for Boris's name and found that he is mentioned three times, in the prosecutor's summaries of KGB interrogation records. In 1976, the KGB's 'Senior Especially Serious Cases Investigator' in the Latvian Soviet Socialist Republic, questioned a former Arājs Kommando member named J. Bedelis. Bedelis worked as Arājs's chauffeur, he witnessed the Kommando members arresting Jews, Latvians and Russians, imprisoning them and then taking them to execution sites. Bedelis personally transported Arājs to Biķernieki Forest, where he watched the Kommando murder thousands of people. 'Together with Arājs, he usually drove Kinslers there, whose first name he did not know and who, as he recalled, had the rank of lieutenant,' the prosecutor writes.

Many testimonies date from Arājs's Hamburg trial. Indeed, the indictment from that trial had been appended to the case file, as had the relevant witness statements, including documents from Jānis Edwards Zirnis, the crank from Ludwigsburg whose alert had led to Arājs's final arrest. The prosecutor includes a summary of Ella Medalje's 1976 testimony, in which she describes how she was forced to clean Cukurs's office at the Kommando's headquarters, how she once bumped into him and he told her that she did not look like a Jew. She describes how, after she pleaded for her life in the forest and was mercifully spared, it was Cukurs who drove her and three other women to SS headquarters. 'On the next day, they were interrogated by Jeckeln himself, who asked how they had ended up in the forest,' the prosecutor writes. 'She responded that she was married to a Jew, an accountant by profession. Then at the office, she had to name the address where she would be living and later she secured documents [attesting] that she was a Latvian and remained alive in this way.' Portions of the 1979 verdict against Arājs are also quoted, for during his trial Arājs repeatedly described driving to the Rumbula Forest 'with his deputy Cukurs'.

The verdict gives the initial impression that the prosecutor has left no stone unturned: he refers to Cukurs as 'the accused', he quotes the testimonies of Jewish survivors provided by the Simon Wiesenthal Foundation, from the Latvian Jewish Community and from the Eichmann and Arājs trials. Eliezar Karstadt, the survivor who told the Israeli judges about Cukurs, is mentioned ever so briefly. In 1975 he wrote to Simon Wiesenthal, the famous Nazi hunter, offering to provide testimony against both Arājs and Cukurs. Also mentioned are the testimonies that Alperovitch helped collect – the accounts of Abram Shapiro, David Fishkin, Max Tukacier and several others. As is Miriam Kaicners. Law, like memory, is a milieu de rencontre. As I read through the verdict, I encountered so many familiar names.

Documents from the Soviet Extraordinary Commission are quoted at length before they are declared untrustworthy: they could not be verified as 'proof' because they had 'not been recorded according to the procedure defined by the Criminal Procedure Law'. The signatures could not be verified, their provenance could not be ascertained, the prosecutor claimed. The same went for the nine survivor testimonies sent from Vienna by the Wiesenthal Foundation, several of which were fatally 'unsigned'; besides, the prosecutor explained, Cukurs had himself 'completely repudiated and also disproved all of the charges expressed against him by these persons, of which he was aware at the time, as false'.

Only Cukurs's own words seemed to have been taken at face value. Provided by the 'Herberts Cukurs Memorial Fund', one document contained his refutation against 'Jewish Accusations'. Written in Portuguese and dated 20 June 1960, the letter states that he had 'not murdered a single Jew, let alone 500', that he did not smoke or drink, and as for those who were detained and killed at the Arājs Kommando headquarters, well, 'as far as he knew, the past of the prisoners was examined, the innocent released and the guilty, including women and men, together with the investigative materials were passed on to German officials'.

Wikipedia, the online encyclopaedia edited by volunteers, is cited on numerous occasions in the decision as a source of information.[2] Contemporary works of non-fiction on Israeli spy operations are also referenced. Meanwhile, the interrogation record of a former Arājs Kommando member who claimed to have witnessed a battalion led by Cukurs burn fifteen Soviet villages and kill forty Soviet partisans was dismissed as 'general and not concrete in its essence'. The testimonies of survivors are discarded wholesale, read as dubious, inconsistent and procured outside the strict procedures of criminal law. That included Ella Medalje's claim that Cukurs had driven her back to Riga from the Rumbula massacre: 'it can be concluded that he had arrived at Rumbula for a time on 8.12.1941, possibly even on two occasions, at the time that a mass shooting campaign of Jews was taking place there – that he drove Arājs there and back as a chauffeur, and also drove four rescued women from there in the same way,' the prosecutor writes. 'But from these documents, it is not possible to make any kinds of substantiated conclusions about H. Cukurs' role and participation in this campaign.' The prosecutor accepted that Cukurs had been in the forest during the massacre, but chose to believe that all through the night and into the early hours of the morning he had simply sat safely in his car, only emerging in his capacity as a 'journalist', to procure information about what was going on. And, though the Latvian criminal code holds participating or belonging to a criminal organisation punishable by up to twenty years in prison, the prosecutor had been unable to determine that Cukurs had definitively belonged to the Kommando. 'It should be noted that in these criminal proceedings, H. Cukurs's service during the German occupation period, from 1941 to 1943 inclusive, has not been established in a documented way,' the decision reads. All that the prosecutor had been able to determine was that Cukurs had agreed to 'work on the repair of motor vehicles for several Latvian institutions', including the Arājs Kommando, where he had supervised the mechanics. 'He had duties of a technical nature only and he only turned up there a few times a week, which is why he could not command anyone nor take part in any missions,' the decision concludes.

The legal opinion, James Boyd White writes, 'is always fictional, and this helps, really: the victor never wholly wins, the loser never wholly loses. What the judgement will mean after all ... is still open, as the trial and judgement themselves become the elements of a story: perhaps in a court of appeals, perhaps just in the neighborhood.'[3] No verdict holds absolute authority until the public court of opinion says it does. For the logic of any verdict, White argues, 'should always be defensible in other terms, in the language of the community itself'.[4]

In Latvia, the right-wing newspapers rejoiced at the prosecutor's decision. The Cukurs family began making plans to bring their paterfamilias's ashes back to Latvia. They wanted him to be buried in the Brethren Cemetery, a solemn space reserved for the nation's martyrs, heroes and soldiers. The Prosecutor, Monvīds Zelčs, offered quotes to the media, participating in interviews in which the Cukurs family also featured. 'The point is not whether we can blame him or not, but about what can be proven,' he told the daily newspaper *Latvijas Avīze*. 'We have evaluated this case as well as can be done after almost eighty years. Neither the corpus delicti, nor the objective nor subjective side of the case has been determined.'[5]

Corpus delicti is an old and entirely sensible legal provision. Its name encapsulates its meaning: "the body of the crime". It was introduced into European law in 1678, when Sir Matthew Hale, in his *Pleas of the Crown*, wrote, 'I would never convict any person of murder or manslaughter, unless the fact were proven to be done, or at least the body found dead.'[6] Over the centuries that followed, Hale's dictum became known as the 'corpus deliciti rule', designed to prevent people from being 'convicted of imaginary, non-existent crimes'.[7] In his 1875 *Lectures on Jurisprudence*, John Austin defines 'corpus delicti' as 'a collective name for the sum or aggregate of the various ingredients which make a given fact a break of a given law'.[8] Austin saw this corpus as a collection of evidence pointing to a singular transgression. To this day, the term operates in this manner, acting as a mechanism by which the 'fact' of a crime is established, and prevents individuals from committing 'legal suicide' – confessing to a capital crime that cannot otherwise be proven to have occurred – by mandating that all extrajudicial confessions must be corroborated 'to guarantee truthfulness'.[9] In other words, the corpus delicti rule is one standard of evidence against which testimonies and confessions must be measured. It is a safeguard against false accusations and imagined crimes, an acknowledgement that law makes provisions for and admits to the possibility of its own fraudulent use.

During the Soviet period, the corpus delicti rule was often invoked in rehabilitation cases. 'The most common formulation that accompanied rehabilitation reports – "in the absence of a corpus delicti (za otsutstviem sostava prestupleniia)" – rejected convictions on the precise grounds that the proffered evidence failed to demonstrate the commission of a crime,' Casper writes. 'The party-state thus took it upon itself to admit not only that repressed individuals were innocent, but that the very charges with which they had been impugned had no grounding in reality.' By invoking the rule in the Cukurs case, the prosecutor seemed to be locating Cukurs in a long line of posthumously rehabilitated souls. The wording of the decision seemed to suggest that the problem wasn't just that it could not be proven that Cukurs had personally fired his gun or given direct orders to kill; it was also that there was no *body found dead*, no evidence that a murder had been committed at all.

In the context of the Holocaust, it occurred to me that there is a sense in which the corpus delicti rule takes on a sinister double meaning. The *body of the crime* was not just one body but millions of bodies. Jews, communists, partisans, Roma – they were neatly ushered to their deaths and either shot, gassed, or buried alive, their remains burned and their graves chemically destroyed. Millions were killed without a trace – their bodies would never be *found dead*. Those who did leave traces, corpses and skeletons that their captors had not managed to destroy, were photographed, recorded, archived and presented as evidence. There was never any question that their bodies met the standard of juridical proof. But what of all the others? The disappeared others, the bodies cannot be counted: they are why to this day the total number murdered in many concentration camps is unknown. Some estimates admit they may be off by a couple of thousand, others as many as a hundred thousand. The difference between the actual and estimated murders may never be resolved.

What does it take to meet the standards of juridical proof, to turn fragments of evidence into unyielding facts? What kind of torturous thinking does this require? As I mulled over these questions, I thought back to the infamous libel trial against the Holocaust historian Deborah Lipstadt, held at the British High Court of Justice in 2000. David Irving, a serial Holocaust denier, sued Lipstadt for calling him as much. In court, Irving tried to further his denialist agenda, promising that he would prove that the 'gas chambers shown to the tourists in Auschwitz is [sic] a fake built by the Poles after the war'.[10] He trotted out blueprints of the gas chambers, trying to argue that they could not have possibly destroyed so many bodies. In one session, Irving argued that the elevator of Auschwitz's crematorium #2 did not have the capacity to operate when piled with corpses 'six or seven high'. Lipstadt's defence team called the architectural historian Robert Jan van Pelt to counter his claims. Irving pressed him to calculate 'how long it would take to load two thousand bodies, go up one level, remove them, and return to the bottom,' Lipstadt writes in her account of the proceedings. Van Pelt hoped the judge would intervene, but he said nothing. 'For what seemed like an unbearably long time, the two debated the procedure for loading and unloading bodies,' Lipstadt writes. A journalist in the audience went home and re-did their calculations. 'Ten minutes for each batch of 25, I tapped in. That makes 150 an hour, which gives 3,600 for each 24-hour period. Which gives 1,314,00 in a year. So that's fine. It could be done. Thank God the numbers add up. When I realized what I was doing, I almost threw the little machine across the compartment in rage,' he writes. Lipstadt felt similarly: 'Irving, despite his record of distortions and interventions, had beguiled both of us into taking his theories – if only for a moment – seriously.'[11]

One must engage with lies in order to refute them. 'The logic of proof is the logic of the murderer,' Marc Nichanian argues.[12] To correct a lie is also to repeat it, to contribute to its spread. In *The Historiographic Perversion*, Nichanian traces how the mechanisms of denial worked to erase the Armenian Genocide. Some of the perpetrators did face trial, but the records of those proceedings were later destroyed.[13] The survivors dedicated the rest of their lives to collecting and archiving their testimonies. They thought this would make a difference. The result was catastrophic. They had trapped themselves inside the logic of the denier, Nichanian explains. 'They had to prove their own death.'[14] Along the way, the annihilation of their families went from a fact to a historical question.

Where does one find the way out? How to escape this murderous logic, this suffocating, closed loop? Humanists and romantics, like James Boyd White, might suggest that our salvation lies in storytelling, in narrative. Perhaps this is indeed the case – after all, here I am, trying to construct yet another one, quoting victim testimonies and interviewing survivors. But Nichanian argues that even this is not enough. No narrative is great enough to foreclose the possibility of denial. Only law can do this, he claims. 'All genocidal projects of the twentieth century have been first of all challenges to law,' he writes. 'In some exceptional circumstances, law has taken up the challenge.'[15] The verdict in the Cukurs case was not one such instance.

That summer, I wrote to the prosecutor once more, to ask for a follow-up interview in Riga. His press secretary asked for written questions, so I asked: Why did he issue the decision when he did? How did he decide which pieces of testimonial and archival evidence to exclude? Could I access the volumes of evidence he had compiled? How did he understand the term corpus delicti, and what role had it played in his decision?

The press secretary responded the next day. The prosecutor was 'quite busy with another case for the next three weeks' and did not have time to meet. Instead, he sent written answers: he had closed the case because he had finally received responses from the relevant nations, with the exception of Israel, and had completed his evaluation of the case file. As for his reasoning, he said that the decision contained his justifications. The law of criminal procedure forbade him from sharing the evidence files. He did not respond to my question about corpus delicti, but he did conclude quite clearly: 'This criminal case has been terminated on a rehabilitative basis.'[16]

I asked the leaders of the Jewish community what they made of the ruling. The prosecutor had not conducted a full investigation, they claimed. They believed that he had applied different standards of evidence to the submitted materials, giving full credence to Cukurs's claims and none to those of his colleagues and accusers who spoke of his participation, none to the Jewish survivors who claimed to have seen him at work. The verdict was a 'scandalous document' in the eyes of the Jewish community. It could not stand. They were preparing a formal appeal; they had hired a lawyer pro bono. They were trying to do everything quietly, careful not to attract too much attention to themselves as they began pushing back against the state. 'It's a question of patriotism,' a prominent member told me. He did not want to go on the record; for the time being, they were focused on trying to keep things quiet. They had confidence that the verdict would be overturned. If it wasn't, well, then they would consider turning it into an international affair. Officially, they maintained that Latvia had one of the lowest levels of anti-Semitism in all of Europe. But they could easily choose to tell a different story.

22

Road of Contemplation

One stormy summer day in July 2019, six months after I received the full text of the prosecutor's decision, I boarded the tram near my apartment in Riga and rode north. It was a trip I had been putting off for too long, one that I had kept telling myself could wait. The publication of the prosecutor's decision, and the flurry of press that followed, meant that the time for waiting, for putting off, was no longer. Soon after news of the decision, the headlines began: 'Will Herberts Cukurs be reburied in the Brethren Cemetery?' one read.[1] Another reported that 'Discussion on the reburial of Cukurs' had 'resumed' following the termination of the criminal proceeding.[2] In 2011, the Cukurs family had petitioned the authorities to grant them the honour, and had been told that 'no decision has been made and the matter has been postponed due to conflicting views'.[3] Like the question of his guilt, the matter of his internment had been deflected for as long as possible. Now that the prosecutor's decision had been made public, I feared that would soon change. The ghost hero was after his prized plot.[4]

The tram deposited me near a street lined with flower kiosks, their bright carnations and roses protected by a series of small tin roofs. I had arrived outside the city's sprawling burial complex, a cluster of several cemeteries, each one marked with its own script and stonework. The Brethren Cemetery, where Cukurs's family would like to see him interred, anchors the complex. To approach its imposing entrance one must first pass by a number of old burial grounds, among them the famous Rainis cemetery, where Jānis Rainis, Latvia's national poet, lies entombed, and a small, almost invisible Muslim cemetery marked only by a crumbling white gate and two small plaques inscribed in Arabic and Russian. An expansive park, full of lush and intersecting plots; some have been overgrown and forgotten, others have been glorified and well groomed.

The Brethren Cemetery is a 'quasi-sacred' space for Latvians, a national necropolis for its fallen heroes.⁵ Its monumental entrance is marked by an impressive, brutalist limestone gate bearing the national coat of arms. This is one of the oldest elements of the burial ground, the stone already pockmarked and discoloured, well on its way towards disintegration. '1915' and '1920' are engraved on either side of the crest, along with two crosses: the dates bookmark Latvia's long fight for its first period of liberation. Reliefs of four ancient horsemen flank the entrance columns. Three of their heads are bowed, hands at their reins. One of them solemnly stares straight ahead, confronting the mourners who pass through the gate.

In 1936, Latvia's authoritarian pre-war president Kārlis Ulmanis formally dedicated the Brethren Cemetery a national memorial, but it had been used as a burial ground for over a decade before that. The necropolis had been born with the nation; it had provided a place where those who fought and died in its successive, formative wars could be buried. It took twelve years to build the stone structures of the spare cemetery, which would serve as a designated resting place for the nation's greatest heroes and unknown soldiers. Periods of construction coincided with waves of the heroic dead. The first men buried there fought with the 12th Russian Imperial Army in the First World War, battling German forces on a small strait of land that became known as 'Death Island', one of the first places where chemical weapons were used in warfare.⁶ Designed to exemplify the unique history and pagan culture of the Latvian people, the cemetery represents the conversion of Herder's poetic imagination of the nation into something far more militaristic. This was where the Cukurs family hope their paterfamilias will one day be buried.

I hurried through the gate and found myself standing alone on a wide, open walkway lined with linden trees. This was the Road of Contemplation, the long path separating the world of the living from that of the dead, a symbolic River Styx. 'The living on one side, and the dead on the other,' a guide to the cemetery explains. Every year, Latvians walk the five kilometres separating the Freedom Monument in the city centre to the cemetery. They carry candles, flowers and flags as they proceed, each step reminding them of their own inexorable march towards death, each step bringing them closer to the fallen. The university fraternities march in groups, the Lettonia men wearing their green and yellow caps. The Road of Contemplation is only 200 metres long, but in some sense it spans the entire nation.

I picked up my step as I walked down the exposed path, thinking the whole time of why I had come, and what exactly I was doing in a country that my family had all but abandoned. Why did I care where a dead man might be buried? Why was I preoccupying myself with the finer points of the Latvian criminal code, concerning myself with the details of an obscure investigation? Before the verdict was issued, I had spent many months wondering how the prosecutor would rule, and what evidence he would privilege in his decision. I had been curious to see how he would approach the difficult task he'd been assigned, to look back upon his nation's past and regard it in the same way as the prosecutors at Ludwigsburg: not as history, but as crime. Now, I knew.

The Road of Contemplation deposited me on a terrace lit by an eternal flame, still glowing despite the rising winds. Across the way, a sombre statue of a woman in mourning came into view. This was Mother Latvia, the symbol of the nation. She holds the national flag and a bronze wreath of oak leaves. Her head is tilted down, towards the two fallen soldiers at her feet, still clutching their swords. To approach her, one must walk past rows of graves. The heroes of the war for independence, the dead of 1917 and 1918 and 1919, they lie closest to Mother Latvia. Then come the generals of the Second World War, their riflemen buried several paces away. The further one strays from Mother Latvia and her dead sons, the more one begins to see tombstones written in Russian, graves from the Soviet period, the dead marked with a star instead of a cross.

Each step towards Mother Latvia forces the traveller to consider their direction of movement: away from the living and towards the heroic dead, away from the graves the nation has forgotten and towards those it has chosen to exalt. Walking down the pathway lined with linden trees, I thought of how easy it was for visitors to remain oblivious to the small memorial in copper, steel and glass that stands outside of the cemetery's vast, wooded expanse. 'In Memory of the Victims of the National Socialist Concentration Camp "Riga-Kaiserwald"and Its Subordinate Camps', its inscription reads. It marks the spot where Eliezar Karstadt, the man who uttered Cukurs's name in the Eichmann trial record, and more than 18,000 other Jews from all over Europe were imprisoned after the ghettos were destroyed.

The Kaiserwald memorial was created by the Latvian sculptor Solveiga Vasiljeva. It was erected in 2005, just after Latvian joined the European Union. The relevant dignitaries attended the consecration: 'May this monument give us hope that we shall be able to learn from the crimes of the past,' the German ambassador remarked. 'Latvia must not hide the dark pages of [its] history,' the Latvian president said. They laid flowers before the memorial, they issued a press release: 'Only Germans worked in the Mezaparks camp administration and [as] guards; unlike the Salaspils concentration camp, there were no Latvians in either the interior or outside guard,' it concludes. No Latvians contributed to the making of this death camp, they wanted the world to know.[7]

The Riga Cemetery Agency oversees burials at the Brethren Cemetery. Every year they receive dozens of requests for reinterment. In a public television spot that aired shortly after the prosecutor's decision was issued, Cukurs's daughter Antinea Dolores Rizzotto, the prosecutor Monvīds Zelčs and the head of the cemetery agency, Guntars Gailitis, were each interviewed in turn.[8] Rizzotto told the reporter that, since the 1950s, she had been haunted by her father's reputation. 'For over sixty-nine years, we have been known as a murderer's family. This is something terrible

... I cannot walk with my head held up. It is extremely painful. I would like to clear our name.' Using derogatory language, she explained that her family turned to the prosecutor and asked him to try to prove that he had killed a single Jewish person: 'Please prove at least one. And they couldn't prove it. I know that he was good to Zhids and to other people – that can be proven.' (Remember what Nichanian argues: *the logic of proof is the logic of the murderer*.) She told the host that her father 'deserves' to be buried in the Brethren Cemetery, 'to clean his name as wrongly accused', Rizzotto said. 'The way I see it, if those Zhids themselves don't clean it then others have to do it. That is the truth.'

When the prosecutor appeared before the camera, he explained, once again, that the evidence did not suffice, that it did not matter if Cukurs was living or dead, that neither he nor his corpse could be tried. '[I]f Cukurs were alive now, would I be able to raise the indictment based on the materials as they are right now? To send it to the court? It is practically impossible.'

Finally, Gailitis was asked to speak about the possibility of reinterment. It wasn't up to him whether Cukurs would be reburied in the Brethren Cemetery, he explained. He did not want to be in the centre of this controversy; he did not want to be the one with the final say. He did not want to say 'yes' or 'no'. 'Everyone thinks that Gailitis is some genius who can decide what and how. Gailitis doesn't decide,' he told the journalist. He listed all the organisations that have to sign off on burials: not only the Brethren Cemetery Committee, but also all branches of the military, the defence ministry, and more. 'If it is a sensitive subject, then the Foreign Ministry needs to be consulted, and the historians,' he explained. His message was clear: Cukurs would not be reburied, and he was not the one to blame. (The historians were later consulted: they did not recommend reburial.)[9]

I turned to leave the cemetery, passing the Eternal Flame and running down the Road of Contemplation, trying to beat the rain. The limestone gate loomed before me once again. It is slowly falling apart – natural limestone begins decaying after only about a hundred years. As I approached its faded stones, I could not help but think of another immortal gate, the one that appears in Franz Kafka's parable *Before the Law*.

The parable tells the story of a countryman who travels a great distance to plead his case before the law. He walks and walks and walks until he finally arrives at its gates, only to find a gatekeeper standing guard. Though the gates are wide open, the gatekeeper will not let him through, not 'at this moment'. The man waits. He grows older, he begins to die, but he remains at the gate. When he is so old that he can no longer move, he asks the gatekeeper a final question: 'Everyone strives to attain the Law,' says the man, 'how does it come about, then, that in all these years no one has come seeking admittance but me?' The gatekeeper responds: 'No one but you could gain admittance through this door, since this door was intended for you. I am now going to shut it.'"[10]

Who, in the legal thicket that I had wandered into, occupied the cursed position of Kafka's man from the country? Was it Cukurs, whose case was continuously in limbo, never quite making it into the courtroom, yet also never fully dismissed? Was it the dead witnesses, the survivors and their children, the accusers whose testimonies the prosecutor had refused to admit? Was it the onlookers, the inheritors, the hangers-on, people like me who had discovered these proceedings and could not look away? I imagined us all standing together, crowding before the gates of the law, trying to peer past the gatekeeper and seeing only further obstacles, stronger gatekeepers, endless gates.

In Kafka's parable, the man from the country cannot defy law without risking incurring its wrath – 'I am powerful,' the gatekeeper reminds him. To stand before the gate is to confront law's incredible capacity for destruction: 'Legal interpretation takes place in a field of pain and death,' Robert Cover writes. '[T]he normative world-building which constitutes "Law" is never just a mental or spiritual act. A legal world is built only to the extent that there are commitments that place bodies on the line.'[11] Bodies demarcate the entrances to law, and bodies are ultimately what law seeks to control, be they living or dead.

Kafka's parable never reveals what the man from the country has come to plead. Perhaps, like *The Trial*'s protagonist Joseph K., he does not know what the law wants from him or of what crime he stands accused. Joseph K. knows only that 'proceedings' have been 'instituted' against him, and no more. Perhaps the crowd that I imagine assembled before the gate, the crowd in which I stand craning my neck, does not know what law wants from us either, or what we, in turn, want from law. What do we want the prosecutor to deliver? Absolution, culpability, finality, a clean bill of historical health? If the prosecutor had reached a different conclusion, if he had determined that Cukurs bore some share of the guilt, would that have been enough? Or would the only acceptable option have been for the prosecutor to have thrown up his hands in the face of history, to refuse to take on the case, to leave the messy business of judgement to the historians?

In Kafka's writings, law never fully reveals itself. And yet its presence is always felt, its operations always in motion. The literary scholar Katrin Trüstedt points out that the inaccessibility and obfuscation of the law, and K.'s perpetual inability to appear before it, 'suggests that Kafka's writings themselves belong to some kind of preliminary stage', that the *prozess* described in *The Trial* is more akin to pre-trial proceedings than to 'the actual oral trial'.[12] K.'s legal process is full of secrets and stops and starts: 'The procedures never come to the stage of a main trial where a person appears, a case is made and debated, and a verdict is reached,'[13] Trüstedt writes. The Cukurs case, technically, was also a pre-trial proceeding, a protracted investigation into the possibility of a trial. Its details and origins were similarly opaque. Not even the prosecutor knew who exactly had instigated the case, who had sent over the first trove of documents, when and why. He did his best to make this terrible case finally go away, to clear it from the docket. And yet it persisted. The legal matter would not conclude so cleanly. The public court of opinion had yet to rule.

I couldn't help but wonder if, as in *The Trial*, there would be no moment of revelation, no jury or final judgement. In this indefinite suspension of legal procedure, I suspect that somewhere lurks the slightest hint of relief.

PART III

Why isn't everything over? Why can I question you? Why are you there like a space in which I am still lingering and with which I feel connected?

Maurice Blanchot, *The Last Man*[1]

For me Latvia became a riddle only some ten years later, when a half truth, long unspoken in my family, acquired outlines, when, like wormholes, those penetrations into space and time, into new spaces and a new time, it began to create shortcuts toward a journey, that often dangerous and destructive journey the end of which cannot be seen. But, some years later, all that rubbish, all that rot and rubble settled and we began to step over it, softly at first, trying not to disturb the dust, then we collected shards of that past, all those splinters, we buried all that debris and moved on.

Daša Drndić, *EEG*[2]

23

The Appeal

In a small office on an upper floor of the Jewish community's headquarters in Riga, Ilya Lensky, director of the Museum "Jews in Latvia", labours away. The quotation marks are part of the museum's name, a curious and revealing grammatical choice. The nation and its subjects, squashed together between twin sets of double inverted commas, as if 'Jews' and 'Latvia' could only be made to fit together speculatively, their pairing merely an idea or historical curiosity, not a living, breathing reality.

The museum occupies the third floor of an imposing pre-war building in the city centre. Built in 1914, it housed a Jewish theatre, club and library during Latvia's first bout of independence, functioning as a central gathering place for the community. In its auditorium, Herberts Cukurs once addressed a crowd of curious Latvian Jews, telling them of his journey to Palestine, of what they might find there. The Soviets used it as a *Dom Politprosvesheniya*, a 'House of Political Education',[1] and the Nazis turned it into an officers' club. After the Soviet collapse in 1991, the building was returned to the Jewish community and put to use as a meeting place and documentation centre. Under the direction of a Holocaust survivor and historian named Marģers Vestermanis, a skeleton staff set about collecting family archives, picking up the scraps of the successive occupations, creating a record of what had been destroyed and what remained.

Today, to walk into the small museum is to encounter a long and dark history. The exhibition proceeds chronologically, beginning with documents from the eighteenth and nineteenth centuries illustrating the restricted conditions of Jewish life in Riga, including an 1810 leaflet from the Riga Jewish Community, entreating their Christian neighbours to 'recognise Jews as competent members of society'. Among the reports of pogroms are also glimmers of fellow feeling: a Latvian composer collects Jewish folksongs, now preserved in the state folklore treasury; a Jewish composer translates Latvian folksongs, or dainas, into Yiddish. A small exhibition features Latvian dainas in which Jews appear. The poems are inscriptions of otherness; as Herder observed, the nation drew its borders through its songs. One goes: 'The Jews walked grumbling, / When the sun was up high; / The poor little peasants / Had finished threshing rye.' And another: 'Only Jews, only Jews, / Where dear mother sent me to / I heard no more lovely songs, / Nor kind, good words for which I long.'

Lensky's office is a few doors down from the exhibition hall. He has a thick shock of dark hair, a warm face, a scholarly demeanour, an encyclopaedic memory. He belongs to the generation of Riga Jews raised after the collapse of the Soviet Union, a young custodian of what remains of the nation's Jewish community. He was one of the first people I wrote to when I discovered this peculiar case. He had helped assemble evidence for the prosecutor, pulling reams of testimonies and documentation from the museum's holdings and sending it down the street for examination. (The museum is located on the north side of the city centre esplanade, the prosecutor's office on the south. A beautiful park separates the two buildings.) After the prosecutor's decision was issued, I started speaking with Lensky more regularly. He was busy preparing the appeal, gathering more testimonies, analysing the verdict's many oversights and obfuscations. He was willing to grant that perhaps it was just the oversight of a single prosecutor that had produced the verdict. He paraphrased the historian Uldis Neiburgs, who had told the press: 'It's not like Cukurs was just in Rumbula, picking flowers.'

'Basically, the prosecutor said, no, he *was* just picking flowers there,' Lensky explained. 'He was there for unknown reasons, not because he was a member of a genocidal organisation.'

Whenever I visited Lensky's office in Riga, full of stacks of files and books, he would update me on the status of the case, and I would tell him what I had found in other archives. He had pored over every line of every testimony, he knew where survivors had misremembered and embellished their stories, and where they had adhered strictly to the horrible truth. He hated the idea that the prosecutor's office had been charged with issuing a verdict on what had really happened in the past. Cukurs's guilt was for historians, not prosecutors, to judge. 'What are they going to do, arrest his ashes?' he asked during one of our many talks. But as long as the case remained a concern of the Prosecutor General, Lensky would continue to track its progress. One day, he sent me a colour-coded spreadsheet of sixty witnesses whose testimonies had been submitted as evidence during the Arājs trial. The admitted testimonies were in green, the excluded ones in red. He thought the prosecutor might have a harder time ignoring testimonies that had already been accepted in German courts; it had fallen to him to try to track the original testimonies down. If the prosecutor had excluded testimonies without signatures and affidavits of their origins, well, then, Lensky would get him exactly what he was asking for. He would allow the prosecutor no further excuses.

In an émigré newsletter, the *Latvian Jewish Courier*, Lensky sometimes publishes updates on his work. In one edition, he and David Lipkin, a lawyer and Jewish community board member, co-authored a status report titled 'RECENT DEVELOPMENTS IN THE CUKURS CASE'. For his day job, Lipkin is an in-house lawyer at a Latvian manufacturing and development firm. After the verdict came down, he had taken on the Cukurs case pro bono, representing the Council of Jewish Communities of Latvia as they prepared an appeal. In their first co-authored *Courier* article, Lipkin and Lensky summarise what the verdict argues, and what had to be done about it. The Council had been 'shocked' by the verdict's 'content and conclusion,' they write. 'The prosecutor, who made the Decision without any reasonable grounds, ignored and rejected as unsuitable for use in the investigation numerous testimonies of eyewitnesses that establish Cukurs's guilt in killings and other crimes against the Jewish population of Latvia during World War II, while recognising as true Cukurs's own testimony stating that he had never killed or committed any other crime against Jews.'

In a report in a subsequent edition of the *Courier*, this time titled 'The Case of Herberts Cukurs: A Brief Introduction to Sources: Enough Evidence to Consider Cukurs Complicit', Lensky gives émigré readers a sense of the available evidence. He is admirably forthcoming about the fact that some testimonies are unreliable, smattered with patently fabricated and embellished facts. For example, the testimony that a survivor named Rafael Schub provided to Michelson's Committee for the Investigation of Nazi Crimes in the Baltic Countries, in London, claims that Cukurs burned the Great Choral Synagogue, sterilised Jewish men in Bauska and forced 1,200 Jewish people in Kuldiga to drown themselves in the wide rapid of Venta Lake. Yet Cukurs had not yet joined the Arājs Kommando when, in the first days of the group's existence, they burned the Great Choral Synagogue. Moreover, 'Schub was not in Bauska at the time nor was he in Kuldiga,' Lensky writes, so he could not have witnessed the events he describes. Schub was known for being a fabulist and a gossip, and his depositions had been dismissed in prior legal cases, including at the Arājs trial. He was one of the many survivors who, quite understandably, wanted to see Cukurs in the dock, and he was willing to bend the truth to make it happen. 'Therefore, although we have an authentic document with good provenance coming from the "free world", its content and legal history have been fully discredited,' Lensky wrote.[2] 'This said, we want to emphasise that we consider Holocaust history to be tragic and bloody enough to have no need for inflation or exaggeration. We also consider the sources we have to be sufficient to answer, with certainty, the question about Cukurs's participation.'

Lensky and Lipkin had wasted no time after receiving the verdict. If the prosecutor insisted upon discounting the words of dead witnesses, they would find the few remaining living survivors and see if the prosecutor's office would dare to ignore them, too.

Lipkin flew to Tel Aviv to depose two nonagenarian survivors, both of whom remembered seeing Cukurs convoying prisoners to their deaths in Rumbula Forest. They also tried to track down the children of Cukurs's victims, who might testify to what their parents saw. It took them little more than a month to submit their appeal. They petitioned the Prosecutor General to reopen the case because they had uncovered new facts, new documents and new witnesses that the prosecutor had not taken into account.

In April 2019, Lipkin sent a formal appeal to the Prosecutor General's office. The document begins with the criminal case at hand, Nr. 12812000506, and states that it is being submitted on behalf of two individuals whom the prosecutor had not encountered before: Jehuda Leo Feitelson, of Jerusalem, and Paul Semenoff, of Auburn, California. These two men, he argued, had information that the court was obligated to hear. When I read through the text of the appeal, I too encountered their names for the first time. But I would soon become well acquainted with each of their stories.

A month later, in May, Lipkin's appeal was rejected. The new evidence, the prosecutor reported, did not disclose 'any new crucial facts'. It proved that Cukurs had been in the Riga ghetto, 'but did not prove that Cukurs killed people or committed any other crimes; that the witness had seen Cukurs convoying the prisoners of the Riga Ghetto did not constitute a new development'. That could have been the end of it, but Lensky and Lipkin persevered. 'It's clearly a political decision, either of the prosecutor himself, or of someone who has influence over him,' Lensky explained. Nearly everyone I spoke to understood that the Prosecutor General was trying to close the case as quickly and quietly as possible, to get this politically incendiary criminal investigation off the docket. But the Jewish community of Latvia wasn't about to play along, not on those terms, not if it meant that Cukurs would be permanently, posthumously absolved of all sins. 'If he wants to do it the painful way, we can do it the painful way,' Lensky told me, speaking of the prosecutor. He wanted the agents of the law to look at the evidence before them and see not what they wanted to see, nor simply what was politically convenient to see, but what was actually there. He wanted them to behold the totality of testimonies and understand them for what they were – imperfect records of a persecuted people, crying out for an almost infinitesimal acknowledgement of their immense pain, of all that they had lost, and at whose hands.

*

In July 2019, I met Lipkin for the first time in a Riga coffee shop. He arrived sporting a suit and a buzz cut, a trim and fit man who, I would soon learn, spends his free time competing in Iron Man competitions and triathlons. He told me that he had only picked up the case five months prior, in February. I had been following its progression for longer than he had, but I needed him to bring me up to speed on the latest legal state of play. He was hell-bent on not letting the prosecutor's first decision stand. He walked me through the logic of the first appeal and told me he was already well into preparing a second one. He would submit more new evidence; he would not let up. He had been chosen as the legal counsel for the last survivors and their descendants, and he felt the full moral weight of that responsibility. Lipkin argued that the prosecutor's verdict was illegal for two reasons: first, because he had not conducted an adequate investigation, and, second, because he had not consulted all the available evidence. 'The head prosecutor can reopen the case on either of those grounds,' he explained. He was operating in uncharted legal waters: 'You won't find in Latvia any precedents about this,' he said. The independent nation had never attempted to try one of its own Nazi collaborators.

So Lipkin had been spending time reading about other Nazi prosecutions, in other times and other nations. He went through the records of the Eichmann trial, he found the original testimony from Eliezar Karstadt, the man who had called the court's attention to the existence of Herberts Cukurs. He planned to resubmit Karstadt's testimony with his second appeal. The prosecutor had only dismissed Karstadt's statement to Simon Wiesenthal – Lipkin thought the authorities would have a harder time dismissing witness evidence that had been presented before

an Israeli court. The Eichmann and Cukurs cases had been linked
from the beginning, and so they would remain linked until the
bitter end. It struck Lipkin that, just as Eichmann had been tried
for his logistical role in the Holocaust, for conveying millions of
Jews to their deaths, so, too, should Cukurs be held accountable
for participating in the same crime, albeit on a much smaller
scale. The prosecutor did not dispute that Cukurs had been
in the ghetto while Jewish people were being assembled to be
transported to Rumbula. And there was ample evidence attesting
to the fact that Cukurs had convoyed prisoners of the Riga ghetto
to their deaths. The conveyance, Lipkin argued, was an 'integral
part of the Rumbula Action'. Yet somehow the prosecutor had
not registered this act as a crime.

As we sat with our coffee, I asked Lipkin where he saw the case
going over the next several years, and how he thought it might end.
He told me that, if the prosecutor refused to reopen proceedings,
he could appeal it before the European Court of Human Rights,
in Strasbourg, where member states have lately been turning to
settle their intractable memory disputes. He seemed to harbour
an unshakeable hope in the possibility of attaining justice through
law – a lawyer's lawyer through and through. His stridency made
me recall Nichanian's claim that genocide is at its root a challenge
to law, a challenge which only law has the muscle to respond to
and refute. I want to believe that this is possible, I want to share
in Lipkin's unshakeable hope. But I can't help but worry that,
even if he succeeds, too much irrevocable damage has already
been done.

A few weeks later, I woke up to a flurry of emails from Riga.
Lipkin's appeal had at last been accepted. In a press release, the
prosecutor's office had announced that the previous decision
had been annulled, and that the 'pre-trial investigation has been
re-opened'.' An internal investigation had found that 'the decision
to terminate the criminal proceedings was made prematurely,
before all possible investigations and procedural actions provided
for in the Criminal Procedure Law were used in obtaining and
examining evidence, therefore it was revoked'. In other words, the

first prosecutor had not done his job thoroughly enough, and while it may once have appeared politically expedient to close the case with such a fumbling decision, the situation had changed. The investigation had been assigned to another prosecutor. The case against Cukurs was open once more.

24

Race for the Living

By the time the criminal investigation was formally reopened, in September 2019, I had been following its progress for over two years. I remained bewildered that, so many decades after the Second World War, questions of complicity, culpability, rehabilitation and restitution were still making their way through the courts. It was a naïve bewilderment, but a motivating one. I had come to think of the Cukurs case as a race for the living: for the verdict to be fully overturned. Lipkin and Lensky knew that not only did they have to overwhelm the prosecutor with new evidence, but they also had to ensure that the survivors they had found would live long enough to testify. The two names on Lipkin's initial appeal – Jehuda Feitelson and Paul Semenoff – came from two different generations, the former a survivor himself, the latter the son of one. They seemed to represent a changing of the guard, the anxiously awaited transition from first-generation to second-generation survivors, from memory to post-memory. It was on behalf of both of these generations that Lipkin had filed the appeal. It was for them that it had to succeed.

For over a half-century, Jehuda Feitelson kept a notebook in his desk drawer. He had started writing in it in the 1950s, when, after a long and arduous journey, he had finally managed to settle in Israel and set up a new life. He was a young man, nineteen years old, when the Nazis invaded Latvia. 'We did not – at least I did not – understand what was about to happen,' he wrote in his notebook. 'On the first few nights, we were careful not to be seen on the streets. Armed Latvian groups, allegedly assisting police, removed tenants who they thought were Jews, or whom the doormen told them were Jews. The Jewish men were supposedly taken to work and they disappeared without a trace.' His parents, Isaac and Vera, settled their family in Bauska. The whole family was soon moved into the Jewish ghetto.[1] On the night of 30 November 1941, he watched as his aunt and her two young children were marched to their graves. Eight days later, it was his parents' turn. 'I did not get to see my parents in their last days, but the horror of people walking and being shot and falling on the side of the street in the snow has haunted my dreams for many years and is engraved in my memory forever.' Another image remained engraved in his mind: the SS men and their 'Latvian assistants' surveying the ghetto with pleasure. In his notebook, Feitelson recreated the scene, noting one eerily familiar face: 'I saw the killer Cukurs among them.'

He survived only because he was strong enough to work, kept on as a slave labourer throughout the war, kept alive long enough to be deported to Germany with the retreating Nazi forces. 'The Jews were on the bottom of the ships, the Germans were on the top,' his son Eran told me. Feitelson was sent to a labour camp, where he was soon liberated by American soldiers. He was one of the lucky ones.

After that, it was up to him to decide where to restart his life. With his family and home destroyed, there was no reason for him to return to Bauska. 'He didn't want to go back to Latvia. He felt that the Latvians, essentially, were for the Germans,' Eran said. He did not think it would be safe for him there. So, with a group of friends, he sneaked onto a train bound for Belgium, and from there headed to the South of France, where he had learned that Zionist organisations had clandestinely laid on ships bound for Palestine. Feitelson's, like many others, was intercepted by British forces, and he ended up spending three days dangling his legs off the prow of a Turkish trawler, waiting for permission to dock. He would go on to fight with Israeli forces in the 1948 war, to get his PhD in chemistry, to marry, to join the chemistry faculty at the Hebrew University of Jerusalem. In his notebook, he wrote down his memories of the family he had lost, of Latvia, of the German occupation. He did not hide it from his sons, but he did not tell them about it either.

Things changed in the 1990s, after the Soviet Union fell. In 1998, Jehuda decided that it was time for him to return to Latvia, to see what remained. 'He took a long while until he was ready to go back there,' Eran told me. 'He had severe, strong feelings about it, but he wasn't the kind of person who would express them outwardly.' In 2001, he returned with his sons to show them the old family home in Bauska, the empty plot where the town synagogue once stood, the mass graves, and in Riga, the exact place where he saw his mother alive for the last time.

It occurred to him that there should be a memorial at the site of the old Bauska synagogue, once a bustling centre of Jewish life, where he had prayed before its luxurious holy ark as a young man. So he joined forces with a South African-born American businessman named Yehudi Gaffen, whose family had also lived in Bauska before the Holocaust, to try to make it happen. It was a long and painful process trying to convince the town council to cooperate. For many years, they made no progress. Meanwhile, the memorial to Latvians who died fighting with the Germans went up elsewhere in town. Yehudi and Jehuda, two of Bauska's exiled sons, continued to press forward with their mission, frustrated but undeterred. The obvious ease with which the SS memorial went up, and the protracted battle they fought just to get a simple sculpture up in the empty lot where the synagogue once stood, well, 'that kind of tells the story,' Eran said.

Yehudi Gaffen and Jehuda Feitelson travelled to Bauska together to visit their former familial village. 'One of the things that stood out for me in my conversations with Jehuda was that I think I have way more enmity against the killers and murderers than he did,' Gaffen told me. 'He was almost matter-of-fact about it.'

On that trip, they went to visit a woman who remembered Feitelson from school. 'We went up to her apartment and she pulled out an album to show pictures of him and her together in the classroom,' Gaffen said. 'And as we were turning the pages, there was a man in an SS uniform. I asked her, "Who's that?" And she said, "That was my husband."' Feitelson took it in his stride. 'He had an amazing acceptance of it all, without hatred,' Gaffen said.

In 2017, the synagogue memorial finally went up.[2] Dignitaries from Latvia, Israel and the United States convened at the site later that month for the unveiling; a Yizkor prayer was recited, recalling the dead. A stone pillar, carved in the shape of the book of life, now immortalises the long history of the town's vanished Jewish community. 'Dedicated to the Jews of Bauska, who for centuries lived here and built this city,' it begins, in English and Latvian. Four sculpted figures representing the murdered mark the perimeter of the site, their bodies fashioned from rubble – all that remains of the synagogue – and encased in strips of steel. Jehuda Feitelson was by then too frail to make the journey, but he took pleasure in the success of his project.

Not long afterwards, Lipkin went to visit him at home in Jerusalem. 'By the time they came to collect his testimony, he was already quite frail,' Eran, who was present during the visit, told me. 'It's a pity they didn't get it earlier, but, you know, his views were very clear about it.' Feitelson told his visitors that he had seen Cukurs in the ghetto, that he recognised his face from the newspapers, that his memory of that encounter was not uncertain. 'During the aforementioned events, to which I was a witness, observing from the window of the cellar of 4-storey building at the corner of Ludzas and Līksnas streets, among the Latvians and Germans, convoying the Jews from Riga Ghetto to the killing site in Rumbula, I have recognized Herberts Cukurs, who has been managing these deeds,' he told them.[3] He was aware of the rehabilitation campaign, of how Cukurs was being re-embraced in Latvia. He told them it was a good thing he had been murdered. 'The fact that people were taking this criminal and turning him into a hero was, for him, a sore point,' Eran explained. Lensky and Lipkin forwarded his affidavit to the prosecutor. They hoped that Feitelson would live long enough to testify again, this time before law enforcement authorities.

Jehuda Feitelson died in February 2020, aged ninety-seven. He did not live to be deposed by law enforcement authorities in person.

Perhaps this is a blessing: he did not live to see his testimony denied. Feitelson is immortalised as 'Witness 1' in the ongoing investigation. The prosecutor's office reviewed and rejected his initial affidavit, claiming that not only did it not reveal any new facts, but also that, even though he may have seen Cukurs in the ghetto on the day of the Rumbula massacre, that does not mean Cukurs was involved in convoying Jews to their deaths. 'The Prosecution Office maintains that Witness 1 learned after the war that people were being led to be killed; accordingly, his affidavit does not testify to anything but the fact that Cukurs was present at the Riga ghetto, which is not proof of guilt,' Lipkin explains. 'The logic of the Prosecution office seems to be: if the witness did not see someone pulling the trigger, then the person cannot be considered complicit in the genocide.'

25

The Violinist's Son

On 5 October 2020, Paul Semenoff arrived at the FBI's Sacramento Field Office, a modern building in a north-east suburb of the city. A soft-spoken, middle-aged broker with a white goatee, he had spent months – years, even – waiting for this moment, anticipating it, preparing for it, wondering why it had taken so long to arrive. His father had entrusted him with information before he died – stories of expulsion, terror, theft and murder. Now, finally, seventy-five years after these events, the time had come for Semenoff to speak these stories into the record.

He had been summoned to the Sacramento Field Office to provide his testimony in the Cukurs case. The Latvian Prosecutor General had sent a formal request to the US Department of Justice to collect Semenoff's witness statement, and the FBI had been tasked with the job. The meeting at the FBI was the result of many years of logistical negotiation and legal manoeuvring, and both Lensky and Lipkin hoped it would have a significant effect on the case. In Paul Semenoff they had found a living link to the crimes in question; he had not seen the crimes occur with his own eyes, but he was a witness all the same.

Like many children of immigrants and exiles, Semenoff blends into his surroundings seamlessly, a triumph of the assimilated American Dream. About a year before his appointment with the FBI, we met for coffee at a corner café in Sacramento. It was a bright, cold winter day in California, and as we began to talk he apologised – he had made an emergency trip to the dentist earlier that morning and was still feeling the effects of his treatment. I ordered a drink, found a seat by the window of the busy café and asked him to tell me his story.

His father, the legendary Sasha Semenoff, died in January 2013. I say 'legendary' because that is precisely what he was – a man who defied all expectations, whose name everyone knew, whose exploits, misfortunes and joys encapsulated all that was great and terrible about the twentieth century. Sasha is the little boy depicted in the terrible musical described in Chapter 20, the pitiable child left clutching his teddy bear as his own father is shot offstage, his real sorrow turned into a saccharine spectacle. Sasha said he had watched as Cukurs took over his family's apartment, and he claimed to have seen him in uniform, doing the bidding of the Arājs Kommando. But he was no longer alive to give his own testimony, and so his son had been tasked with relaying his father's words.

The younger Semenoff grew up in Las Vegas, where his father was a fixture on the strip's music scene, a charismatic figure who everyone knew as 'Frank Sinatra's favourite violinist'. (Sinatra used to ask Sasha to serenade him at the blackjack table.[1]) He was a character, a mensch. At a young age, he had learned that to entertain is also to survive. Born Abram Shapiro in Riga, he was a critical witness in the Cukurs case, for he had repeatedly sworn that he encountered Cukurs during the war several times, and that he had seen him perpetrate dreadful crimes. Shapiro is one of the primary witnesses whose depositions appear again and again in the archives, taken at different times and translated into different tongues. In a 1948 affidavit collected by the Central Committee of Liberated Jews, Shapiro reports that, on 2 July 1941, Cukurs and several other Latvian SS volunteers came to the Shapiro family apartment, arrested his father and took him away to the Central Prison, where he was shot. In his 1983 memoir, Shapiro describes how he was forced to play the piano while Cukurs and his colleagues drank themselves into oblivion. When Cukurs had had enough of his piano playing, Shapiro was sent to the Riga ghetto and conscripted to work in the garage at the Arājs Kommando headquarters.[2] His 1948 testimony contains a critical passage in which Shapiro describes Cukurs personally murdering two Jewish men from his work detachment:

> I worked with a Jew named Lutrins in Cukurs's garage. That day the Jews were forced out to stand at the roll-call and everyone was ordered to be there. Two other people from our brigade hid with us in the garage, and we saw how the people who stood at the roll-call were beaten, put into trucks, and taken away. One of the guards said that our brigade wasn't at the roll-call. Cukurs ordered us to stand in front of him and said that my colleague Lutrins and I were allowed not to participate because we were working on the car. The two others – Leitman and another one, whose name I don't remember – were terribly beaten by the Latvian guards under Cukurs's orders. Later, I saw Cukurs take out a gun and cold-bloodedly shoot the two Jews from our work brigade. Since that day I did not go to work anymore because I felt fatally threatened.[3]

The prosecutor needed evidence that Cukurs had personally pulled the trigger, that he had killed Jews with his own hands. He needed evidence of the corpus delicti, the body found dead. That was what Shapiro's testimony provided. It was one of the critical accounts copied out in Meidad's memoir, an explanation of why Mossad had pursued Cukurs in the first place. The problem was that Shapiro had offered slightly conflicting accounts of his encounters with Cukurs: he 'has shown a certain inconsistency in his testimony,' Lensky explains in the *Courier*. In his 1948 affidavit, Shapiro describes how his father pleaded with Cukurs for help; in his 1983 memoir, his father is not mentioned as being inside the apartment when Cukurs came to confiscate it. Because of this partial contradiction, and because all of Shapiro's testimonies had been given in out-of-court settings, the prosecutor had dismissed his claims as inadmissible and unverifiable. On their own, none of his many testimonies could be considered. But Lensky and Lipkin hoped that in the figure of his son they might have found someone who could meaningfully back up Shapiro's claims.

Like Alperovitch, Shapiro had attracted the attention of the revisionists. He appears in the 2011 documentary directed by a well-known ultra-nationalist, filmed in response to the National Geographic adaptation of Meidad's memoir. The ultra-nationalist tracks down Abram Shapiro in Las Vegas to ask him about his testimony against Cukurs. 'Mossad did not kill him because he was a good guy,' Shapiro tells him. He is seated in some kind of casino, pink and purple neon lights glowing behind his face. 'They had more evidence than me. They knew what Hitler did, what Cukurs did.' When the ultra-nationalist tells him that Mossad cited his testimony in their explanation of the murder, Shapiro doesn't believe them at first. 'Mossad did not do it because of my testimony!' he says, laughing. 'Mossad said that in the book?' He appears to be delighted by the news. He throws his head back, he rests his hand triumphantly upon the buffet.

But the ultra-nationalist interprets this differently: 'From our Las Vegas expedition we found out that Abram Shapiro had never given such a testimony. Supposedly, this testimony was documented by the legal department of the liberated Jews in Germany. This same organization has also putatively documented two other testimonies. What is this organization? We couldn't find out. It is unknown whether such an organization ever existed.'[4]

Paul Semenoff grew up listening to his father's stories. The only reason Shapiro survived the Holocaust was because while he was being transferred from a work camp in Latvia to Stutthoff concentration camp in occupied Poland, a German soldier saw him holding a mandolin and asked him to play 'La Paloma', a Spanish pop tune. 'I don't know what would have happened if I hadn't known the song,' he told the *Las Vegas Sun* in 2009.[5] His music saved his life.

As a young man, Paul accompanied his father to gigs across the gambling city, playing the bass and guitar in his father's famous band. 'From my earliest childhood, I remember the name of "Cukurs", and the fact that he was a monster, and that he was directly responsible for my grandparents losing where they lived, and ultimately their lives,' he told me. 'Then there's the horrific part about my father having to go back and watch Cukurs pick over my grandparents' apartment, and entertain him while he was doing whatever he was doing there.'

In 2019, a man named Ivar Brod, one of the leaders of the emigré Latvian Jewish community, and the editor of the *Latvian Jewish Courier*, contacted Paul to tell him about the Cukurs case, and to ask him if he would be open to meeting with the lawyer handling the appeal. Paul agreed, and soon he found himself on the phone with David Lipkin, who asked him if he would be willing to testify to what his father saw and suffered. 'I have to speak the truth of what I know,' Paul told me. 'I'm not trying to sell anyone ... I'm not trying to hold anything back. It is what it is. It happened, he told me it happened, I remember it from my earliest recollections, it's part of me.'

At first, it seemed to Lipkin that Paul would have to return to Riga to provide his testimony to the prosecutor in person. 'Initially, he said, we want you to come over here, and there might be some buzz about Shapiro's son coming back.' Lipkin imagined that Paul could participate in press interviews that would help stoke public interest in the case. 'But I don't care about any of that stuff,' Paul told me. 'All I want to do is go over there and do what my dad would have done.'

That was easier said than done. The case stalled for over a year, caught in the crosshairs of transatlantic bureaucracies. Paul knew that the Latvian prosecutor had asked US authorities to depose him, but months and months later the call had not come. Lipkin was keeping him apprised of the case's development abroad, such as the fact that the Israeli government had yet to cooperate with the Latvian Prosecutor General's request for information and depositions. 'It's like nobody gives a damn,' Paul told me. 'Nobody in the Israeli government is doing anything about it, which is a little disappointing. It's rather disheartening, that nothing is moving forward.' He had even deputised a distant cousin, a former Miss Israel, to intervene, to try to petition her political acquaintances to move the case forward. He was worried that the second living witness, a man named Menachem Sherman, would die before his deposition, just as Jehuda Feitelson had. 'One of my biggest fears is that this guy is going to die,' Paul told me. A dead man's deposition is worth less than a living man's, no matter how diminished his memory may be, no matter how advanced in age; this disparity is just one of the many great iniquities separating the living and the dead.

Two agents sat down with Paul that day in Sacramento. They asked him a series of questions: what had his father told him about Herberts Cukurs? What had his father witnessed first-hand? They wrote his answers down on a yellow legal pad, and told him that their report would be sent back to the DOJ and, from there, back to the prosecutor in Riga. Paul went home, knowing he had finally done his duty.

26

'God bless their souls'

I was walking in South Berkeley one afternoon in the spring of 2019 when my phone rang. I had emailed Helga Fisch, the daughter of Miriam Kaicners, for the first time earlier that day, asking if she would be open to speaking with me about her mother Miriam's story. I did not expect to hear from her so quickly. I answered the phone and heard Helga's rich, accented voice for the first time, and quickly ducked into a coffee shop to take notes.

I had procured her email from an unexpected source: the Cukurs family themselves. In 2018, Cukurs's great-granddaughter, Laura Rizzotto, had been chosen to represent Latvia in that year's Eurovision Song Contest. Born and raised in Brazil, Rizzotto had retained Latvian citizenship through her grandmother Antinea. Her Eurovision nomination meant that her family heritage was being highlighted in the press. The young girl was having to answer for her great-grandfather's crimes, and the family wanted to shield her from these accusations. Asked by a journalist about her 'interesting family roots' and how 'being a descendant of Herberts Cukurs has affected her life', Rizzotto had explained how, having been born three decades after his death, she had learned everything about him from her grandmother, how she was grateful that, because of him, she had both Latvian and Brazilian citizenship.[1]

I knew that I had to interview the Cukurs family at some point, and the easiest way to get in touch presented itself via Laura Rizzotto's professional website. I filled out the press contact form on the site, and soon received a response from 'Laura Rizzotto's Team', stating that Cukurs's daughter, Antinea, might be open to an interview with me, but only after I had already spoken with several people. The list included the ultra-nationalist filmmaker, the author of *You Will Never Kill Him* and Andrew Ezergailis, author of *The Holocaust in Latvia*. Helga was the only one on the list with whom I had not yet been in touch. (After I had completed all these steps and reiterated my request for an interview, I received no response. The Cukurs family refused to speak with me for this project.)

On the phone, Helga launched right in: 'My mother never talked about her experience during the war,' she told me. After her break with the Cukurs family, Miriam had married a Jewish man whose family had settled in Brazil in the 1920s. Helga was the youngest of Miriam's three children, two daughters and a son. Miriam drew a heavy curtain over her past; she never told her children about Cukurs, and they did not know enough to ask.

'She felt betrayed – she had a history of betrayal,' Helga told me. 'Never trust someone who isn't Jewish, that's how we were brought up.' Miriam had passed away recently, and Helga was just beginning to sift through her mother's past, to finally begin to understand her own inheritance.

Helga only found out about the whole Cukurs saga a few years ago, when a Brazilian doctoral researcher named Bruno Leal called her. 'Did you know that your mother came to Brazil with this man who was the Hangman of Riga?' he asked. Helga started researching. 'Knowing what I know now, it clarifies how my mother was, her survivor's guilt,' she told me. 'I think, deep inside, she realized that she was in cahoots with a Nazi.' Like so many children of survivors, Helga had taken up the unhappy task of reckoning with all that her mother saw, and what she chose not to see. 'The last time I saw her, I said, "Mom, what happened with the family that saved you?" She said, "God bless their souls."'

Helga and her husband had recently retired and moved from New York City to Aspen, Colorado. She told me that she had finally resolved to understand as much of her mother's story as she could. She was in touch with the Cukurs family, she was planning a trip to Riga. Cukurs's daughter Antinea had agreed to meet Helga and to show her the farmhouse in Bukaisi where Miriam had lived with the family. 'I've been kind of stalling,' Helga told me. 'I realise that his daughter is getting older and older. It came to a point where I just thought, "What am I waiting for?"'

Already, she was starting to make sense of how her mother lived, and beginning to reckon with Cukurs's complicated and somewhat contradictory persona. She had read all about Eichmann, she knew how seemingly normal he was, how he had appeared to live a peaceful, domestic life while systematically destroying millions of people. 'Eichmann went home and hugged his kids as well. He had another life, outside the camps,' she told me. 'I cannot point fingers, I cannot say yes or no, I can only go off of the written statement that my mother gave to the Jewish organisation in Brazil. This is the only historical account that I believe I will ever get,' she said. She had typed up her mother's deposition and translated it into English. She understood that it might be an imperfect record, but it was all she had. 'It is someone giving a statement about something from the past that you cannot prove – there could be gaps, there could be euphemisms, whatever. But I still see this as my mother's story.'

Helga was grateful that Antinea was open to showing her around, but sensed that it wouldn't be a simple meeting. She told me that she sensed there was 'some resentment from the family', some lingering discomfort with Miriam's story. 'Talking to his daughter, who is nine years younger than my mother, I can tell that the family was a bit bothered that he went to all these lengths to save my mother. But the fact that he saved my mother is all I can hang on to.'

The Cukurs family told her about the prosecutor's investigation. She knew that the initial decision argued that there wasn't any evidence to suggest that Cukurs had personally killed anyone, and that he himself had been 'killed in vain', she said. She knew that the Cukurs family had celebrated the verdict, that they were petitioning for his reburial in the Brethren Cemetery. 'I was talking to someone recently, a Jewish lady, who said, "Listen. Mossad would not have gone to kill someone if they did not have evidence." '

I got the sense that Helga understood better than anyone that this history was not black and white, that it would not lend itself to simple answers. 'The problem is, you don't know what you will do to survive,' she told me. 'There are the heroes that died in the process, and there are people who did what they had to do.'

We hung up and agreed to stay in touch. I offered to help her with the arrangements for her trip – she had never been to Riga before. I asked her if she would be interested in meeting with representatives from the Jewish community there, who might be able to tell her more about her mother's pre-war life. She said yes, of course. She wanted to speak to anyone who could help her collect the million missing fragments that Miriam had left behind, things unsaid, stories untouched.

In Riga, Ilya Lensky and David Lipkin looked forward to Helga's arrival. They hoped that she might agree to serve as a witness in their appeal. She was uniquely positioned, they believed, to testify to Cukurs's complicated character, to acknowledge what he did for her mother and also to speak about the hell he had wrought for others. Helga's life story was intimately intertwined with the facts of the Cukurs case, even if she knew almost nothing of the details. The least they could do was try to secure her testimony.

But neither of them had realised just how little Miriam had told her family. In Riga, Lensky led Helga on a tour of the city, he showed her what remained of the old Jewish ghetto and the building where her mother had been detained before Cukurs saved her. The trip had been transformative. 'It's crazy how life can change overnight,' she said. 'I had never before understood what a "ghetto" was.' Lensky had explained how quickly it had been formed, he had shown her where the barbed wire had been, how the Jewish community had been confined. 'It must have been horrendous. My mother said, "May your eyes never see" – that's what I did.' Helga had seen. She remembered what Miriam had described to the Federation of Brazilian Jews, how after the first transport from the ghetto, Miriam happened to see an area strewn with luggage and blood and corpses. 'So we know what would have awaited,' Helga said.

The Cukurs family, too, had hoped Helga would testify on their behalf. One day, 'out of the blue', Laura Rizzotto's father, Rodolfo, called Helga and asked her to make a statement defending Cukurs. 'I said, "Rodolfo, I'm sorry, I know nothing",' Helga said. Since then, I've learned more.'

In Riga, Cukurs's daughter Antinea took Helga on a different tour. Together, they travelled to the farmhouse in Bukaisi, which now operates as a small museum dedicated to Cukurs's accomplishments in aviation. I find it listed on a map of regional tourist attractions, open Tuesday through Sunday, 10 a.m. to 5 p.m., by appointment only. A journalist from a right-wing paper accompanied them on the trip to document Helga's triumphant homecoming. Antinea had not asked Helga's permission to bring a journalist along, nor did she send Helga the article that was then published chronicling the visit.[2] Helga left a note in the guestbook at the museum: 'Thank you for showing me the house where the Cukurs family hid my mother during the German occupation of Latvia,' she wrote. 'A beautiful home, where my mother lived among the Cukurs family embraced by all.'

Helga went to Riga to make her own discoveries, to add colour and contrast to the outlines of her mother's life. She was filling out her own story, not contributing to someone else's. 'I went to Riga with a question: was he that bad?' she explained. She had been reading through documents, watching video testimonies about his crimes. 'All of these people cannot be making it up,' she said. She believed that Cukurs would not have survived if he hadn't collaborated. She had been struck by how Antinea led her around the farmhouse, how she described the opulence in which the family had lived out the war. Helga knew what it would have taken to live like that. 'You couldn't survive if you weren't playing their game,' she said. 'They had a very nice home.'

The story of Miriam Kaicners complicates Cukurs's story, but it does not absolve his ghost. It is understandable that the family would cling to an image of their paterfamilias as Miriam's saviour, her ticket to survival. Other descendants of perpetrators have made similar claims, suggesting that their ancestors could not have participated in massacres because they also had saved several Jews, as if two things cannot be true at once. The suggestion is always the same: saving a few excuses the slaughter of the whole. This is a narrow understanding of complicity, an attempt to whittle down the share of the guilt.

I met Helga in person a few months after her trip to Riga. I happened to be in Aspen on an assignment, and she agreed to meet me for a coffee while I was there. We met at a small European café near the base of Aspen Mountain. When Helga arrived, I was struck by her elegance: deep brown eyes, a heart-shaped face and rich brown hair. Beautiful, like her mother. She seemed at home in Aspen, with its famous mix of elite high culture and frontier air. I learned that she had come to the US from Brazil in her early twenties to enrol in a master's course in industrial design in New York, and had stayed in the country, started working, married a surgeon, retired comfortably.

We begin trading information, leaning towards one another, cautious but also eager to conspire. I tell her about my grandfather, she tells me about Miriam. We both record the conversation. It occurs to me that we've had similar upbringings, both of us growing up in Jewish communities, both of us knowing that there was something that our families preferred to leave unsaid. I listen as Helga tells me what she thinks of Cukurs, of how she has come to regard her mother's moral compromises and strategic silences. 'Most of the time, she was two hours away from Riga, and he would go in for his day job,' she tells me. 'I don't think Eichmann's wife knew what he was doing during the day.'

Perhaps there was a moment when Miriam began to suspect that Cukurs was using her as an alibi, as living proof of his goodwill. Perhaps she realised what he was doing when he was not at the farmhouse, that he was not as generous or as kind to the other Jews he encountered. Maybe she only realised it when he wore his SS uniform during their flight from Latvia to Germany at the close of the war. 'Sometimes you don't want to know, and you don't ask,'

Helga tells me. 'You think, "as long as I'm surviving, as long as I'm getting out of Latvia"', it might be okay not to know. There were rumours that Miriam had been Cukurs's mistress, but Helga could not believe there was any truth to them. During the war, her mother had lived with the family for four years, working as the children's tutor. Helga understood that her mother did what she had to do, but she could not believe that she would have done *that.*

I asked her what she thought about the whole saga now that she had walked Riga's city streets and spent more time with Cukurs's family. What did she think of his assassination? 'The diatribe of the family is that Israel has no evidence, that Mossad killed an innocent man,' she says. 'I asked Ilya [Lensky], "What does that mean, there is no evidence?" and he said, "Of course there is evidence."' He had dedicated himself to collecting all of it, he had an encyclopaedic knowledge of Cukurs's life and crimes. He had sent Helga filmed testimonies, including one from Abram Shapiro. It was to the Shapiro apartment that Cukurs had brought her mother after whisking her away from the prison.

Helga knew that Paul Semenoff had agreed to testify in the appeal. She saw the similarities between their two positions, she understood why Lipkin and Lensky had hoped that she might be able to help their case. But her mother had done all she could to protect Helga from the past. The result was that she felt she did not know anything about what had really happened. 'Paul had contact with his father throughout his life, so he will testify to what his father said,' Helga explained. 'My mother never talked to me about it, so I am not a source.'

27

One Witness, No Witness

Testis unus, testis nullus. One witness, no witness. A principle of evidence, a universal law. Or is it just another legal fiction? In Jewish law, the same rule holds: 'Even if we see two [people] enter a room, one runs out and the other is found inside dead with a knife in his back, we do not have conclusive evidence that A murdered B,' the Chabad Rabbi Tzvi Freeman writes. 'If two witnesses did not see it, we have only a probability.[1] Once it has been witnessed, it is a fact.' It is one of the oldest teachings in the Torah, from the book of Numbers: 'If anyone kills a person, the murderer shall be put to death on the evidence of witnesses. But no person shall be put to death on the testimony of one witness.'[2]

Every legal system comes with its own evidentiary rules. It is left to the men and women who serve the law – judges, lawyers, prosecutors, clerks – to interpret those rules, to use their discretion to determine what kinds of claims they will listen to, and which ones they will ignore. The prosecutor's decision in the Cukurs case seemed to undermine the very status of survivor testimony, refusing to take testimony seriously as a repository of knowledge and a record of the past. After a half-century dedicated to collecting survivor testimonies, and ensuring they were properly, carefully recorded, filmed, translated, archived, the verdict suggested that, while these efforts were all well and good for historical or memorial purposes, they were useless before the law. They did not meet the required standards of evidence so their claims would not be considered, neither in whole nor in part.

Lipkin and Lensky had two last hopes. The first was that the man they referred to in public as 'Witness 2', Menachem Sherman, a ninety-six-year-old survivor living in Ramat Hasharon, in Tel Aviv, would stay alive. He was the last living eyewitness, the 'last man', as Maurice Blanchot might say. Sherman had testified in an affidavit that he had seen Cukurs in the Riga ghetto, where he had been imprisoned in 1941, when he was fifteen. 'He recalled in his affidavit that Cukurs frequented the Riga Ghetto, always wearing the military uniform,' Lipkin explains in the *Courier*. Sherman said he had seen Cukurs murder people on three separate occasions. He remembered the exact times and locations of these murders, 'and also where he himself was located at that point, and how he happened to witness these,' Lipkin writes. During one of these episodes, Sherman watched as Cukurs tried to force a Jewish man to beat a young child in the ghetto. When the man refused, Cukurs shot them both.[3] This testimony the prosecutor's office accepted.

The second hope was more of an idea: if the prosecutor's office would not take the testimonies of dead survivors seriously on their own merit, perhaps they would change their minds if they heard from the man who had collected many of them in the first place. During one of our conversations in Riga, Lensky described this man to me: he had been the secretary of the Central Committee of Liberated Jews, in Munich. He had corresponded with fellow survivors around the world, collecting testimonies against Cukurs, he had been involved in their transcription and translation. He had been in a rush to collect these accounts, because the British were supposedly preparing a trial of the men who had created and then destroyed the Riga ghetto. And he was still alive. 'His name was Edward Alperovitch, but now he goes by Edward Anders,' Lensky said. 'Do you know him?'

Evidently, I was still living in a closed loop. I told them that not only did I know Alperovitch (now Anders), but that I had met him in California and that we had continued our correspondence.

Lipkin asked me to relay a request on his behalf: might Anders be willing to testify on behalf of the Jewish community, to vouch for the conditions under which Shapiro's 1948 testimony, and others like it, were collected? The Prosecutor General's office had determined that many of the survivor testimonies had been collected by amorphous groups without clear authority, and therefore determined that they lacked legal credibility. To Lipkin and Lensky, Anders seemed to be the last living person who could counter that damning claim.

Up to this point I had not been an active participant in the case. I had tried to maintain my posture as an observer. I could never have claimed to be impartial, but I was an observer all the same. Lipkin, too, had maintained his stance as a lawyer: there was a limit to what he could tell me while the case was ongoing. But neither of us was sure when – if ever – it would end.

Anders had sent me all his correspondence regarding the Cukurs case, every email he had written and received from 1998 to 2021. As I read through these files, I discovered how much authority he held over the historians of the subject. They all wrote to him, sending him their articles, asking him for details, verifications, recollections. 'About Cukurs. Yes, one possibility is that he was a linear combination of good and bad. That is not uncommon: some notorious SS-men loved Mozart or otherwise showed a more humane side. Few people are all black or all white; shades of gray are more common,' he wrote to one of them in a 2014 email. 'Another possibility is more cynical. In history there are several examples of mass murderers who spared a few potential victims so they could go home and tell their people what fate awaits them if they don't surrender. A more recent variant are mass murderers who spared a few victims to testify for the defense if the murderer's side lost the war. (Dead men tell no tales, but survivors do.) In a fair number of cases a few victims were spared because before the war they or their fathers had been good to the future murderer. That fits in your category of dark gray rather than jet-black murderers.'[4]

When another historian emails him asking about the precise number of Jews who were murdered, and what Cukurs might have been doing in the Arājs Kommando's garage, Anders responds courteously: 'With so many killer groups competing with each other, it surely is difficult to get a reliable number ... I do not know how much work was involved in maintaining the vehicles of the Arājs Kommando. If it was a full-time job then Cukurs could at most be a passive deputy, knowing little about Arājs's job, but (as the most prestigious officer) ready to succeed him if he got killed. On the other hand, he was present at the clearing of the ghetto on 30.11.41, accompanied the victims to Rumbula, and apparently killed a number even if he never went to the actual execution site. If he visited only a single execution at Biķernieki and listened to the talk of active members at dinner and at drinking parties, he would know enough to succeed Arājs,' he wrote. 'I think the assassination by Mossad was a very bad idea, even a crime. He should have been put on trial. And the documents of Mossad should have been made public in 1965.'

Reading through his correspondence, I learned of how doggedly Anders was fighting to ensure that the Latvians who had hidden and rescued Jews were properly honoured. He waged a one-man campaign to see that a dead corporal named Kārlis Avots, who had served in a Latvian Police battalion and who had smuggled a woman and her three-year-old child out of the ghetto, was recognised for his good deed. Yad Vashem, the Israeli institution that is the final authority on these matters, had initially named Avots as one of the Righteous Among the Nations, but had later revoked the award. Anders was still fighting. He was so committed to ensuring Avots got some honour that he decided to create his own award, one that would honour Latvia's 'Silent Heroes' – those who had saved any of their fellow citizens from deportation and death, during any one of the occupying regimes. 'I shall continue to fight for Avots as long as there is hope,' Anders wrote in one email.

I relayed Lipkin's request to Anders, and received a characteristically prompt and decisive response:

'The lawyer is on a quixotic mission impossible, to find new, credible witnesses against Cukurs,' his email began. 'Please tell him that I lived in Liepaja during the war, have never seen Cukurs, and hence have no first-hand evidence against him,' he wrote. He suggested that relying upon reputable historical works on the Holocaust in Latvia would be a more fruitful approach. 'If I give him my address, this will result in several pairs of messages thanking me but trying against all odds to squeeze some usable information out of me. Life is too short for that.'

He wrote that, in his opinion, Mossad should have gone looking for Arājs instead of Cukurs. At the time, he explained, the British were planning to try a number of men from the Riga ghetto, and, as Anders put it, 'unrealistically asked for witnesses who had seen [Arājs] pull the trigger'. Finding none, the case against him collapsed. They had to let him go. 'Mossad should have looked for Arājs who lived with his wife under her maiden name in Frankfurt, who was easily traceable even by a rookie,' Anders wrote. 'He was arrested after a couple of Latvian ex-soldiers betrayed him for two bottles of beer, served seven years in a comfortable German prison, and died peacefully in his bed. So why keep bringing up Cukurs and his gruesome execution?' Recollections change over the courses of decades – he had seen it happen himself, over the many hours he spent comparing testimonies taken nearly a half-century apart. Those who were 'looking for witnesses against Cukurs seventy-nine years later,' Anders wrote, were 'making fools of themselves'.

He had a point. The Latvian prosecutor, like the British prosecutors before him, had tried and failed to find witnesses who had seen the dead defendant pull the trigger. Finding insufficient evidence from the living, and unverifiable evidence among the dead, the first prosecutor had figured that his job was done and the case was closed. One witness, no witness.

But the Cukurs case was not an ordinary criminal investigation. It would not simply go away. His execution marked his case as unique, an affair unlike any other. The first, critical difference between his case and Arājs's is that Arājs did, eventually, end up in prison. There were no loose ends to tie up in his case, no ambiguities about the extent of his complicity, no question marks to exploit. The second is that Lipkin was not 'bringing up' the case of his own accord – he was responding to an investigation in motion, attempting to contest revisionist history, to safeguard the very records that Anders had helped create. Anders was right that it would have made far more sense for Mossad to go after the leader of the killing squad than one of its henchmen. But Cukurs was in many ways an easier target. He lived in the open, his whereabouts well known, his history well documented, his movements surveilled. He was killed in an act of vengeance, murdered before his trial instead of after. Now, the vengeance that was won by the act of his murder may yet be undone.

28

Foreign Fred

On the website of the Federal Security Service (FSB) of the Russian Federation, the successor organisation to the NKVD and the KGB, there is a 'web reception' portal. Visitors are invited to select from a drop-down menu of options: requests for government services, for government information, for the transfer of important information to operative units, for information on the FSB's educational outfits and academies, for archival records. To click on this final option is to encounter a revealing list of options, a drop-down menu of fates and misfortunes, an index of unresolved histories:

- Requests pertaining to military service in the state security agencies and troops (VChK-OGPU-NKVD-NKGB-MGB USSR, MSB-AFB-MBVD-MB-FSK-FSB of Russia).
- On the work of civilian personnel in state security agencies and troops.
- On the application of repression and rehabilitation of victims of political repression in criminal cases of state security agencies.
- For questions about the passage of state inspection by servicemen of the Red Army after their release from captivity, from concentration camps and forced labour in Germany and other European countries during the Great Patriotic War.

- On the participation of security personnel in the partisan
  movement in the temporarily occupied territory of the USSR.
- On the participation of Soviet citizens in the European
  resistance movement during the Second World War.

A colleague directed me to this portal. You might not expect the
FSB to have a web reception service, he said, but it's there. Might as
well try to see if anything will come of it. Direct descendants have
the right to petition for family documents, even if they have yet
to be declassified. My colleague had used it himself, to get records
about his grandfather's internment in a penal colony. He had sent
in his own birth certificate, and his father's, to prove he was a direct
descendant, he had indicated where he thought the files might be
held. By law, requesters are entitled to receive a response within
thirty days. The online oracle worked for him: within a month, he
received his grandfather's personal file, records of his repression and
death. Maybe, he said, the oracle would work the same way for me.

I was not hopeful, but I had to try. The portal seemed to be
my best chance at getting information out of the Central KGB
archive, which is not accessible to researchers. The first problem: to
which category of unfortunates did my grandfather belong? Did
he qualify as a military or civilian officer? Hadn't he been both?
Was he formally repressed, before he disappeared? Did he qualify
as someone involved in the 'partisan movement in temporarily
occupied territory'? There were some accounts, none of them
verified, that suggested he had joined a Soviet partisan unit after
the Arājs Kommando was dissolved and its members reassigned
to combat battalions, that he had killed a Latvian forest fighter.
I had not paid them much attention – these seemed to be a wrinkle
too far. But I wondered if I should mention these rumours in my
request.

I deliberately left this business until the very end. To send in
my written request for information seemed a mere formality, a
way of confirming what I already knew. And yet, there was still a
chance that something new would turn up, the stubbornest sliver

of hope. How much does the archive know? How much can the oracle reveal?

My father had already checked the relevant archives in Germany, Latvia and the US. From the CIA, he received a polite bureaucratic response from the agency's 'information and privacy coordinator'. 'We have completed a thorough review of your request and have determined in accordance with Section 3.6(a) of Executive Order 13526, the CIA can neither confirm nor deny the existence or nonexistence of records responsive to your request. The fact of the existence or nonexistence of such records is itself currently and properly classified and is intelligence sources and methods information protected from disclosure by Section 6 of the CIA Act of 1949 ...'

To confirm or deny the existence of any records pertaining to my grandfather would risk breaching the agency's intelligence sources; an odd but not completely unusual response, a standard answer used to swat away any requests that even approach sensitive information. In 2004, under the Nazi War Crimes Disclosure Act, the CIA declassified reams of documents about Latvian war criminals, several of whom it had recruited as spies. The visas, fingerprints, reports of these men are now downloadable online. There are over a dozen documents on Cukurs, even more on Arājs. The American agencies collected and summarised what their European colleagues had already documented and what newspapers had already reported. They kept tabs on these cases, but they did not seem to have actively investigated either man. Cukurs's file consists of second-hand reports and news clippings: 'Eichmann Unit Linked To Death Commandos', from the 5 May 1961 *Evening Star*. 'Israeli Envoy Linked to Killing of Latvian Nazi in Montevideo', from a March 1965 issue of the *New York Times*. But there was nothing on Boris, apparently, at least nothing that could be confirmed or denied.

On the evening my father showed me this letter from the CIA he also pulled out another letter from his files, one that I had never seen before. It was a rough photocopy, addressed to someone else, dated 6 November 1994. The author was named

Marģeris Vītoliņš, a former KGB agent and illustrator of some renown. A Latvian émigré, an acquaintance of my father's, had sent this former agent a photograph of my grandfather and asked if he recognised his face. The agent wrote back: 'Of course! It was not in London, nor in Hamburg that I met this man, but in Riga! He was sent there to be a "Foreign Fred",' a man from abroad, an agent with no traceable history. The letter goes on to explain that, years ago, Vītoliņš had discussed the case of Boris Kinstlers with one of his former superiors, an elderly man named Albert Bundulis, once the deputy chief of the KGB in Latvia. Bundulis had told him that the real name of this 'Fred' was 'Spakovskis' or 'Svakovskis'. Here, then, was the genesis of the rumours behind the novel about my grandfather. Who knew if it was true? Vītoliņš died in 1996. His source, Bundulis, died in 1988. I am too late. The agents are dead, but the rumours live on. Online, I can google their KGB registration cards, their life histories and read unsourced accounts of their deceits and betrayals. But I cannot ask them about Boris.

I filled out the FSB request form. I put down all the necessary personal information about myself and my family, I attached my grandfather's KGB registration cards, his curriculum vitae, his reported date and location of death: Sillamäe, Estonian SSR, April 1949. Then I sent my small plea into the void.

I may never find out who my grandfather was, or what happened to him, or how he came to be the subject of so much strange intrigue. After all these years, I am not sure how much all the remaining question marks matter. I do not think I want to know everything about Boris Kinstler. What I have already learned is quite enough.

On 29 December 2020, the oracle's response arrived in my email. A one-page letter from the Central Archive of the FSB, signed earlier that day in Moscow. A merciful missive, short and sweet:

> We would like to inform you, that in the Central Archive
> of the FSB of Russia there is no information or materials

pertaining to your grandfather, Kinstlers (Kinstlera) Boris Karlovich, b. 1918.

Deputy Head of the Archive
N. A. Ivanov

29

Baltic Troy

An Italian scholar, Felice Vinci, has advanced the theory that the world of Homer's epic tales did not take place in Greece, on the islands and archipelagos of the Mediterranean Sea, but instead in the Baltic. His evidence is anecdotal: that in the *Iliad*, Trojan men are described wearing heavy cloaks and furs fit for a colder climate, that Baltic amber is a frequent finding in Mycenaean tombs, that Homer never actually describes Crete as an island. Ancient Troy, Vinci claims, was really located in the Finnish village of Toija, 100 kilometres west of Helsinki; Thebes, near Stockholm, Lemnos on the Swedish island of Lemland, Crete along the Polish Baltic coast, Hellas in present-day Estonia, Achilles's home of Phthia along the border of Latvia and Russia. The whole mythical ancient world, relocated to colder Nordic climes. In the pagan mythologies of the Scandinavian cultures, Vinci finds traces of Greek myth. Kurland, a western region of Latvia, used to be called 'Curetia', which he argues is derived from 'Homer's Curetes, whom Greek mythology links to Zeus's birth. As to Zeus himself, just in that region there is "the figure of a supreme god called *Dievas* in Lithuanian and *Dievs* in Latvia. In local folklore he curiously shows features typical of Hellenic Zeus." [1]

It is a ridiculous idea, but also an entrancing one. It is true that Troy has never really been found.[2] Homer sings of its complete destruction, of how the great city of 'half-god mortals' was obliterated, 'made all smooth again', submerged beneath the sand. The patron saints of romantic nationalism, Goethe and Herder, did not care where Troy truly lay, or whether it had existed at all. Its landscape was always unfurling before them wherever nations went to war, wherever catastrophe came to unfold. 'In the blink of an eye, the world is thrown off keel,' the scholar Wai Chee Dimock writes of Homer's rendering of the Trojan catastrophe. 'Everything that once anchored it, everything once taken for granted, is irretrievably lost.'³ After the Second World War , the destruction of Troy took on a new meaning. 'This was a time when the *Iliad* was being read as an allegory of the Nazi destruction of Western civilization, and of Jews in particular,' the classicist James Porter writes.⁴ In Europe, as in mythical Troy, all was irretrievably lost, obliterated, erased, buried beneath the earth.

The ruins of the Great Choral Synagogue in Riga do not look like they are from eighty years ago, but from a thousand. Its remains were razed and buried after the war, when Soviet authorities turned the space into a park. They installed park benches and an impressive, orderly line of trees. After the Soviet Union was itself obliterated, excavations of the site began and soon the synagogue's old foundations began to peek through the soil. Today, the few recovered fragments of the synagogue's Romanesque-style arches have been pasted into a series of roughly reconstructed walls. They blend into their new, artificial enclosure almost seamlessly; pass by the ruins too quickly and you will miss the carved, curled floral detail among the blackened stone, the twin leafy ornaments, the odd corner curlicue. Skip over the metal menorah and memorial signs and you might even mistake it for the remains of an ancient aqueduct or fortifying wall.

Every year on 4 July a small crowd gathers before these ruins. They wear suits and ties, they gaze at the assembled dignitaries: the president, the prime minister, the defence minister, the Israeli and German ambassadors, the head of the Jewish community and the lone survivor with his cane. Men and women arrive from the embassies, national flags pinned to their lapels and flowers in their hands. Retirees watch the spectacle from the park benches, their eyes following the dignitaries as they stride in unison towards the memorial and bend down to place their wreaths.

In 2019, I stood among the crowd and listened to the then president proclaim:

> Let us remember that on 4 July 1941, the terrible events of
> the Holocaust began with the burning of the synagogue. The
> Holocaust in Latvia would not have happened if Nazi Germany
> and the USSR had not destroyed Latvia's sovereignty. Sadly, the
> so-called Arājs Kommando was also involved in the genocide
> organised by the occupying Nazi authorities. According to
> the Latvian Commission of Historians, it killed about 26,000
> civilians. These are serious and unjustifiable crimes against
> humanity and against Latvia's future, and their investigation
> cannot be undertaken using a simplified approach.[5]

Was that final line a warning, a message? If so, to whom? Was the new prosecutor assigned to the case supposed to hear it and take heed? The crimes of the Arājs Kommando, the president said, were not only crimes against humanity but crimes against the future. Because of their actions – their complicity, their zealousness, their terror – their nation would never know a future unencumbered by the past. No matter how many investigations, trials, historical commissions and memorial ceremonies were undertaken, nothing could spare future generations this unseemly inheritance. This, the president lamented.

When the speeches were over, the wreaths laid and the photographs taken, the crowd dissolved. The dignitaries disappeared around a corner and into their cars, the embassy staffers chatted on their way back to their desks. A small group lingered around the lone survivor, the ninety-six-year-old Margers Vestermanis. When he was nineteen, he escaped from a death march by running into a forest. He lived out the war with Soviet partisans; he dedicated the rest of his life to documenting all that had been lost.

One of my mother's old friends, Dmitry, lingered with the others. His father was Peter Krupnikov, the historian who worked as a translator during the trial of Friedrich Jeckeln, who had later led Jeckeln's daughter around the trial chamber. Dmitry, a successful businessman, was now overseeing the Jewish community's restitution campaign, working to reclaim religious and communal properties that were nationalised during the first Soviet occupation. Dmitry introduced me to Vestermanis, explaining that I was the daughter of one of his old friends, that my last name was Kinstler. Vestermanis did not miss a beat. '*You are the granddaughter!*' he said. Out came a rush of remembrances: he said he once danced with my grandmother Biruta, that she had been his dentist. Boris, he said, was the smartest man in the Arājs Kommando. He was the one who had been writing back and forth between the Latvians and the Germans. 'And then he became a KGB agent,' Vestermanis said. 'Somewhere, it is written that he was sent to Belarus and then he disappeared.'

I asked him where it was written, but he did not remember. Many Arājs Kommando members had been sent to Belarus towards the end of the war, mobilised alongside German regiments trying to hold back the Soviet advance. It was possible that Boris had been sent there during the war, but none of the records I've been able to find suggest as much. I thanked Vestermanis for telling me, and we agreed to speak again after he had recovered from the day's exertion.

Vestermanis, like everyone else in the Jewish community, had been following the progress of the Cukurs case. When I called him a few days later to ask him what he thought of it, he told me that the investigation was just a folly of the prosecutor's office, a politically motivated misstep. He was one of the few people alive who had witnessed the whole arc of this terrible story. He, too, had been asked to testify against Cukurs, but declined. He had no evidence to offer, for he had never personally encountered Cukurs during the war. But he had seen something else: in early sixties, he had worked in the state archives, he had gone over all the files about the Arājs Kommando, about the creation and destruction of the Riga ghetto. He noticed that a few files were missing: the records of the 6th and 9th Police Precincts of Riga, to which members of the Arājs Kommando had been assigned. It was not unusual for files to be incomplete – during the Soviet period, important and sensitive files were moved from the periphery to the centre, from Riga to Moscow. The prosecutor had taken note of this gap in the archive in the text of his decision: 'The archive cannot provide other information about H. Cukurs's service in the German army and his activities during the Second World War, as the relevant documents from the period of German occupation have not been preserved in full, and this information is not in the existing ones,' he wrote.

But why had these particular files been spirited away? Vestermanis drew a reasonable conclusion, the same one that a fair few familiar with this strange story had already drawn: Soviet authorities had been preparing another judicial process, their very own 'world trial', an emulation of Israel's proceedings against Eichmann. They had planned to prosecute Cukurs, and so they had set about compiling the necessary evidence. That was why the police precinct files were missing, Vestermanis deduced. Perhaps it was also why Israeli forces went after Cukurs in the first place.

His suspicions once again raised the spectre of a trial that never came to pass, the ghost hero's ghost trial. What would this trial have achieved? Would some new, definitive evidence have emerged? The idea of this ghost trial kept coming up in my conversations about the case: no matter what side of the issue people were on, they all seemed to agree that the prosecutor would have no business investigating Cukurs's guilt a half-century after his death if there had been a trial while he was alive. If this suspected Soviet trial had succeeded in the past, none of this would be happening in the present.

The belief in this trial was a counter-factual indulgence, a desire for a history carved in stone, a history that does not shift with the political sands. The evidence for it, like the evidence of a Baltic Troy, is purely anecdotal. It is an appealing idea because it invites historical speculation – if there had been a trial, there would have been no rushed court martial in Shangrilá, no assassination, no telegrammed verdict.

In a way, the assassination succeeded beyond the assassins' wildest dreams. If we accept Mossad's claim that the killing was an attempt to prevent a statute of limitations from precluding further Nazi prosecutions, a murder meant to expand the parameters of legality and explode the historical boundaries of law, then they got precisely what they wished for. The statute of limitations for Nazi crimes was infinitely deferred, not only in Germany but throughout Europe. These crimes remained prosecutable long enough for a new generation to get their law degrees and apprenticeships and come into power, a generation unscathed and untouched by the world war. For this generation – my generation – the events of the past century will always be somewhat occluded, surrounded by an ever-thickening haze. It is easier for them to look back upon the crime scene of history and find insufficient evidence, to throw up their hands. The expanding reach of law cuts both ways: a crime that can still be tried can also still be pardoned.

30

The Antonym of Forgetting

'To define force – it is the x that turns anybody who is subjected to it into a thing. Exercised to the limit, it turns man into a thing in the most literal sense: it makes a corpse out of him. Somebody was here, and the next minute there is nobody here at all.'
　　– Simone Weil, 'The Iliad, or the Poem of Force', 1940

This book began with a question: 'Is it possible that the antonym of "forgetting" is not "remembering", *but justice?*' I wish Yerushalmi, the great Jewish historian, had been more specific: justice of what kind? If he is correct about this antonymic opposition, then what do we mean when we say 'Never Forget'? We cannot simply mean 'Always Remember', for remembering has proven itself to be a crude and insufficiently capacious commitment. Memory can trap its devotees in its own closed loops. It unlocks its own murderous logics.

The story of Herberts Cukurs, of the long afterlife of his assassination, is a story of justice deferred, delayed, circumvented, undone. It is an illustration of the difficulties of reconciling the parallel tasks of the judge and the historian, who are 'linked by the shared belief that it is possible to 'prove, according to given rules, that x did y', as the historian Carlo Ginzburg writes. 'The paths of judge and historian, which run side by side for a certain distance, eventually and inevitably diverge.' They must go their separate ways, follow different plotlines.

What does it take to prove that x did y? The judge and the historian each have their own methods. The academics cannot decide. Is it the narrative or the evidence that satisfies our will to know? Is it the plot that makes the proof, or the proof that makes the plot? Another endless loop. A colleague gently reminds me that 'x did y' is the most basic kind of plot.

It now seems like no accident, no mere trick of fate that my guide in Uruguay, Marcelo Silva, was himself a judge, a man who spends day after day determining if x did y, and what penalties x should face. As an emissary of the law, he was trained to look at evidence in one way; as a painter, he had taught himself to regard it in a slightly different light. In his investigation into the assassination, he writes, 'as a rational man, and as a man of the law, I would have liked to see Herberts Cukurs sitting in the chamber of a German Criminal Court, outlining his defence with his lawyer. I would also have liked the Holocaust survivors to give their personal testimonies face to face [with the perpetrator] and thus fulfil their thirst for justice.'[1]

In Montevideo, I asked him to elaborate upon why he thought there should have been a trial for Cukurs, why the assassination was a far cry from a sufficient form of justice. He responded with a kind of commentary on the function and power of the judicial process: 'Before they go to trial, facts are just facts,' he said. 'At trial, facts are transformed into evidence, into proof. If there is no trial, facts are just indices. They can be called true or false, but they are not yet proof.'

It was a somewhat muddled formulation – evidence generally precedes and *proves* the facts – but Silva was expressing the widely held belief that law possesses the power to transform reality, that legal rulings and the deliberative processes that precede them shape the contours of our lives. Like many legal scholars, he believed that the 'facts' that exist before a trial are of a different order from the 'proofs' that a trial can produce. Speaking with him made me recall the many conversations I had had with the survivors, descendants and historians who have dedicated their lives to preserving the hard-won facts of the Holocaust, who see the facts of history slipping out from under them, carried away by the cresting tides of revisionism, ultra-nationalism and denial. Feitelson, the scientist who made sure to give his deposition before he died; Alperovitch, the cosmochemist who traced the movements of battalions as he had once traced meteors; Vestermanis, who noticed the missing police files in the archive, who lamented, in his 2021 address on Holocaust Remembrance Day, that 'the malefactors usually try to hide their wrongdoings, while here certain circles are proudly cherishing this gruesome legacy'.[2] Then there were the second and third generations, carrying out their duty, stewarding the memories they had inherited as best they could: Paul Semenoff, Helga Fisch, Ilya Lensky, David Lipkin, Dmitry Krupnikov.

All over the globe, Second World War-era cases are still winding their way through the courts. In Germany, the heirs to the Prussian monarchy have sued for their familial treasures;[3] a historian has been litigated for uncovering illicit love affairs in concentration camps;[4] nonagenarians still find their way into the dock. They are let off with light sentences, in the miraculous event that they survive long enough to hear them. In Amsterdam, a former FBI agent has supposedly determined who really betrayed Anne Frank. His team mobilised forensic analysis, they created a virtual model of her hiding place, they referred to it as a 'cold case'.[5] In January 2022, they revealed the identity of the man whom they suspect is responsible. The historians disagree with their findings.[6] Will the ghost go to trial? A perpetrator's name adorns the Vilnius street where, a few years ago, a significant collection of Jewish texts was unearthed from a pre-war genizah. In Poland, to study the Holocaust and even to hint at accusation and collaboration, can lead to three years in prison, to a series of defamation suits.[7] On judges' desks and in litigation offices, the testimonies of dead survivors are being picked apart; depending on what side they are on and in what country they practise, lawyers are either lamenting that they can no longer cross-examine the eyewitnesses or are silently thankful for their deaths. A dead witness can be much more easily impugned than a living one. (Remember what Edward Anders wrote: 'Dead men tell no tales, but survivors do.')

Survivors have been telling the story of the Holocaust for the better part of a century, and still the judges ask for proof. Throughout Eastern Europe, not only in Riga but also in Vilnius and Kyiv and Warsaw, forensic investigators are still looking for the mass graves. Their general locations have long been known, but the investigators want to know their precise contours, the exact slant of their soils. They will make 3D visualisations of their findings; they will upload them to the internet and show them to the world. Will these proofs be enough?

As I was in the final months of revising this manuscript, wondering where my plot went, which one I had ended up following (if any plot at all), I received a series of unexpected messages. The first was from Dmitry Krupnikov, my mother's old schoolmate, whose father had led Jeckeln's daughter around the trial chamber. 'Had an interesting meeting today,' he wrote to me on WhatsApp. 'Can you talk?'

I called him immediately. A young woman had texted him earlier that day. She was one of Cukurs's great-granddaughters. (Not the one who represented Latvia in Eurovision.) She asked Dmitry if he would be willing to speak with her. Her family had told her stories about their paterfamilias, about how he had been unfairly persecuted and maligned. She told Dmitry that she wanted to hear 'the other side of the story'.

Dmitry told Lensky what had happened, and together they invited the great-granddaughter to visit them at the headquarters of the Jewish community, in the same building where Lensky's museum lives, where, once upon a time, Cukurs himself had addressed an adoring crowd. They sat with her for two hours, they showed her photographs and documents, they told her what they knew: that it was not accurate to call Cukurs the 'butcher' nor the 'hangman' of Riga; that it was true that many of the specific, gruesome crimes of which he had been accused could not be verified; that, nevertheless, his culpability in genocide and war crimes went far beyond a reasonable doubt. Just as Dmitry's father had explained what happened to Jeckeln's daughter, now Dmitry was explaining what happened to Cukurs's great-granddaughter.

First the father, now the son. First the daughter, now the great-granddaughter. Where do these stories end? What responsibilities attend their transmission, so many generations on? How do we know when we've got to 'Z'?

The second message I received was from Anders. He wanted me to know that he had received a bad diagnosis, that his heart was losing strength. He was sending me his files, anything and everything he thought I might need in the future. He wanted me to have the original versions, the ones he himself had typed out, not the translations. 'As people in the Romantic era would say, 'mit meinem Herzblut geschrieben'. *Written with my heart and soul.* He wished me luck.

The third was from my father. He had read the manuscript; he had no corrections. He gave me his blessing, but he warned: 'Be ready for attacks from all possible sides.' And then, on Whatsapp, he sent me a series of photographs. One of them I had never seen before. In it, my grandfather stands in full German uniform, his cap in his arms and what looks to be a Lettonia crest patched into his sleeve. His hair is slicked, his gloves in his hands. The photograph commemorates some kind of official meeting; Boris stands next to a man in a suit and tie. They look towards each other as if they have been told to politely converse. It is a terrifying image, my grandfather in his Nazi outfit. My father has had it all this time. Maybe he did not want me to see it – maybe he did not want to pass on this particular part of the story. Maybe I did not ask if it existed because I did not want to know. Or maybe I am only now learning which questions to ask, and to discern all that their answers demand.

Notes

OPENING EPIGRAPH

1 The Drifter, *Nation Magazine*, 25 January 1928, p. 96

PROLOGUE

1 "25 years of Soviet Latvia," Harvard Library. https://library.harvard. edu/collections/25-years-soviet-latvia

2 Uldis Berzins, 'Summer Rain.' https://latvianliterature.lv/upload/ ll_authors/36/Uldis_Berzins.pdf

3 Nicholas Dames, 'Coming in from the Cold: On Spy Fiction', *N+1*, Issue 31, Spring 2018. https://nplusonemag.com/issue-31/reviews/ coming-in-from-the-cold-2/

4 Armands Puče, *Jūs nekad viņu nenogalināsiet* (Riga: Mediju Nams, 2015).

5 Maria Tumarkin, *Axiomatic* (Oakland: Transit Books, 2019), p. 144.

6 'Prokuratūra joprojām izmeklē Cukura iespējamo līdzdalību ebreju nogalināšanā', *Delfi.Lv*, 14 April 2011, https://www.delfi.lv/news/ national/criminal/prokuratura-joprojam-izmekle-cukura-iespejamo-lidzdalibu-ebreju-nogalinasana.d?id=38010303

7 Ibid.

8 Kristīne Sutugina, Press Secretary, Prosecution Office of the Republic of Latvia, 'Reply to the email message dated 26 April 2016 of the "Politico Europe" journalist Linda Kinstler, with request to provide information on the progress of investigation conducted by the Prosecution Office into so called Herberts Cukurs Criminal Case.' Riga, 6 May 2016.

9 Marc Nichanian, *The Historiographic Perversion*, trans. Gil Anidjar (New York: Columbia University Press, 2009) (originally published as *La Perversion Historiographique*, Paris: Lignes-Léo Scheer, 2006), p. 1.

10 Ibid, p. 11.

11 Maria Todorova writes that Lavabre's *milieu de rencontre* is 'a place of exchange, a place of communication. Collective memory, [Lavabre] explains, is not the simple adding up of individual recollections.' ('Introduction: Similar Trajectories, Different Memories', *Remembering Communism: Private and Public Recollections of Lived Experience* (Budapest: CEU Press, 2014), p. 7.

12 Yosef Hayim Yerushalmi, 'Postcript: Reflections on Forgetting' (an address delivered at the Colloque de Royaumont, 3 June 1987), in *Zakhor: Jewish History and Jewish Memory* (University of Washington, 2011), p. 117.

13 Ernest Klein, Dictionary entry: זָכַר, Klein's Comprehensive Etymological Dictionary of the Hebrew Language, (Toronto: Tyndale House Publishers, 1987). Accessed via Sefaria.

PART I

1 Friedrich Nietzsche, "On the Uses and Disadvantages of History for Life", *Untimely Meditations* (1874; Cambridge University Press: Cambridge, 1997) https://doi.org/10.1017/CBO9780511812101.007.

2 Aleksandrs Pelēcis, 'Sibīrijas Grāmata' (trans. from the Latvian by Karl Jirgens), *Descant* 124, Spring 2004. Vol. 35, No. 1, p. 63.

I THE POLICE ACADEMY, DECEMBER 2019

1 Marcelo Silva and Linng Cardozo, *El Mossad y La Ejecución de Herberts Cukurs en Uruguay* (Montevideo: Carlos Alvarez, 2010).

2 'Uruguay: Man in the Icebox', *Time* magazine, 19 March 1965, http://content.time.com/time/subscriber/article/0,33009,833564-1,00.html

3 'Die Spinne: Informationen Bundeskriminalamt', VWI-SWA Cukurs, Herbert, Protokoll Die Spinne 1965.

4 'Nazi eagle in Uruguay auction "should go to museum",' BBC, 22 July 2020. https://www.bbc.com/news/world-latin-america-53486061

5 Anton Kuenzle and Gad Shimron, *The Execution of the Hangman of Riga: The Only Execution of a Nazi War Criminal by the Mossad*, trans. Uriel Masad (London: Vallentine Mitchell, 2004), p. 127.

6 Silva and Cardozo, *El Mossad*, pp. 150–53. Original text: G. M. Gilbert, *Nuremberg Diary* (New York: Farrar, Straus, and Giroux, 1947).

7 The final line of Shawcross's speech reads: 'The father – do you remember? – pointed to the sky, and seemed to say something to his boy.' 'One Hundred And Eighty-Eighth Day', Saturday, 27 July 1946, Nuremberg Trial Proceedings, Vol. 19, The Avalon Project, Yale Law School Lillian Goldman Law Library. https://avalon.law.yale.edu/imt/07-27-46.asp

8 Sir Hartley Shawcross, 'Closing Statement by the British Prosecution', 26 July 1946, Robert H. Jackson Center. https://www.roberthjackson.org/nuremberg-event/closing-statement-by-the-british-prosecution/

2 BORIS

1 See 'Wansee Conference and the "Final Solution"'. US Holocaust Memorial Museum, Washington DC. https://encyclopedia.ushmm.org/content/en/article/wannsee-conference-and-the-final-solution

2 Steve Naragon, 'The Herder Notes from Immanuel Kant's Lectures', Manchester University, June 2021, https://users.manchester.edu/FacStaff/SSNaragon/Kant/HerderNotesComplete/BeginHere.htm

3 Johann Gottfried von Herder, 'Correspondence on Ossian', in Burton Feldman and Robert D. Richardson, comps, *The Rise of Modern Mythology* (Bloomington: Indiana University Press, 1975), pp. 229–30. Also quoted in Svetlana Boym, *Future of Nostalgia*, (New York: Basic Books, 2001), p. 12.

4 Johann Gottfried von Herder, *This Too a Philosophy of History for the Formation of Humanity* [an early introduction]. In M. Forster (ed.), *Herder: Philosophical Writings*, Cambridge Texts in the History of Philosophy (Cambridge: Cambridge University Press, 2002), pp. 268–71.

5 Richards Plavnieks, *Nazi Collaborators on Trial During the Cold War: Viktors Arājs and the Latvian Auxiliary Security Police*, Series: The Holocaust and Its Contexts (London: Palgrave Macmillan, 2018), p. 36.

6 *Dienas Lapa*, 14 October 1886. 'Mums der par dzīvu pierādījumu, cik ļoti var stiprināties kāda maza, nicināta tautiņa, pie viņiem mēs skaidri redzam, ko panāk caur izmanību, pacietību un savstarpēju ciešu kopību.'

7 Lettonia Facebook page, https://www.facebook.com/lettonus/
8 'Lettonia, 1870/1882', https://lettonia.lv/
9 'Lettonia – pajumte un aizstāvība latviešu studentiem, kas pulcējas, lai augtu tautiskā garā un tēvzemes mīlestībā.' https://lettonia.lv/parlettoniu/
10 'Valsts prezidenta balvas mazpulkiem', *Zemgales Balss*, Nr. 200, 6 September 1937. http://periodicals.lndb.lv/periodika2-viewer/?lang= fr#panel:pa|issue:114041|article:DIVL143
11 Plavnieks, *Nazi Collaborators*, p. 36.
12 Andrew Ezergailis, *The Holocaust in Latvia 1941–1944: The Missing Center* (Washington DC: United States Holocaust Memorial Museum, 1996), p. 177.
13 'During occupation,' Lettonia, https://lettonia.lv/vesture/gara-vest ure/okupacijas-laiks/
14 Czesław Miłosz, 'The Problem of the Baltics', *Captive Mind* (New York: Vintage International Edition, 1990), p. 229.
15 The precise number of minutes it took for one occupying regime to give way to another has been disputed. The historian Andrew Ezergailis estimates that Bauska changed hands in under thirty minutes, and that most Latvian towns switched from Soviet to German control in a matter of hours. Inesis Feldmanis characterises these estimates as a 'radical view' and a 'a rather simplified interpretation of the period of interregnum between the departure of the last Red Army troops (the old occupants) and the arrival of the first Wehrmacht soldiers (the new occupants)'. See Inesis Feldmanis, 'Latvia under the Occupation of National Socialist Germany 1941–1945', *The Hidden and Forbidden History of Latvia Under Soviet and Nazi Occupations 1940–1991*, Symposium of the Commission of the Historians of Latvia, Vol. 14., Institute of the History of Latvia, Riga, 2005.
16 Plavnieks, *Nazi Collaborators*, pp. 29–30.
17 Ezergailis, *The Holocaust in Latvia 1941–1944*, p. 178.
18 Plavnieks, *Nazi Collaborators*, p. 30.
19 Rudīte Vīksne, 'Members of the Arājs Kommando in Soviet Court Files', *The Hidden and Forbidden History of Latvia Under Soviet and Nazi Occupations 1940–1991*, Symposium of the Commission of the Historians of Latvia, Vol. 14, Institute of the History of Latvia, 2005, p. 195.
20 Lawrence L. Langer, 'The Dilemma of Choice in the Deathcamps', *Centerpoint*, Vol. 4, No. 1, (1980): 222–32.

21 Franziska Exeler, ' "What Did You Do During the War?" Personal Responses to the Aftermath of Nazi Occupation', *Kritika: Explorations in Russian and Eurasian History*, Vol. 17, No. 4 (Fall 2016), p. 809.

22 Bernhard Press, *The Murder of the Jews in Latvia 1941–1945*, trans. Laimdota Mazzarins (Chicago: Northwestern UP, 2000), p. 46.

3 CUKURS

1 'SECRET, 1 March 1955, File 1686, CUKURS, Herberts, declassified and released by the CIA, Nazi War Crimes Disclosure Act, 2003.'

2 The Cukurs family has made scans of these news clippings publicly available via their blog 'The Eagle of Baltic Sea', http://herberts-cuk urs.blogspot.com/

3 Fernando Esposito, *Fascism, Aviation and Mythical Modernity* (London: Palgrave Macmillan, 2015), p. 3.

4 Ibid., p. 330.

5 A bronze bust of Lindbergh's likeness sits in the Smithsonian National Portrait Gallery, in Washington DC; his name adorns luxury bags and Las Vegas kiosks; he has his own entry in a children's book my nieces like to read, a compilation of historical adventurers. None of these cultural artefacts make note of his Nazism.

6 The house is currently listed as a tourist attraction on an English-language guide to the region of Tervete. http://www.tervetesnovads. lv/wp-content/uploads/2015/08/Welcome-to-Tervete.pdf

7 Aldis Purs and Andrejs Plakans, 'Cukurs, Herberts (1900–1965)', *Historical Dictionary of Latvia*, 3rd edn (New York: Rowman & Littlefield, 2017), p. 82.

8 Ezergailis, *The Holocaust in Latvia 1941–1944*, p. 182.

9 Uldis Neiburgs, 'Latvian Military Formations During World War II,' *(Two Sides): Diaries of Latvian Soldiers in WW II*, Vita Zelče and Uldis Neiburgs, eds. Kārlis Streips, trans. Riga: Apgāds Zelta Grauds, 2018 (2011), p. 49.

10 Ezergailis, *The Holocaust in Latvia 1941–1944*, p. 182.

11 Ibid., p. 183.

12 Ibid., p. 192.

13 Frida Michelson, *I Survived Rumbuli*, trans. Wolf Goodman, US Holocaust Memorial Museum, 1979 (1973), pp. 77–8.

14 Ibid, pp. 223–4.

15 I'm grateful to Edward Anders for sending me a copy of Cukurs's account, which he, in turn, received from Ezergailis.

4 THE KOMMANDO

1 Rudīte Vīksne, 'Members of the Arājs Kommando in Soviet Court Files', 2005, p. 191. (see ch. 2 footnote 19)

2 Ezergailis, *The Holocaust in Latvia 1941–1944*, p. 224.

3 Vīksne, p. 193.

4 *Ibid.*

5 Uldis Neiburgs, *(Two) Sides: Diaries of Latvian Soldiers in WWII*, Vita Zelče and Uldis Neiburgs, eds., trans. Kārlis Streips (Riga: Apgads Zelta Grauds, 2018).

6 Plavnieks, *Nazi Collaborators*, p. 81: 'Both in terms of chronology and number of convictions, the Soviet Union was the leading post-war prosecutor of Arājs Kommando members. A total of 356 former members of the Latvian Auxiliary Security Police are known to have been captured, tried and convicted by the Soviets. Almost all of them were apprehended between 1944 and 1950. After peaking in 1947 with eighty-seven convictions, the number of suspects dwindled to a trickle in the 1950s and 1960s, with individual years seeing one, two, three, or sometimes no arrests at all. In 1967, the Soviet Union captured its final former Kommando member.'

7 'It has not been established either how many of Arājs men survived World War II, because it is known that many of them were killed in battles against the Soviet partisans and the Red Army. Several suicides have also been registered …' Vīksne, p. 189.

8 Lieutenant Vasilchikov, «Протокол Допроса». Interrogation of Jānis Rainisovich Brencis, Riga, 24 December 1946, Extraordinary State Commission to Investigate German-Fascist Crimes Committed on Soviet Territory, Cases in the Latvian SSR, 1941–1946, Fond 93 (Op. 2–18), Accessed via USHMM.

9 Vīksne, p. 190.

5 'THE TRIAL BEGINS'

1 Musya Glants, *Patchwork Stitched by Memory (Loskutnoye odeyalo shhitoye pamatyu)* (Boston: IM Press, 2021), p. 103.

2 Plavnieks, *Nazi Collaborators*, p. 86.

3 Daša Drndić, *EEG* (New York: New Directions, 2019), pp. 284–5.

4 *The People's Verdict*, p. 37. Quoted in Ilya Bourtman, '"Blood for Blood, Death for Death": The Soviet Military Tribunal in Krasnodar, 1943', *Holocaust and Genocide Studies*, Vol. 2. Issue 22, 2008, p. 256.

5 'The Execution of Fascists in Krasnodar, July 18, 1943.' https://www.youtube.com/watch?v=Z1DEjCrYeRY

6 Arieh J. Kochavi, 'The Moscow Declaration, the Kharkov Trial, and the Question of a Policy on Major War Criminals in the Second World War'. *History*, Vol. 76, No. 248, 1991, pp. 402–3. www.jstor.org/stable/24421381

7 Michael J. Bayzler and Frank M. Tuerkheimer, 'The Kharkov Trial of 1943: The First Trial of the Holocaust?', *Forgotten Trials of the Holocaust* (New York: New York University Press, 2014), p. 40.

8 'Kotvetu nemetskikh ubiits!', KZ, 16 December 1943. Quoted in Jeremy Hicks, 'Soul Destroyers: Soviet Reporting of Nazi Genocide and its Perpetrators at the Krasnodar and Kharkov Trials', *History*, Vol. 98, No. 4 (332), 2013, pp. 530–47. www.jstor.org/stable/24429506.

9 'Universal Newsreel outtakes', Moscow, Kharkov, Paris, 1943, RG-60.1905, Steven Spielberg Film and Video Archive, United States National Archives and Records Administration, Motion Picture Reference, https://collections.ushmm.org/search/catalog/irn557804

10 Bayzler and Tuerkheimer, *Forgotten Trials*, p. 23.

11 Barbara Shapiro, '"Fact" and the Proof of Fact in Anglo-American Law (c. 1500–1850)', in *How Law Knows*, Austin Sarat, Lawrence Douglas and Martha Umphrey, eds. (Stanford: Stanford University Press, 2007), p. 42.

12 The entire Soviet manufacturing and propaganda apparatus was relocated during the war years. Eliahu Gordon, whose father Frank Gordon appears in this chapter, told me that his grandfather, Joseph, had a strange job for an evacuee: the Soviets were producing propaganda films about the war effort from the evacuation zone in Almaty, and for production purposes needed their men to learn to look and sound like Wehrmacht troops. Joseph Gordon was fluent in German, so it became his job to teach the Soviet soldiers how to properly pronounce 'Heil Hitler!'. He joined them on set as an extra, dressed up in SS garb. 'It's absurd, but it's true,' Eliahu told me. 'So, it's a very Jewish story.

13 Bayzler and Tuerkheimer, *Forgotten Trials*, p. 32.

14 Il'ia Erenburg, 'Standartnye ubiitsy', KZ, 18 December 1943, p. 3.

15 Bayzler and Tuerkheimer, *Forgotten Trials*, p. 27.

16 Rīgas Latviešu biedrība, https://www.rlb.lv/sakums

17 G. H. Bennett, 'Exploring the World of the Second & Third Tier Men in the Holocaust: The Interrogation of Friedrich Jeckeln: Engineer and Executionner', *Liverpool Law Review*, 2011, Vol. 32, p. 16.

18 'Карта с данными об уничтожении евреев айзантцгруппой A на оккупированной территории СССР', 1941–1942, Central Archive of the FSB, Ф. К-72. Оп. 1. Пор. 12. Л. 61. https://victims.rusarchives.ru/karta-s-dannymi-ob-unichtozhenii-evreev-ayzantcgruppoy-na-okkupirovannoy-territorii-sssr-1941-1942

19 Пётр Крупников, *XX век: прожитое и пережитое. История жизни историка, профессора Петра Крупникова, рассказанная им самим* (Saint Petersburg, Алетеия Publishers, 2018).

6 COME TO THIS COURT AND CRY

1 The United States Holocaust Memorial Museum has a special training programme that pays for American judges, prosecutors and government attorneys to come together to study Nazi laws, to see how it was that the German judiciary enabled and sanctioned genocide. They study Nazi contract law, family law, the progression of fascist decrees. They ask themselves: 'What can judges do to ensure that the kinds of failures that led to the Holocaust do not happen in this country?' See: https://www.ushmm.org/outreach-programs/judiciary

2 'Second Day, Wednesday, 11/21/1945, Part 04', in *Trial of the Major War Criminals before the International Military Tribunal*. Vol. II, Proceedings: 11/14/1945-11/30/1945. [Official text in the English language.] (Nuremberg: IMT, 1947, pp. 98–102). https://www.roberthjackson.org/speech-and-writing/opening-statement-before-the-international-military-tribunal/

3 Ibid.

4 Robert H. Jackson, 'Introduction', in Whitney R. Harris, *Tyranny on Trial: The Evidence at Nuremberg* (College Station, Texas: Texas A&M, 1999), pp. xxxv–vi.

5 Francine Hirsch, *Soviet Judgement at Nuremberg: A New History of the International Military Tribunal After World War II* (New York: Oxford UP, 2020), pp. 71–2.

6 Christiane Kohl, *The Witness House: Nazis and Holocaust Survivors Sharing a Villa During the Nuremberg Trials* (New York: Other Press, 2010), p. 46.

7 Ibid.

8 Robert H. Jackson, 'Opening Address for the United States', *Nazi Conspiracy and Aggression*, Vol. 1, United States Office of Chief of Counsel for the Prosecution of Axis Criminality, US Government Printing Office, Washington DC, 1946, p. 140. https://play.google.com/books/reader?id=vb9GAQAAMAAJ&hl=en&pg=GBS.PA1

9 'It was, and remains, a point of pride among Latvians everywhere that the "Viesturs Company", a guard detachment at the Nuremburg Trials, was composed of Latvians in American uniform', the historian Richards Plavnieks writes. Plavnieks, *Nazi Collaborators*, p. 119.

10 For a scholarly history of the massacre at Katyn and its aftermath, see Alexander Etkind, Rory Finnin, et al., *Remembering Katyn* (Cambridge, UK and Malden, MA: Polity Press, 2012).

11 Hirsch, *Soviet Judgement*, p. 153.

12 Lawrence Douglas, 'History, Memory and Crimes Against Humanity: A Response to Todorov', *Salmagundi*, no. 128/129, Skidmore College, 2000, pp. 320–26, http://www.jstor.org/stable/40549287.

13 Another, Hitler's deputy Martin Bormann, is sentenced to death in absentia. He was thought to be at large until 1973. 'Is Bormann alive or dead? We do not know. There are persistent rumors that he is alive in South America, but so far he has not been identified there. Recently Gen. Reinhard Gehlen, former Nazi, former chief of the German Federal Intelligence Service, declared publicly, from his own certain knowledge, that Bormann, even while serving Hitler, had been a Russian spy; that after Hitler's death he had gone to Russia; and that he had since died in Russia. For this story there neither evidence nor probability', *New York Times*, Sunday 14 January 1973. Bormann's remains were found and identified in Berlin that year. He died in 1945 while fleeing Berlin. https://www.nytimes.com/1973/01/14/archives/martin-bormann-was-last-seen-definitely-in-a-tank-in-berlin-on-may.html

14 'International Military Tribunal: The Defendants', *Holocaust Encyclopedia*, US Holocaust Memorial Museum, Washington

DC. https://encyclopedia.ushmm.org/content/en/article/
      international-military-tribunal-the-defendants
15 Hirsch, *Soviet Judgement*, pp. 64–5.
16 Allie Brudney, 'The *I.G. Farben Trial:* Evidentiary Standards and
      Procedures and the Problem of Creating Legitimacy', *Harvard
      International Law Journal*, Vol. 61, No. 1, Winter 2020, p. 257.
17 Roman A. Rudenko, 'Final Statement', International Military
      Tribunal, 29 July 1946, University of Georgia Law Digital Commons,
      https://digitalcommons.law.uga.edu/cgi/viewcontent.cgi?
      article=1008&context=imt
18 'One Hundred and Eighty-Ninth Day, Monday, 29 July 1946,
      Morning Session', *Nuremberg Trial Proceedings*, Vol. 19, The Avalon
      Project: Documents in Law, History and Diplomacy, Yale Law
      School Lillian Goldman Law Library, https://avalon.law.yale.edu/
      imt/07-29-46.asp
19 Robert H. Jackson, US Chief of Counsel, IMT, 'Closing Arguments
      for Conviction of Nazi War Criminals', *Temple Law Quarterly*,
      pp. 85–107, https://www.roberthjackson.org/wp-content/
      uploads/2015/01/Closing_Argument_for_Conviction_of_Nazi_
      War_Criminals.pdf

7 THE COMMITTEE MEN

1 In 1948 the 'Association of Baltic Jews in Great Britain' was located at 310
      Regent Street, London, W1. It relocated to New Cavendish Street the
      next year. 'Committee for the Investigation of Nazi war crimes in Baltic
      countries: correspondence', File 539/7, 1948–1950, Wiener Library.
      https://wiener.soutron.net/Portal/Default/en-GB/recordview/
      index/74671
2 'Field Reference: WCG/C/461/FIS; Legal Reference:
      WCG/15228/2/C.2087/Legal; Index to List of Accused – Riga Ghetto
      Case', Committee for the Investigation of Nazi Crimes in the Baltic
      Countries, Wiener Library, microfilm accessed 22 July 2019.
3 One announcement published in the classifieds of the information
      bulletin of the Association of Jewish Refugees in Great Britain reads
      as follows: 'WAR CRIMINALS: The Association of Baltic Jews in
      Great Britain, 42 Theobald Rd., London, W.C.1, is collecting evidence
      of war crimes committed against Jews in the Baltic States and appeals
      to all people who have any evidence to offer to pass it on to their

office, where a list of war criminals responsible for the "liquidation" of the Ghettoes, especially in Riga, and their photographs are also available.' 'Postal Announcements', *AJR Information*, June 1948, Vol. III, No. 6, p. 7.

4 'The notifications about the trees and the Jews are also given in Latvian on the same page', Nadine Fresco, *On the Death of Jews: Photographs and History*, Sarah Clift, trans. (New York: Berghahn Books, 2021), p. 47.

5 Email from Edward Alperovitch to author, 29 June 2021.

6 I'm grateful to Molly Krueger for translating the letter from Yiddish. I shared an image of this letter, which clearly contains his signature, with Alperovitch in June 2021. He responded, via email, as follows: 'I did not write this letter as my active vocabulary of Yiddish has always been pathetically small. Probably one of the Board members wrote the Yiddish version on the basis of my German draft. Certainly Latvian Jews would be the main source of witnesses against Cukurs, but it took another good 10 years to capture and kill Cukurs.' Email from Edward Alperovitch to author, 29 June 2021.

7 Valerie Geneviève Hébert, *Hitler's Generals on Trial: The Last War Crimes Tribunal at Nuremberg* (Kansas City: University Press of Kansas, 2010).

8 Appendix C. 'Copy of the letter of Major F. Elwyn Jones, M.P., dated 18th May, 1949, to Mr. E. Michelson'. Committee for the Investigation of Nazi Crimes in the Baltic Countries. Wiener Library, File 539/7.

9 Plavnieks, *Nazi Collaborators*, p. 116.

8 THE VICTORY DAY PARADE

1 Institute of Anatomy and Anthropology, Theatrum Anatomicum, Rīga Stradiņš University, https://www.rsu.lv/en/institute-anatomy-and-anthropology

2 Linda Kinstler, ' "A Partial Freedom": What Latvia found in the KGB Archives', *New York Review Daily*, 5 March 2019, https://www.nybooks.com/daily/2019/03/05/a-partial-freedom-what-latvia-found-in-the-kgb-archives/

3 Robert Burns, *A Theory of the Trial* (Princeton: Princeton University Press, 1999), p. 86.

4 'ENSV Riikliku Julgeoleku Komitee eriteadete materjalide kollektsioon', ERAF.131SM.1.190, March – June 1949. Estonian National Archives, Tartu.

9 A DEPOSITION

1 Letter from Jewish Federation of Rio de Janeiro to Committee for the Investigation of Nazi Crimes in the Baltic Countries, 4 August 1950. Yad Vashem, M.21.1, War Criminals' Section, Legal Department at the Central Committee of Liberated Jews, Munich, File 584.

2 Telegram from World Jewish Congress, London, to Federação Sociedades Israelitas, 23 September 1950, Yad Vashem. Documentation about Trials of War Criminals, O.4. 154.

3 Miriam Kaicners, Deposition before the Jewish Federation of Rio de Janeiro, 14 August 1950. I'm grateful to Helga Fisch for sending me the original Portuguese document as well as an English translation.

4 Bruno Leal Pastor de Carvalho, 'O "Homem Dos Pedalinhos" Herberts Cukurs, O Estado Brasileiro E A Questão Dos Criminosos Nazistas No Brasil do Pós-Guerra (1945–1965)', Doctoral Dissertation at the Universidade Federal Do Rio de Janeiro Instituto de Filosofia e Ciências Sociais Programa de Pós-Graduação em História Social, Rio de Janeiro, 2015, p. 136.

5 Tom Bower, *The Red Web: MI6 and the KGB Master Coup* (London: Aurum Press, 1989).

6 VWI-SWA, Cukurs, Herbert, Document 011, 1944.

10 THE CRIME COMPLEX

1 Joseph Berman, 'Reese Report', 1950, 'Committee for the Investigation of Nazi War Crimes in Baltic Countries: correspondence', Ref. 539/7, The Wiener Holocaust Library.

2 Zentrale Stelle der Landesjustizverwaltunge zur Aufklärung national-sozialistischer Verbrechen, Justiz in Baden-Würrtemberg, https://zentrale-stelle-ludwigsburg.justiz-bw.de/pb/,Lde/Startseite

3 Patrick Tobin, *Crossroads at Ulm: Postwar West Germany and the 1958 Ulm Einsatzkommando Trial*. Dissertation submitted to the faculty of the University of North Carolina at Chapel Hill, Chapel Hill, 2013, p. 37.

4 Ibid., pp. 64–6.

5 'Ein interessanter Arbeitsgerichtsprozeß', *Schwäbische Donau-Zeitung*, 26 May 1955; 'SS-Oberführer wieder "aufgetaucht"', *Ulmer Nachrichten*, 25 May 1955. Quoted in Tobin, *Crossroads at Ulm*, p. 108.

6 Tobin, *Crossroads at Ulm*, p. 191.

7 Nellmann, 'Zentrale Ermittlungsbehörde muss Klarheit über NS-Verbrechen schaffen', *Stuttgarter Zeitung*, 3 September 1958. Quoted in Tobin, *Crossroads at Ulm*, p. 342.

8 Linda Kinstler, 'The Last Nazi Hunters', *The Guardian Long Read*, 31 August 2017, https://www.theguardian.com/news/2017/aug/31/the-last-nazi-hunters

II MR PEARLMAN'S NON-FICTION

1 Wolfe died in 2014 after a long career as an archivist and historian. Robert Wolfe, 'The CIA and Adolf Eichmann: Worldwide Media Bit on an Erroneous Sound Bite', https://www.archives.gov/iwg/research-papers/eichmann.html.

2 https://www.ilholocaustmuseum.org/wp-content/uploads/2016/08/OF-Text-Panel-and-Artifact-Checklist.pdf

3 *Saturday Review*, 8 April 1961, quoted in Yosal Rogat, *The Eichmann Trial and the Rule of Law*, Center for the Study of Democratic Institutions, Santa Barbara, CA, 1961.

4 Ofer Aderet, 1 July 2012, 'Mossad agent who helped abduct Eichmann dies at 93', *Haaretz*, Tel Aviv, https://www.haaretz.com/.premium-mossad-agent-who-helped-nab-eichmann-dies-1.5191437?v=1604414458083

5 'Rafi Eitan, a team member who planned and executed this and many other field operations, would later classify the capture of Eichmann as "one of the simpler operations that I did".' See Martin Kramer, 'The Truth of the Capture of Adolf Eichmann', *Mosaic*, 1 June 2020. https://scholar.harvard.edu/files/martinkramer/files/the_truth_of_the_capture_of_adolf_eichmann_mosaic.pdf

6 Hannah Arendt, *Eichmann in Jerusalem: A Report on the Banality of Evil* (New York: Penguin, 1963), p. 240.

7 'Operation Finale: The Capture & Trial of Adolf Eichmann', Exhibition credit list.

8 Moshe Pearlman, *The Capture of Adolf Eichmann* (London: Weidenfeld and Nicolson, 1961). Pearlman would go on to publish a spate of books on Israeli themes, including *Ben Gurion Looks Back in Talks with Moshe Pearlman* (New York: Simon & Schuster, 1965).

9   Pearlman, *The Capture of Adolf Eichmann*, p. 104.
10 Ibid., p. 10
11 Ibid., pp. 35–9.
12 Arendt, *Eichmann in Jerusalem*, p. 279. See also Judith Butler, 'Arendt's Death Sentences', *Comparative Literature Studies*, Vol. 48, No. 3, Special Issue Trials of Trauma (University Park: Penn State University Press, 2011), p. 295.
13 Arendt, *Eichmann in Jerusalem*, p. 279.
14 Rogat, 1961, p. 37.
15 Arendt, *Eichmann in Jerusalem*, p. 263.
16 'The Eichmann Trial', Yad Vashem. https://www.yadvashem. org/yv/en/exhibitions/eichmann/eichmann-trial.asp#proof-of-guilt
17 Shoshanna Felman, 'A Ghost in the House of Justice: Death and the Language of the Law', *Yale Journal of Law & The Humanities*, Vol. 13, Issue 1, New Haven, 2001. https://digitalcommons.law.yale.edu/cgi/viewcontent.cgi?article=1240&context=yjlh
18 The Trial of Adolf Eichmann, Session 29, The Nizkor Project. http://www.nizkor.org/hweb/people/e/eichmann-adolf/transcripts/Sessions/Session-029-03.html
19 Associated Press, 'Latvia Tale: 100,000 Jews Slain', *Salt Lake Tribune*, Saturday 6 May 1961.
20 Arendt, *Eichmann in Jerusalem*, pp. 244–8.
21 *Hatalyan (The Hangman)*. Directed by Natalie Braun, Torch Films, 2010. https://www.torchfilms.com/products/the-hangman
22 For a scholarly engagement with Shalom Nagar's role in the execution, see Itamar Mann, 'Hangman's Perspective: Three Genres of Critique following *Eichmann*', *The Oxford Handbook of International Criminal Law* (Oxford: Oxford University Press, 2019).

12 SHANGRILÁ

1 Anton Kuenzle and Gad Shimron, *The Execution of the Hangman of Riga: The Only Execution of a Nazi War Criminal by the Mossad*, Uriel Masad, trans. (London: Vallentine Mitchell, 2004), p. 100.
2 Katherine Verdery, *The Political Lives of Dead Bodies: Reburial and Socialist Change*, New York, Columbia UP, 1999. P. 52–53, 112.
3 Silva and Cardozo, *El Mossad*, p. 106.
4 Arvida Andersona, 'Kominters mēģina rādīt Latviešu Eichmani', *Latvija Amerikā*, Nov. 30, 1960, Issue 96.

5 Ibid.

6 Ronen Bergman, *Rise and Kill First: The Secret History of Israel's Targeted Assassinations* (New York: Random House, 2018).

7 Aderet, 'Mossad agent who helped abduct Eichmann dies at 93', *Haaretz*, Tel Aviv.

8 Kuenzle and Shimron, *The Execution*, p. xiv.

9 During his time in Brazil, Cukurs appears to have moved between Rio de Janeiro and São Paulo; the main family compound was outside of São Paulo. A 2 July 1960 AFP report notes that he had moved to Rio to distance himself from the Jewish community of São Paulo, which was militating for his arrest. Yad Vashem, M.21.1, War Criminal's Section, Legal Department at the Central Committee of Liberated Jews, Munich.

10 Kuenzle and Shimron, *The Execution*, p. 7.

11 Ibid., p. 8.

12 Ibid., p. xx.

13 Robert A. Monson, 'The West German Statute of Limitations on Murder: A Political, Legal, and Historical Exposition', *American Journal of Comparative Law*, Vol. 30, No. 4, Autumn 1982, p. 610.

14 Kuenzle and Shimron, *The Execution*, pp. 93–8.

15 Ibid., p. 106.

16 Ibid., Chapter 15, 'Judgement Day', pp. 121–8.

13 PAST AS PRELUDE

1 'Report Mengele condemned another Nazi to death in doublecross plot', *Jerusalem Post*, 13 October 1977.

2 'Cukurs traveled with a certain shadow over his destiny', *O Cruzeiro*, 3 April 1965. I am grateful to René Bienert at the Vienna Wiesenthal Institute for Holocaust Studies for sending me scans of the Brazilian tabloid coverage.

3 Silva and Cardozo, *El Mossad*, p. 216.

4 Because the bottom half of the trunk has been irretrievably lost, I cannot verify this for myself – but based on all the existing photographs of the trunk, including ones from the Uruguayan police investigation, there do not appear to have been breathing holes. But, again, it may not matter – one can dream up a million alternative scenarios in which Cukurs could have been spirited away alive.

5 K-ZETNIK, TZOFAN: EDMA 32 (Hakibbutz Hameuchad
   Publishing House Ltd, 1987), translated in KA-TZETNIK 135633,
   SHIVITTI: A VISION 16, Eliyah Nike De-Nur and Lisa Hermann,
   trans. (Harper & Row, 1989). Quoted in Felman, 'A Ghost in the
   House of Justice'.
6 Maurice Blanchot, *The Last Man*, trans. Lydia Davis (UBU
   Editions, 2007), p. 8. Originallly published as *Le Dernier Homme*
   (Paris: Gallimard, Coll. Blanche, 1957).

PART II

1 Ivars Lindbergs, trans. from the Lavtian by Eva Eglāja-Kristsone,
   'VĒSTULE ŠVEIKAM NO GRĀFA MIĶEĻA AMĀLIJAS DĒLA',
   Jauna Gaita, 1968, No. 70, 28–29. https://jaunagaita.net/jg70/JG70_
   Dzeja.htm#Ivars_Lindbergs
2 Uldis Bērziņš, trans. from the Latvian by Ieva Lešinska, Kevin
   M. F. Platt, ed., 'In Defense of Informers' (Tjärn, 1990). https://
   latvianliterature.lv/upload/ll_authors/36/Uldis_Berzins.pdf

14 ARON KODESH

1 Uldis Neiburgs, 'The History of the Occupation of Latvia', Museum
   of the Occupation of Latvia, Riga, http://okupacijasmuzejs.lv/en/
   history/nazi-occupation/the-latvian-legion-and-16-march
2 In 2015, the Latvian interior minister urged civilians to avoid the
   area surrounding the Freedom Monument on the day of the
   commemorative march. The *Baltic Times* staff, 'Latvian Interior
   Minister urges people to avoid Freedom Monument today', *Baltic
   Times*, Riga, 16 March 2015. See also, Reuters staff, 'Latvian SS
   veterans march in defiance of ban', Reuters, 16 March 2009, https://
   www.reuters.com/article/us-latvia-march/latvian-ss-veterans-march-
   in-defiance-of-ban-idUSTRE52F3UB20090316
3 'Jēkabpils Municipality, the Turning to Zasa', Holocaust Memorial
   Places in Latvia, Center for Judaic Studies at the University of Latvia,
   Riga, 2021. http://memorialplaces.lu.lv/memorial-places/zemgale/
   jekabpils-municipality-the-turning-to-zasa/
4 'Bauska Municipality, Bauska', ibid. http://memorialplaces.lu.lv/
   memorial-places/zemgale/bauska-municipality-bauska/

5 Nikolay Koposov, *Memory Laws, Memory Wars: The Politics of the Past in Europe and Russia*, Cambridge, Cambridge UP, 2018, p. 304.

6 Dace Dzenovska's *School of Europeanness: Tolerance and Other Lessons in Political Liberalism in Latvia* (Ithaca: Cornell University Press, 2018) is an indispensable account of this phenomenon.

7 Ministry of Finance of the Republic of Latvia, 'Official conversion rate', 2013.

8 When Riga hosted the annual Nato Summit, in 2006, thousands of Latvian handwoven mittens were distributed to attendees. According to one account, the weavers were expressly forbidden from including the Latvian Thundercross in their designs, for fear that it would be taken the wrong way. https://latvians.com/index.php?en/CFBH/Zimes/zimes-10-rhetoric.ssi

9 Santa Vaļivahina, 'The non-implemented vision "Karosta-Culture Port"', *Scientific Journal of Latvia University of Agriculture; Landscape Architecture and Art*, Vol. 10, No. 10, pp. 49–58. https://llufb.llu.lv/Raksti/Landscape_Architecture_Art/2017/Latvia-Univ-Agricult_Landscape_Architect_Art_VOL_10_2017-49-58.pdf

10 Aaron Eglitis, 'Artistic quest ignites historic fire', *Baltic Times*, Karosta, Latvia, 15 June 2005, https://www.baltictimes.com/news/articles/12900/

11 Aaron Eglitis, 'Kirsteins kicked out of People's Party', *Baltic Times*, Riga, 1 June 2005, https://www.baltictimes.com/news/articles/12804/

12 The MP returned to parliament in 2014 and four years later joined the Latvian delegation to the NATO parliamentary assembly. In 2006, a year after the exhibition, Kristine Briede won an award from the Latvian Ministry of Culture for her work at K@2.

13 Rob Hamelijnck and Nienke Terpsma, 'Conversation with Carl Biorsmark about "The presumption of Innocence", a documentary in the making on Herberts Cukurs, the Lindbergh from the Baltics', *Fucking Good Art*, Riga Audio Edition, 12 August 2007. https://www.fuckinggoodart.nl/Archive/fga18.html

14 Glants, *Patchwork Stitched by Memory*, p. 103.

15 J. Correspondent, 'Synagogue bombing stuns Latvian leaders and Jews', *Jewish News of Northern California*, 10 April 1998.

15 BEFORE THE LAW

1 'Ģenerālprokuratūra arī pēc atkārtota lūguma no Izraēlas nesaņem informāciju par Cukuru', *Delfi.Lv*, 21 March 2015. https://www.delfi.

lv/news/national/criminal/generalprokuratura-ari-pec-atkartota-luguma-no-izraelas-nesanem-informaciju-par-cukuru.d?id=45724002

2 Prosecution Office of the Republic of Latvia, June 06, 2016. "Reply to the e-mail message dated 26 April 2016 of the "Politico Europe" journalist Linda Kinstler, with the request to provide information on the progress of investigation conducted by the Prosecution Office into so called Herberts Cukurs criminal case."

3 'Criminal Procedure Law', *Latvijas Vēstnesis*, 74, 11 May 2005; Latvijas Republikas Saeimas un Ministru Kabineta Ziņotājs, 11, 9 June 2005, https://likumi.lv/ta/en/en/id/107820-criminal-procedure-law

4 Samuel Casper, 'The Bolshevik Afterlife: Posthumous Rehabilitation in the Post-Stalin Soviet Union, 1953–1970', *Publicly Accessible Penn Dissertations*, 2724, 2018, p. 5.

5 Drindic, *EEG: A Novel*, trans. Celia Hawkesworth (New York: New Directions, 2019), p. 86.

6 Casper, 'The Bolshevik Afterlife', p. 22.

7 Lon L. Fuller, *Legal Fictions* (Stanford: Stanford University Press, 1967), p. ix.

8 Ibid., p. 21.

9 Harriet Flower, *The Art of Forgetting: Disgrace & Oblivion in Roman Political Culture* (Chapel Hill: University of North Carolina Press, 2006), p. 21.

10 Serge Dauchy, 'Trois procès a cadavre devant le Conseil souverain du Québec (1687–1708): Un exemple d'application de l'ordonnance de 1670 dans les colonies', January 2000, https://halshs.archives-ouvertes.fr/halshs-01133366/document

11 Guy Vidal, 'Les Procès aux Cadavres', from 'L'histoire du Poitou Protestant, des humanists réformateurs a 1787', ouvrage collectif, Editions Maison du Protestantisme Poitevin, http://guy.vidal.pag esperso-orange.fr/Thomas_MARCHE/proces_cadavres9.htm

12 Dauchy, 'Trois procès', January 2000.

13 James Boyd White, *Heracles's Bow: Essays on the Rhetoric and Poetics of the Law* (Madison: University of Wisconsin Press, 1985), p. 117.

16 THE PLOT

1 Interview with Armands Puče conducted by author, Riga, 18 April 2016.

2 Puče, *Jūs nekad viņu nenogalināsiet.*

3 Throughout the novel, Boris's last name is spelled 'Kinslers'. I have used my familial spelling for consistency.

17 FORGOTTEN TRIALS

1 Plavnieks, *Nazi Collarorators*, p. 129.
2 Ibid., pp. 130–31; excerpts from StaH. 213–12 Staatsanwaltschaft Landgericht-NSG-0044-01. 'Arājs Verfahren.' Sonderband 2, pp. 282–3. Leonhard Manfred Schwarz, 'An der Staatsanwaltschaft Stuttgart', Flensburg-Murwik, 2 July 1973.
3 Plavnieks, *Nazi Collaborators*, p. 131. Plavnieks speculates on possible candidates for the mystery correspondent.
4 Ibid., p. 142.
5 Ibid., p. 133.
6 Ibid., pp. 133–4.
7 Ibid., p. 165.
8 Ibid., p. 137.
9 Ibid, p. 142.
10 Ella Medalje, *The Right to Live*, trans. David Silberman (Riga-Moscow: Russian Holocaust Library, 2011), pp. 29–31.
11 Plavnieks, *Nazi Collaborators*, p. 145.
12 'Examination Protocol", «Комитет Государственнои Безопасности При Совете Министров Латвиискои ССР» Case #40563, Delo No. 48, Riga, February 16, 1976, 3:30 p.m. p. 6. Zentrale Stelle der Landesjustizverwaltungen zur Aufklarung nationalsozialistischer Verbrechen (Central Office of the Judicial Authorities of the Federal States for Investigation of National Socialist Crimes), Record Group B 162 of the Bundesarchiv, Germany, Accessed via USHMM.
13 'War crimes case of Viktor Bernhard Arājs"', RG-06.009.03, U.S. Department of Justice, Office of Special Investigations, USHMM, Microfiche, p. 89.
14 Ibid., p. 151.
15 Ibid., p. 199.
16 Plavnieks, *Nazi Collaborators*, p. 157.
17 'Fragen Nach Gräben', *Der Spiegel*, 24 December 1978, Issue 52, https://www.spiegel.de/spiegel/print/d-40348465.html
18 Translation reproduced from Plavnieks, *Nazi Collaborators*, pp. 276–7.

19 Plavnieks, *Nazi Collaborators*, p. 277.

20 Richard J. Evans, 'The Historian as Expert Witness', *History and Theory*, Vol. 41, No. 3, October 2002. https://www.jstor.org/stable/3590689 P. 330.

21 Plavnieks, *Nazi Collaborators*, p. 165.

22 Christopher Tomlins, 'Why Law's Objects Do Not Disappear: On History as Remainder', *Routledge Handbook of Law and Theory* (London: Routledge, 2018), pp. 365–86.

18 AGENT STORIES

1 Caroline Humphrey, 'Stalin and the Blue Elephant: Paranoia and Complicity in Postcommunist Metahistories', in *Transparency & Conspiracy: Ethnographies of Suspicion in the New World Order*, Harry G. West and Todd Sanders, eds. (Durham: Duke University Press, 2003).

2 Alexei Yurchak, *Everything Was Forever, Until it Was No More: The Last Soviet Generation* (Princeton: Princeton University Press, 2006), p. 8.

3 Péter Apor, Sándor Horváth and James Mark, 'Introduction', *Secret Agents and the Memory of Everyday Collaboration in Communist Eastern Europe* (London: Anthem Press, 2017), p. 6.

4 Václav Havel et al., John Keane, ed., *The Power of the Powerless: Citizens Against the State in Central Eastern Europe* (Abingdon: Taylor & Francis, 1979), p. 91.

5 Izabella Tabarovsky, 'Lev Simkin: "The Holocaust Began in Ukraine"', Wilson Centre, Hull, 20 June 2016, https://www.wilsoncenter.org/article/lev-simkin-the-holocaust-began-ukraine

6 Amos Goldberg, 'Rumor Culture among Warsaw Jews under Nazi Occupation: A World of Catastrophe Reenchanted', *Jewish Social Studies*, vol. 21, No. 3 (Spring/Summer 2016) pp. 91–125.

7 A. Anatoliy Kuznetsov, *Babi Yar: A Document in the Form of a Novel*, trans. David Floyd (New York: Farrar, Straus and Giroux, 1970), p. 16.

8 'Только хорошее вспоминается и о директрисе – Нине Дмитриевне Алиевой. Мы знали, что во время войны Нина Дмитриевна была в концлагере Саласпилс, прошла через тяжелейшие испытания, но не сломалась, не озлобилась'. 'Советская Латвия: российский офицер — об учебе в 23-й рижской школе', *Vesti*, 11 February 2020. https://press.lv/post/sovetskaya-latviya-rossijskij-ofitser-ob-uchebe-v-23-j-rizhskoj-shkole

9 'A Child for Hitler', Catrine Clay, Producer, BBC documentary, London, 1992. https://www2.bfi.org.uk/films-tv-people/4ce2b7bc2e77f

10 The two books are *Karakalps* (Warrior) and *Puku Laiks* (Dragon Time), both by Arturs Pormals.

19 THE COSMOCHEMIST

1 Blanchot, *The Last Man*, p. 38.

2 Fresco, *On the Death of Jews*, p. 57.

3 Edward Anders, *Amidst Latvians During the Holocaust*, Occupation Museum Association of Latvia, Riga, 2011, p. 181.

4 'Hunting for a Killer', *Nazi Hunters: The Hangman of Riga*, National Geographic, 2010, https://www.youtube.com/watch?v= eoIkGET7oOg

5 Elita Veidemane, 'Herberta Cukura dēls atklāj patiesību par savu tēvu', *NRA.LV*, Riga, 27 September 2013. https://nra.lv/latvija/103 055-herberta-cukura-dels-atklaj-patiesibu-par-savu-tevu.htm

6 https://www.chicagotribune.com/news/ct-xpm-1994-05-24-9405250 004-story.html

7 Email composed by Edward Anders, 2011.02.08, part of correspondence archive provided to author.

20 THE MUSICAL

1 'ПБК: Премьера мюзикла "Цукурс. Херберт Цукурс"', First Baltic Channel, 13 October 2014, https://www.youtube.com/ watch?v=YAD5NJnFW5o.

2 Maija Spurina, *Cracks in a National Narrative of the Past: Three case studies of collective memory in post-Soviet Latvia*. PhD Thesis published by ProQuest, Publication number: 10258723, 2017, p. 153.

3 '100g kultūras. Diskusija. Vai vajadzīgs mūzikls par Herbertu Cukuru?' *Ltv.lv*, 27 March 2014. https://ltv.lsm.lv/lv/raksts/27.03.2014-100g-kulturas.-diskusija.-vai-vajadzigs-%20muzikls-par-herbertu-cuk.id26808/

4 Spurina, *Cracks in a National Narrative of the Past*, pp. 161–2.

5 Mike Collier, 'Review: Cukurs, Herberts Cukurs', Public Broadcasting of Latvia, 12 October 2014, https://eng.lsm.lv/article/culture/culture/ review-cukurs-herberts-cukurs.a102148/

6 Spurina, *Cracks in a National Narrative of the Past*, p. 166.

7 Ibid, p. 160.

8 'Точки над і. Дело Герберта Цукурса', *Ltv.Lv*, 15 October 2014, https://ltv.lsm.lv/lv/raksts/15.10.2014-%20tochku-nad-i-delo-gerberta-tsukursa.id37092/

9 Rayyan Sabet-Parry, 'Latvian Musical on Nazi collaborator stirs anger', AP News, 30 October 2014, https://apnews.com/article/4779 e20b30e44fbab5bb8b96d2acd46d

10 Spurina, *Cracks in a National Narrative of the Past*, p. 153.

11 Latvian Council of Jewish Communities, 'Ebreju kopiena: Herberta Cukura otrais iznāciens', *Delfi*, 22 October 2014, https://www.delfi.lv/news/versijas/ebreju-kopiena-herberta-cukura-otrais-iznaciens.d?id=45126794

21 THE BODY OF THE CRIME

1 Prosecutor M. Zelčs, 'Decision Re: Termination of Criminal Procedure', Riga, 23 October 2018. I am grateful to Uldis Bruns for his fastidious work translating the complete document into English.

2 The prosecutor might have found a better source to define 'Mossad', for instance: 'Information published on internet encyclopaedia "Wikipedia" (https://lv.wikipedia.org/wiki/Mossad) shows that Mossad is Israel's intelligence service, which was founded on 1 April 1951 and is directly answerable to the Israeli prime minister. It reveals that Mossad's operational activities are connected with secret, special assignments in Israel and beyond its borders.'

3 James Boyd White, *Heracles's Bow: Essays on the Rhetoric and Poetics of the Law* (Madison: University of Wisconsin Press, 1985), p. 186.

4 James Boyd White, *Heracles's Bow: Essays on the Rhetoric and Poetics of the Law* (Madison: University of Wisconsin Press, 1985), p. 191.

5 Viesturs Sprūde, 'Pēc kriminālprocesa izbeigšanas atsākas diskusijas par Cukura pārapbedīšanu Brāļu kapos Rīgā', *LA.LV*, 14 February 2019, https://www.la.lv/paversiens-herberta-cukura-lieta

6 Gordon Linkon, ed., 'The Corpus Delicti-Confession Problem', 43 J. *Crim. L. Criminology & Police Sci.* 214 (1952–1953), p. 214.

7 Ibid.

8 Austin explains that 'corpus delicti' allows for the differentiation of criminal attempts and criminal deeds: 'For want of the *consequence* there is not the *Corpus* of the principal delict. But the *intention* coupled with an act *tending to the consequence* constitutes the *corpus* of the secondary delict styled an "attempt".' John Austin, *Lectures*

on *Jurisprudence, Or, The Philosophy of Positive Law*. The Student Edition (New York: Henry Holt, 1875), p. 228.

9 Linkon, 'Corpus Delicti', p. 217.

10 Deborah Lipstadt, *History on Trial: My Day in Court with a Holocaust Denier* (New York, Ecco, 2006), p. 81.

11 Ibid., pp. 143–4.

12 Nichanian, *The Historiographic Perversion*, p. 47.

13 The first survivors of the Armenian genocide 'did not know that the trials of 1919 in Istanbul, conducted by Turkish military courts under the pressure of English occupiers, would in fact conclude that there was "in existence a plan aiming to exterminate the Armenian people", but also that, in 1922, the issues of the official Turkish journal covering the period of the trials were going to vanish in their entirety – and with them the very minutes of those trials.' Ibid., p. 28.

14 Ibid., p. 28.

15 Ibid., p. 29.

16 Email to author from preses sekretāre, Latvijas Republikas Prokuratūras, 10 July 2019.

22 ROAD OF CONTEMPLATION

1 Gunta Gaidamaviča, '«Kultūršoks»: Vai Herbertu Cukuru pārapbedīs Rīgas Brāļu kapos?' *LSM.LV*, 23 February 2019. https://www.lsm.lv/raksts/zinas/latvija/kultursoks-vai-herbertu-cukuru-parapbedis-rigas-bralu-kapos.a310582/

2 Viesturs Sprūde, 'Pēc kriminālprocesa izbeigšanas atsākas diskusijas par Cukura pārapbedīšanu Brāļu kapos Rīgā', *LA.LV*, 14 February 2019, https://www.la.lv/paversiens-herberta-cukura-lieta

3 Veidemane, 'Herberta Cukura'.

4 Daina S. Eglitis and Michelle Kelso, 'Ghost heroes: Forgetting and remembering in national narratives of the past', *Acta Sociologica*, Vol. 62, Issue 3, 2019.

5 Suzanne Pourchier-Passeraud, trans. Nick Tait, *Arts and a Nation: The Role of Visual Arts and Artists in the Making of the Latvian Identity, 1905–1940* (Boston, Brill, 2015), p. 304.

6 '"Island of Death" Battles Remembered', Public Broadcasting of Latvia, 28 July 2014, https://eng.lsm.lv/article/society/society/island-of-death-battles-remembered.a92779/

7 The US ambassador's speech took a different approach, pointing out exactly how many participants and camp guards were Latvians. Ezra Nathan, 'Holocaust memorial dedicated in Latvia', *Jewish Telegraphic Agency*, 5 December 2002.

8 Interview with Antinea Doloresa Cukurs-Risoto, 'He Has Deserved It'. https://skaties.lv/zinas/latvija/vins-to-ir-pelnijis-herberta-cukura-meita-cer-ka-latviesu-aviators-tiks-parapbedits-bralu-kapos/

9 Viesturs Sprūde, 'Vesturnieku komisija "neieteic" Cukuru Bralu kapiem', *LA.LV*, 4 April 2019.

10 Franz Kafka, *The Trial*, trans. Willa and Edwin Muir; rev. and trans. E. M. Butler (New York: Schocken, 1992 (1937)) p. 214–215.

11 Robert M. Cover, 'Violence and the Word', *Yale Law Journal*, Vol. 95: 1601, 1986, pp. 1604–5. https://digitalcommons.law.yale.edu/cgi/viewcontent.cgi?article=3687&context=fss_papers

12 Trüstedt, Katrin, 'Aporetic Agency: Trials and Metamorphoses', *Conference "Metamorphosis: Human, Animal, Armor"*, Santa Barbara, 4 December 2015. Manuscript on file with the author. p. 11.

13 Ibid.

PART III

1 Maurice Blanchot, *The Last Man*, trans. from the French by Lydia Davis (New Yok: Columbia University Press, 1983).

2 Daša Drndić, *EEG*, trans. from the Croatian by Celia Hawkesworth (Quercus: London, 2018).

23 THE APPEAL

1 'Museum's Building', Museum 'Jews in Latvia', https://www.jewishmuseum.lv/en/menu/39-museum_s_building.html

2 By the 'Free World', he is pointing to the fact that Schub's testimony was taken in the UK, that it cannot be thrown out simply because it was taken by Soviet authorities.

24 RACE FOR THE LIVING

1 'Oral History Interview with Yehuda Levy Feitelson'. United States Holocaust Memorial Museum Collection, Gift of the Holocaust Museum & Center for Tolerance and Education. https://collections.ushmm.org/search/catalog/irn558310

2 'About Us', Bauska Memorial, https://www.bauskamemorial.org/home/about-us/
3 David Lipkin, 'How We Managed To Convince the Latvian Prosecutor's Office to Recall Its Own Decision', *Latvian Jewish Courier*, Vol. 34, Issue 3, December 2020, p. 6

25 THE VIOLINIST'S SON

1 Ed Koch, 'For Sasha Semenoff, Holocaust survivor and longtime Vegas performer, "music was his life"', *Las Vegas Sun*, 11 January 2013, https://lasvegassun.com/news/2013/jan/11/sasha-semenoff-holocaust-survivor-and-longtime-veg/
2 Sasha Semenoff, *Don't Let This Happen Again: A True Story*, Claims Conference Holocaust Survivor Memoir Collection (Washington: USHMM, 1986), https://archive.org/details/bib266041_001_001
3 Abram Shapiro, testimony to the Legal Department of the Central Committee of LIberated Jews, Munich, December 19, 1948. Wiener Library, 'Committee for the Investigation of Nazi War Crimes in Baltic Countries," File 539.
4 'Cukurs.EN', https://www.youtube.com/watch?v=kYXY_6IemJ4
5 Jerry Fink, 'Violin as instrument of survival, happiness', *Las Vegas Sun*, 25 January 2009, https://lasvegassun.com/news/2009/jan/25/violin-instrubment-survival-happiness/

26 'GOD BLESS THEIR SOULS'

1 '"Esmu traka uz mūziku." Laura Rizzotto sirsnīgā intervijā pirms "Eirovīzijas" atlases', *Skaties.LV*, 16 February 2018, https://skaties.lv/izklaide/slavenibas/muziki/esmu-traka-uz-muziku-laura-rizzotto-sirsniga-intervija-pirms-eirovizijas-atlases/
2 Antra Gabre, 'Herberta Cukura izglābtās ebrejietes meita mātes dzimtenē pateicas glābēja ģimene', *NRA.LV*, 23 May 2019, https://nra.lv/latvija/281542-herberta-cukura-izglabtas-ebrejietes-meita-mates-dzimtene-pateicas-glabeja-gimenei.htm

27 ONE WITNESS, NO WITNESS

1 Tzvi Freeman, 'Quantum Reality & Ancient Wisdom', Chabad.org, April 2013.

2 'Witness', Jewish Virtual Library, *Encyclopaedia Judaica*, The Gale Group, 2008.

3 David Lipkin, 'How We Managed to Convince the Latvian Prosecutor's Office to Recall Its Own Decision', *Latvian Jewish Courier*, Vol. 34, Issue 3, p. 7.

4 In another email to a Latvian historian, this one written in 2015, Anders elaborated upon his position on Cukurs: 'As for Cukurs, I too believe that he was a mixture of good and bad. His problems in the Latvian Army suggest that he was undisciplined and impulsive, doing what he wanted to do rather than following rules. That trait may explain his actions in the Arājs Commando, helping kill Jews one day and saving a few Jews (whom he knew or considered pretty) another day. I do not think he was cynical (unlike some other Holocaust participants) and saved a few Jews to serve as character witnesses some day. Instead I believe he was impulsive, and not so deeply committed to antisemitism as some Nazis.'

29 BALTIC TROY

1 Felice Vinci, 'The Nordic Origins of the Iliad and Odyssey: An Up-to-date Survey of the Theory', *Athens Journal of Mediterranean Studies*, Vol. 3, Issue 2, pp. 163–86, https://www.athensjournals.gr/mediterranean/2017-3-2-4-Vinci.pdf

2 The German businessman Heinrich Schliemann claimed to have discovered Homer's Troy, but in fact discovered a palace dating from a thousand years prior. See James I. Porter, 'What Did Homer See?', *Homer: The Very Idea* (Chicago: University of Chicago Press), 2021. See also Easton, D. F., 'Heinrich Schliemann: Hero or Fraud?' *The Classical World*, vol. 91, no. 5 (Johns Hopkins UP, Classical Association of the Atlantic States), 1998, pp. 335–43, https://doi.org/10.2307/4352102.

3 Wai Chee Dimock, 'After Troy: Homer, Euripides, Total War', *Rethinking Tragedy*, Rita Felski, ed. (Baltimore: Johns Hopkins University Press, 2008), p. 66.

4 James I. Porter, 'What did Homer See?' *Homer: The Very Idea* (Chicago: University of Chicago Press), 2021, p. 172.

5 'Valsts prezidenta Raimonda Vejona uzruna Ebrjeu tautas genocidea upuru pieminas dienas pasakuma Gogola iela', Riga, 4 July 2019.

30 THE ANTONYM OF FORGETTING

1 Silva and Cardozo, *El Mossad*, Epilogue.
2 'Holokausta izdzīvojušā uzruna /Marģers Vestermanis/ Address by Holocaust survivor. 4.07.2021. LV/EN', https://www.youtube.com/watch?v=buk3YTtt-UI
3 Madeleine Chambers, "Germany's ex-royal family win legal case against historian," Reuters, 18 February 2021. https://www.reuters.com/article/us-germany-royals/germanys-ex-royal-family-win-legal-case-against-historian-idUSKBN2AI2RI
4 David Batty, 'Court fines Historian over claims of Holocaust survivor's lesbian affair', *Guardian*, 21 December 2020, https://www.theguardian.com/education/2020/dec/21/court-fines-historian-over-claims-holocaust-survivor-lesbian-affair
5 "75 years after the arrest of Anne Frank," Anne Frank House, 1 August 2019. https://www.annefrank.org/en/about-us/news-and-press/news/2019/8/1/75-years-after-arrest-anne-frank/
6 Nina Siegal, "Scholars Doubt New Theory on Anne Frank's Betrayal," *New York Times*, January 18, 2022.
7 Linda Kinstler, 'The Right to A History Without Lies', *Jewish Currents*, 22 March 2021. https://jewishcurrents.org/the-right-to-a-history-without-lies/

Index

Acknowledgements

I could not say, precisely, when I began to work on this book, or whether the work will ever end. I am indebted to all those who helped shape it along the way, through small and large interventions of thought, friendship and generosity; who may not know just what a great help their contributions have been.

There would be no book to speak of without the graciousness of its subjects. Ilya Lensky has been a kind and erudite interlocutor for many years, and his encyclopaedic memory is, as far as I am concerned, a Latvian national treasure. David Lipkin shared his legal strategy and kept me apprised of case developments. Dmitry Krupnikov granted me access to his expansive archive and shared his father's stories from the post-war years. I will always appreciate his periodic reminders that life is, as a rule, stranger than fiction. Helga Fisch trusted me with her mother's story – a story that reminds us that many things can be true at once. Dror and Eran Feitelson shared memories of their father and his journey back to his birthplace. Yehudi Gaffen was a supportive and inquisitive help along the way. Shlomo Shpiro told me about his long conversations with Yaakov Meidad. Eliahu and Frank Gordon kindly shared their own remembrances. Without Marcelo Silva, I would never have been able to understand what happened in Montevideo, or to confront the remaining evidence up close. I will forever admire Edward Anders's lifelong commitment to truth and allergy to imprecision.

Several historical monographs were crucial to the research and writing process. Richards Plavnieks's *Nazi Collaborators on Trial During the Cold War* was instrumental, and I am indebted to Plavnieks for sharing materials, answering questions and reviewing the relevant portions of the manuscript. Francine Hirsch's *Soviet Judgement at Nuremberg* altered how I came to view the IMT. Dissertations by Samuel Casper, Patrick Tobin and Bruno Leal illuminated different aspects of this story. In Riga, Uldis Neiburgs shared his archival findings – what I have been able to learn about my grandfather is in large part thanks to him. Uldis V. Brūns, Toomas Hiio, Mikhail Nakonechnyi and Maija Spurina helped with my research. René Bienert at the Vienna Wiesenthal Institute for Holocaust Studies, Dan Newman at the U.S. Holocaust Memorial Museum, Ainārs Bambals at the Latvian State Archives and the staff of the Wiener Library in London provided archival assistance. *The Holocaust in Latvia* by Andrew Ezergailis was an indispensable source text. Though in his old age Ezergailis became one of Cukurs's staunchest defenders, he remained open to my questions: "Dear Linda! Perhaps, you already know too much!" he wrote me in 2016. "What is the correct way of coming to terms with the Holocaust? Have I done the right thing?" He died in January 2022, as this book was going to press.

I am immensely grateful to the professors and colleagues who set me on this journey, and provided support along the way. At Bowdoin College, Marilyn Reizbaum opened up worlds of meaning, and has offered invaluable guidance and wisdom ever since. At the University of Cambridge, Rory Finnin supported the earliest incarnation of this project. In London, Matt Kaminski told me to get on with it. At Berkeley, Alexei Yurchak and Yuri Slezkine deepened my understanding of the Soviet period and its aftermath, encouraging me to think of it as a story about memory above all. Over lunch at Saul's, Michael Lewis asked for my notebook and jotted down the book's structure, as only a great can do. Judith Butler's Kafka seminar was a revelation.

The Berkeley Rhetoric Department has been a dream of a place to study during the many years it took to write this story. Daniel Boyarin, Samera Esmeir and James Porter broadened my thinking;

Winnie Wong showed me how to take field notes. Ramona Naddaff
has been an incredible intellectual and professional mentor from
day one. Sincere thanks go to her for organising an Art of Writing
Manuscript Workshop for me; and to Andrew Shanken, Harrison
King and Molly Krueger for participating: their comments and
suggestions guided my revisions. Michael Mascuch read and
commented on portions of the manuscript; it is because of him
that I met Edward Anders when I did, a meeting that changed the
course of the work. Marianne Constable taught me how to think
about justice, proof and law's shifting relation to history; her notes
on several early drafts were a critical aid.

I wouldn't have gotten very far without good friends: Genevieve
Barrons, Erica Berry, Amanda Cormier, Kailana Durnan, Katie
Engelhart, Hilary Hurd, Julia Ioffe, Lilia Kilburn, Jacob Mikanowski,
Alice Robb, Madeleine Schwartz, Kyra Sutton, Valerie Wirtschafter
and Tim Wyman-McCarthy provided invaluable feedback, advice
and camaraderie. In Riga, Anna and Marija Kuricina kept me
company, and Sanita Jemberga lent me her fierce investigative
powers. In Montevideo, Diego Zoppolo and Victoria Lorbeer
showed me around their beautiful city, making sure that it wasn't
all work. Camila Alonso was a wonderful translator during my trip.

Grants from the Marshall Aid Commemoration Commission,
the Pulitzer Center on Crisis Reporting and the Berkeley Institute of
Slavic, East European, and Eurasian Studies enabled me to travel to
meet with sources and access archives. David Wolf at the *Guardian*
Long Read commissioned my report on the "last Nazi hunters"
of Ludwigsburg, which is elaborated upon in Chapter Ten. Karl
Jirgens, Eva Eglāja-Kristsone and Ieva Lešinska graciously agreed to
have their translations from the Latvian appear as epigraphs.

Georgina Capel and Simon Shaps believed in this project
from its earliest days, and I'm unspeakably grateful to them, and
to everyone at Georgina Capel Associates for making this book
a reality. At Bloomsbury, Alexis Kirschbaum saw what the book
could become. Jasmine Horsey coaxed it into being; without her
sharp editorial eye, it would be a shadow of itself. Elisabeth Denison
expertly navigated it over the finish line. Richard Collins was an

indefatigable copy editor, Martin Bryant a wonderful proofreader. Phil Beresford created the maps and photo plates. I will always be thankful to them, and to the entire Bloomsbury team, for their contributions.

Over the many years of research and writing, my family has championed and buoyed my work. My in-laws, Jim and Alison Webb, allowed me to use their Maine home as a much-needed writing retreat during the final stages of writing. My sister Carina Yariv taught me how to write in the first place. My father, Olaf Kinstler, trusted me to uncover a difficult history. My mother, Zoya Kinstler, was my co-conspirator and researcher all along. This is their story as much as it is mine. It is dedicated to my family, past, present and future.

Isaac, my first reader and great love, read so many versions of this book that we both lost count. I'm grateful to him for his edits (including of his own acknowledgement), but most of all for his infinite well of good humor, patience and care, for which no words of thanks could possibly suffice.

A Note on the Author

Linda Kinstler is a contributing writer at the *Economist's 1843* magazine. Her coverage of European politics, history and cultural affairs has appeared in the *Atlantic, New York Times, Guardian, Wired, Jewish Currents* and elsewhere. She is a PhD Candidate in Rhetoric at UC Berkeley and previously studied in the UK as a Marshall Scholar. She has received numerous fellowships and awards, and has appeared on NPR, the BBC, CNN and MSNBC, among others. She lives in Washington, DC.

A Note on the Type

The text of this book is set in Adobe Garamond. It is one of several versions of Garamond based on the designs of Claude Garamond. It is thought that Garamond based his font on Bembo, cut in 1495 by Francesco Griff o in collaboration with the Italian printer Aldus Manutius. Garamond types were fi rst used in books printed in Paris around 1532. Many of the present-day versions of this type are based on the Typi Academiae of Jean Jannon cut in Sedan in 1615.

Claude Garamond was born in Paris in 1480. He learned how to cut type from his father and by the age of fi fteen he was able to fashion steel punches the size of a pica with great precision. At the age of sixty he was commissioned by King Francis I to design a Greek alphabet, and for this he was given the honourable title of royal type founder. He died in 1561.